D0402760

ENCOUNTERING THE MYSTERY

Bartholomew I, Ecumenica
Encountering the
mystery : understanding
c2008.

sa   05/19/08

ENCOUNTERING

THE

MYSTERY

Understanding Orthodox Christianity Today

His All Holiness
Ecumenical Patriarch

BARTHOLOMEW

DOUBLEDAY

NEW YORK LONDON TORONTO SYDNEY AUCKLAND

PUBLISHED BY DOUBLEDAY

Copyright © 2008 by The Ecumenical Patriarchate of Constantinople

All Rights Reserved

Published in the United States by Doubleday, an imprint of
The Doubleday Broadway Publishing Group, a division
of Random House, Inc., New York.
www.doubleday.com

DOUBLEDAY and the portrayal of an anchor with a dolphin are registered
trademarks of Random House, Inc.

Book design by Gretchen Achilles

LIBRARY OF CONGRESS CATALOGING-IN-PUBLICATION DATA
Bartholomew, Ecumenical Patriarch of Constantinople, 1940–
Encountering the mystery : understanding Orthodox Christianity today /
by His All Holiness Ecumenical Patriarch Bartholomew.—1st ed.
p.   cm.
Includes bibliographical references.
1. Orthodox Eastern Church. I. Title.
BX320.3.B36 2008
281.9—dc22
2007025597

ISBN 978-0-385-51813-0

PRINTED IN THE UNITED STATES OF AMERICA

1 3 5 7 9 10 8 6 4 2

First Edition

CONTENTS

FOREWORD

To be myself, I need you.
If we do not look one another in the eye,
we are not truly human.

—ECUMENICAL PATRIARCH BARTHOLOMEW[1]

NOT THEORY, NOT PHILOSOPHY, BUT EXPERIENCE

His All Holiness the Ecumenical Patriarch Bartholomew, elected to the See of Constantinople in autumn 1991, is chiefly known to the public for his urgent and courageous statements concerning the present-day ecological crisis. No other church leader has given such emphatic priority to environmental issues, and with good reason he has been called the "Green Patriarch."[2] He is also greatly respected for his commitment to dialogue with other Christians, especially with the Roman Catholic Church, and for his openness to Judaism and Islam. Truly, throughout the sixteen years of his service as leader of the worldwide Orthodox communion, he has striven tirelessly to act as bridge builder.

In the present volume, while having much to say about ecology and dialogue, the Patriarch is concerned to place these two issues in the broader context of Orthodox faith and life as a whole. He does not attempt, however, to provide a systematic and exhaustive account of Orthodox spirituality. That is not his way. He concentrates rather upon the themes that are closest to his heart in his ministry as Patriarch. As the reader of these pages will quickly discover, he speaks with a voice that is gentle yet firm, humble yet authoritative. Above all, his standpoint is compassionate and pastoral.

A great Serbian bishop of the twentieth century, Saint Nikolai Velimirović, has written: "Our religion is founded on spiritual experience, seen and heard as surely as any physical fact in this world. Not theory, not philosophy, not human emotions, but experience."[3] Such also is the approach of the Ecumenical Patriarch. Stressing what he terms "the equal importance of creed and experience," he says:

> *Orthodox Christianity is a way of life* in which there is a profound and direct relationship between dogma and praxis, faith and life. This unity of faith and life means that the reality of the eternal truths lies in their experiential power, rather than in their codification into a set of ideological constructs.[4]

Summing up this experiential stance, Bartholomew states epigrammatically:

> *Truth is beheld; it is not understood intellectually. God is seen; He is not examined theoretically. Beauty is perceived; it is not speculated about abstractly.*[5]

In the present book, the Patriarch remains faithful to this point of view. His words are based not on speculation or academic research—although he holds a theological doctorate—but on his lived experience. It is significant that he illustrates his discussions with personal reminiscences, recalling such moments as prayers in his childhood with his mother, church services on his native island of Imvros, worship as a student at the Patriarchal Theological School of Halki, and the nightly celebration of Compline in the little chapel beside his apartment in the Phanar. Doctrine and life go hand in hand.

There are two main aspects to the Patriarch's spiritual experience, as Deacon John Chryssavgis indicates in his "Biographical Note." First, there is the traditional Orthodox piety acquired in his early years on Imvros, and reinforced by his time on Halki. Second, there is the more wide-ranging awareness that he has gained through his postgraduate studies in the West at Rome, Bossey, and Munich, through his two decades as private secretary to his predecessor, Patriarch Demetrios, and through his continual journeys abroad since his accession to the Patriarchal Throne (for he is an indefatigable traveler). The first of these two things has given him depth, and the second breadth. Together, the two have made him into what he is: a builder of bridges, an opener of doors.

A single master theme binds together everything Patriarch Bartholomew has to say in the pages that follow, and that is his insistence on the value of the human person. As he affirms in the opening chapter, "Each human person is . . . uniquely created in the image of God, never able to be reduced to anything less than a mystery." Characteristically, in words addressed to an environmental symposium in the United States, when singling out what are in his opinion "three particular strengths of Orthodox Christianity most relevant to the world we live in today," he begins by speaking about the person:

> The first strength is Orthodox Christianity's conception of the human being as person. For us, personhood is an ontological category of being. This theological thinking is deeply rooted in our tradition which understands God as a Trinity—a community of persons.[6]

The Patriarch's personalism, it should be added at once, is not merely theoretical, but expresses itself in a down-to-earth and practical manner. He has a gift for friendship, and not least for friendship with children. He has the ability to establish immediate contact with those whom he meets, and he has an excellent memory for faces and names.

There are four leading features in the Patriarch's understanding of the person: mystery, freedom, relationship, wholeness.

MYSTERY

"[N]ever able to be reduced to anything less than a mystery": here is the first distinguishing mark of personhood that Bartholomew is concerned to uphold. Developing the point, he goes on to say in the present work: "The human person can never be defined—it can never be exhaustively or exclusively contained in any single aspect or description"; the most that we can do is to provide an "ostensive perception." We can point, that is to say, to what is signified by being a person, we can give illustrations and examples, but that is all. Since it is indefinable, personhood is by the same token irreducible. The mystery of the fact of being a person cannot be reduced to the facts of the relevant sciences, such as physiology, psychology, or sociology. There is always something more, not to be adequately expressed in words, for the reality of being a person is far greater than any explanation that we choose to give of it. It is an intrinsic hallmark of personalness to be open, always to point beyond. This means that we have no clear conception of the limits of our personhood, of the possibilities as yet latent in our personalness, and of the ultimate fulfillment of being a person. In the words of Saint John the Theologian: "What we are to be in the future has not yet been revealed to us" (1 John 3:2).

As Saint Gregory of Nyssa points out, there is a specific reason for the mysterious and unfathomable character of the human person.[7] This lies in the fact that, as the Patriarch points out more than once, we are formed in the image and likeness of God (Gen. 1:26). Now, an image, if it is to be truly such (as Saint Gregory points out), needs to reproduce the attributes of its archetype. Since God, our archetype, is beyond comprehension, so also, albeit on a different level, is His image the human person. To counterbalance our apophatic theology, we have need to develop also an apophatic anthropology. "The heart is deep" (Ps. 64:6).

FREEDOM

In the words of Søren Kierkegaard: "The most tremendous thing granted to the human being is choice, freedom."[8] Patriarch Bartholomew agrees; and this is the second of the four expressions of personhood to which he wishes to draw our attention. As he declares in this book, "The notion of freedom is critical in Orthodox faith and life." In the important speech that he gave on November 3, 2005, at the London School of Economics, titled "The Role of Religion in a Changing Europe," he highlighted human freedom as precisely the determining constituent of the "European idea":

> Europe, it has often been said, is not simply a geographical area but an idea. What, then, we ask, is the fundamental "idea" that gives unity to Europe, that constitutes the "soul" of Europe, and that the European Union is seeking, however imperfectly, to embody?
>
> The answer can be found in a Jewish saying recorded by Martin Buber in his *Tales of the Hasidim*. "What is the worst thing that the evil urge can achieve?" a Rabbi is asked; and he replies: "To make us forget that we are each the child of a King." As human persons, we are each of us from royal lineage, in the spiritual sense; that is to say, we are each and every one of us *free*.

This notion of personal freedom—of the free dignity and integrity of every single human being—lies at the heart of what we mean by the European idea, and it is the primary guiding principle of the EU.

It is precisely in this perspective that we can begin to appreciate the role of religion in Europe; for personal freedom is fundamental likewise to the Christian doctrine of human personhood. "The truth will make you free," states Christ (John 8:32); "Am I not free?" asserts St. Paul (1 Cor. 9:1).⁹

Without freedom, Patriarch Bartholomew is convinced, there can be no authentic personhood. I am genuinely personal only insofar as I am free:

The human being, as an existential reality, can be a person only when living in freedom. Only in conditions in which the full range of possibilities is open to our free and conscious choice are we able to transform our temporal reality and our selves into the image of the divine Kingdom. Our humanity is realized through the free act of relationship with others. Personhood is a free act of communion that makes heterogeneity and uniqueness fundamental aspects of our humanity.¹⁰

In the last two sentences of this passage, Bartholomew brings in the third aspect of personhood, relationship, to which we shall shortly be turning. But let us for the moment reflect on the main point emphasized in this paragraph, the quality of freedom, of liberty of choice. In Chapter 7 he works out some of the implications of what is meant by this. In the first place, freedom is directly connected with the fact that we are in the image of God. As God is free, so the human person as God's living icon is also free, even though in God's case the freedom is absolute, whereas for us humans it is restricted (but not destroyed) by sin. As a manifestation of the divine image, freedom is not merely a natural trait inherent in our created personhood. It is also, much more profoundly, a gift of grace, containing within itself a spark of the Uncreated. Yet it is not only a gift but also, as the Patriarch puts it, an "unceasing" task, "a gift that is acquired through much spiritual effort." As such, it presupposes a dynamic ascetic discipline; indeed, the main purpose of fasting is exactly to assist us in recovering freedom. To be free is not simply to do what we please, for the only veritable freedom is to do the will of God; "real freedom is obedience."[11]

Furthermore, freedom is indivisible. Defense of my own freedom has always to go hand in hand with respect for the freedom of others. Commitment to the cause of freedom signifies a tireless struggle on behalf of the "poor" of this world, of the oppressed, of the underprivileged, of all victims of discrimination and abuse. This also is crucially important for the Patriarch. "If one member of the body suffers, all the other members of the body suffer with it" (1 Cor. 12:26).

RELATIONSHIP

In speaking of freedom, then, we have inevitably begun to speak also of the third characteristic of personhood, relationship. Personhood, as the Patriarch says in words already quoted, is a "free act of relationship with others . . . a free act of communion." Freedom, in other words, is not only personal but interpersonal, involving "an impulse toward the 'other.' "[12] Freedom is inseparable from love. "As human beings," he writes in Chapter 7, "we cannot be genuinely free in isolation, repudiating our relationship with our fellow humans. We can only be genuinely free if we form part of a community of other free persons. Freedom is never solitary but always social . . . Freedom is expressed as encounter."

Here again, the doctrine of the divine image in humankind is directly relevant to the theology of personhood. We are created in the image of God, that is to say, in the image of God, who is not only one but three-in-one, who is not only a unit but a union or communion of three persons. Just as God the Trinity is a mystery of mutual love, so we humans are created for mutual love. As we proclaim in the Divine Liturgy, "Let us love one another, that with one mind we may confess the Father, the Son and the Holy Spirit, the Trinity one in essence and undivided." The being of God, as Metropolitan John of Pergamon asserts, is "relational being;"[13] and so we humans, as "transcripts of the Trinity," to use a phrase from the hymns of the Wesleys, cannot realize our personhood except in an interpersonal communion that reflects the Triunity of God.

In this connection, let us never forget that the Greek word for "person" is *prosopon*, which means literally "face" or "countenance." We are only truly human, truly personal, if we turn toward other human persons, "facing" them, looking into their eyes and allowing them to look into ours. We are only personal, that is to say, insofar as we greet other persons, joyfully acknowledging them in their otherness. Personhood is social, or it is nothing: "To be myself, I need you." To be a person, then, is to make room for other persons; it is to say to the others, "On this planet created by God for us all, there is room for all of us"—words uttered by the Patriarch as he stood on the site of St. Nicholas Orthodox Church in New York City, beside the ruins of the World Trade Center.[14]

As the Patriarch has regularly stated in his annual encyclical letters for the day of creation (September 1), Christianity involves "applied solidarity."[15] "There is, after all, solidarity in the human race because, made as they are in the image of the triune God, human beings are interdependent and coinherent. No man is an island. We are 'members one of another' (Eph. 4:25) . . . According to Dostoyevsky's Staretz Zossima in *The Brothers Karamazov*, we are each of us responsible for everyone and everything."[16] The human animal is, in Aristotle's phrase, a "political animal," created by God to live in a *polis* or city, in a structured and interactive society, characterized by compassion and mutual obligations. "The ancient Greeks," the Patriarch remarks, "used to say that man, in order to develop, needs the city."[17] In the words of an old monastic dictum dear to Bartholomew, "My brother is my life."[18] Glossing this statement, he adds: *"Every human being is our neighbor."*[19]

Readers of this book cannot fail to notice how often the Patriarch uses such words as "relationship," "encounter," "communion," "sharing," "exchange," and "dialogue." These and similar terms form a golden thread running through the whole of the work and conferring on it a unity of vision. As persons, it is said, we are "created for encounter." Prayer is a "relationship word"; our prayer is "dialogical" in character, for our goal in praying is not only to speak but equally to listen. In fasting, the physical is rendered personal, for it transforms a bodily need, our natural desire for food and drink, into a "mystery of sharing." Indeed, all the Church's sacraments aim at restoring communion and community, alike with God and with our fellow humans. The icon, too, is to be understood in terms of relationship and meeting: serving as a window or door, it enables the worshipper to encounter face-to-face the person who is being depicted. "The icon reminds us that Christianity is a 'religion of faces.' "[20]

Inspired by this theology of relationship and encounter, Patriarch Bartholomew, throughout his years at the Phanar, has given his utmost support to inter-Christian and interfaith dialogue. It is typical of his approach that, when visiting Pope John Paul II at Rome in June 1995, he included in his immediate entourage a leading Turkish philanthropist who is a Muslim. "True dialogue is a gift from God," he insists. While recognizing the obstacles that any serious dialogue has to confront, he remains hopeful. As he says in this book, "Never before in history have human beings had the opportunity to bring so many positive changes to so many people simply through encounter and dialogue." Ours is not only an age of anxiety; it is also an age of dialogue.

Dialogue presupposes freedom; here, as always, the second and the third characteristics of personhood go hand in hand. To illustrate how God himself exemplifies the true spirit of dialogue, Bartholomew likes to quote the words of the second-century *Epistle to Diognetus*: "God persuades, He does not compel; for violence is foreign to Him."[21] In this spirit Bartholomew urges the need for what he calls "humble engagement" and "moderate conversation." He is firmly opposed to all forms of proselytism, that is to say, to the kind of propaganda that uses bribes and threats, encroaching aggressively on the freedom of the other. Any such encroachment is a crime in the name of religion; and, as the Patriarch protests, using the words of the Berne Declaration (1992) and the Bosphorus Declaration (1994), "a crime committed in the name of religion is a crime against religion."[22]

This double appeal to freedom and interrelationship indicates exactly the way in which Patriarch Bartholomew interprets the role of the Ecumenical Patriarchate of Constantinople within the Orthodox world as a whole. The Orthodox Church is a family of some fifteen patriarchates and autocephalous (or independent) churches, which are all united in faith and in sacramental communion but are each self-governing in their own interior life. Within this worldwide communion the Patriarch of Constantinople enjoys an honorary primacy, watching over the universality of Orthodoxy. But, unlike the Pope of Rome, he does not claim a direct and immediate power of jurisdiction, as far as the rest of Orthodoxy is concerned. He sees his position merely as that of elder brother or "first among equals," a phrase frequently used by Bartholomew. The Ecumenical Patriarchate does not seek to impose decisions upon the other Orthodox churches, to command or coerce, nor does it attempt to interfere unasked in their internal affairs. Its vocation is one of presidency, initiative, and coordination. It proposes, but it does not constrain or compel. It is, in the words of the French Orthodox thinker Olivier Clément, "the Church which 'convenes,' " but it always performs this service of convening in full accord and consultation with the other Orthodox churches.[23]

Such was the ideal and the practice adopted by that bold and prophetic figure, the Ecumenical Patriarch Athenagoras, when he convoked the first Pan-Orthodox Conference at Rhodes in 1961, and such has been the policy in the subsequent Pan-Orthodox conferences held at Rhodes, Belgrade, and Chambésy (Switzerland). Athenagoras's successor, Patriarch Demetrios, worked on similar principles, and so likewise has Bartholomew. Both in his contacts with the other Orthodox churches and in his dealings with the Turkish government, Bartholomew has always made it clear that the Ecumenical Patriarchate is "a purely spiritual Institution, a symbol of reconciliation and an unarmed force," to use the words of his Enthronement Address on November 2, 1991.[24]

WHOLENESS

The fourth characteristic of human personhood underlined by Patriarch Bartholomew is wholeness, integration, inclusiveness. The human person is an undivided unity of soul and body, and in our theological anthropology the spiritual is never to be disconnected from the material. Constituting as we do a psychosomatic totality, through our corporeality we humans form part of the physical environment. Our interrelationship as human beings not only embraces all our fellow humans but extends also to the entire created order. It is cosmic in scope. Humankind and the material world form what the Patriarch describes as a "seamless garment." When thinking, then, of the realm of nature, we are to view it always in the light of this relational humanism, not as an "It" but as a "Thou." It cannot be rightly understood except in terms of an "encounter" and in the context of "the mystery of communion."

We humans apprehend our communion with the "seamless garment" of creation above all when we open the eyes of our hearts to the *beauty* of the world: "God saw everything that He had made, and behold, it was *altogether good and beautiful*" (Gen. 1:31).[25] Patriarch Bartholomew often speaks of this cosmic beauty. From his early years, as the essays written in his school days indicate, he has been sensitive to the beauty of nature.[26] This beauty, however, is important for him not simply for aesthetic but also for theophanic reasons, because it points us toward the divine Creator.

The cosmic outreach of our human interrelationship is proclaimed clearly in the Divine Liturgy when the celebrant says, immediately before the consecratory *epiclesis* (the invocation of the Holy Spirit), "Thine own from Thine own, we offer to Thee, in all [things] and for all [things]." *In all things*: our Eucharistic offering includes the animals and plants, the trees and rivers, the mountains and oceans—not only all human beings but the fullness of nature. As a unity of body and soul, set at the crossroads of the universe— as both microcosm and mediator—the human person is priest of creation, called to offer the world back to the Creator in thanksgiving. We are not just "logical" or "political" animals but, much more profoundly, *eucharistic* animals.

The Patriarch's belief in the essential wholeness of human nature, in the cosmic dimensions of our relationality, has made him a keen and committed ecologist. For Bartholomew, the roots of the so-called environmental crisis are not primarily economic or technological but spiritual. It is a crisis not in the environment itself but in the human heart. What is required of us, on the threshold of the third millennium, is not just more sophisticated scientific skills but also, far more fundamentally, repentance, *metanoia*, in the literal sense of the Greek word, which is "change of mind." We need urgently to acquire a new way of looking at ourselves, at the created world, and at God.

As an ecologist, it has justly been remarked, Bartholomew is "anthropocentric" but not "anthropomonist."[27] He is anthropocentric in the sense that he believes the human person to have been set by God at the center of creation, not so as to exercise a selfish and arbitrary domination over nature, but so as to refashion and transfigure the created order, to give it a voice, and so to render it back to God in priestly oblation. But the Patriarch strongly rejects anthropomonism, in the sense of an exclusive concentration on human beings and their selfish advantage, in isolation from the natural environment at its expense and to its detriment.

Indeed, for Bartholomew such exclusive concentration and isolation constitute precisely the essence of secularism. In his eyes, secularism is nothing else than an anthropomonist heresy that separates humanity from God and from the world, ignoring the priestly and eucharistic orientation of personhood. The secularist is one who no longer sees the world as gift of God and sacrament of the divine presence, one for whom the world is no longer transparent but opaque, for whom the human person is no longer priest of the creation but proprietor and autocrat. The Patriarch is quick to add, however, that secularism, understood in this sense, is far from being an exclusively Western phenomenon, but has gravely influenced the "traditional" Orthodox nations as well.

DEEP FOUNDATIONS

This interpretation of human personhood—as mystery, freedom, relationship, and wholeness—possesses deep foundations. Four such foundations call for particular mention. First, as we have already seen, our understanding of what it is to be a person is founded on the Christian doctrine of the Trinity. We are created "in the image of God," in the image, that is to say, of a God who is not only Unity but Trinity, not only personal but interpersonal; and so we humans cannot realize our personhood according to this Trinitarian image except through interrelationship. In the words of Bartholomew, the Trinity is "the symbol of encounter and communion." This is visually expressed in the icon of the Hospitality of Abraham, in which the Trinity is represented in the form of the three angels who visited Abraham and Sarah under the oak of Mamre (Gen. 18:1–2). In many examples, most notably in the celebrated icon of the Trinity painted by Saint Andrew Rublev, the three are not simply sitting in a row but turned toward each other as they engage in reciprocal dialogue. But this is a dialogue, says Bartholomew, into which we humans are also drawn. For while the angels are seated on the three sides of the table, a vacant space is left on the fourth side. "The icon serves as an open invitation to each of us. Will we sit at the table with these strangers?" Only if we accept the divine invitation shall we become true persons after the Trinitarian image.

Second, Bartholomew's appreciation of human personhood is rooted in his Christology. Freedom and interrelationship cannot come to fruition except through self-emptying (*kenosis*), through sacrifice and death after the example of Christ's own death on the Cross. It is very striking that in his Enthronement Address, Bartholomew refers to his future Patriarchal ministry as a crucifixion: he has assumed "the cross of Andrew the 'first-called,' " he says, "in order to be co-crucified with our Lord and His co-crucified Church." He even goes so far as to describe this cross that he will have to bear as "insupportable." But here, as on many other occasions, the Patriarch emphasizes also the unbroken link between Calvary and the Empty Tomb, for having said, "[I]n order to be co-crucified," he immediately adds, "[A]nd in order to perpetuate the Light of the Resurrection."[28]

What the Crucifixion means to Patriarch Bartholomew is evident from his meditation on the Way of the Cross, read by Pope John Paul II in Rome on Good Friday 1994. Here Bartholomew insists uncompromisingly on the total participation of God the Word incarnate in the full range of human suffering:

Human will of Jesus,
in solidarity with all our loneliness,
With our sorrows and our rejections . . .

In Christ, God experiences in a human way
all our agonies,
the immediate agonies of history,
the immense Job-like cry of our destinies.

Glory and praise to you, O Christ,
who become more completely one of us
than we ourselves could ever be . . .

Jesus, the Word made flesh,
has gone the farthest distance
that lost humanity is able to go.
My God, my God, why have you forsaken me? . . .

It is as if the crucified God, for a moment,
finds himself an atheist.[29]

Christ's sacrificial death on the Cross has a particular relevance for the fourth aspect of human personhood mentioned above, wholeness and ecological commitment. There can be no truly theological ecology that does not involve cross bearing. This was the theme in particular of Bartholomew's address at the close of the fourth international and interreligious symposium on the Adriatic Sea (Venice, June 10, 2002), when he spoke of sacrifice as the "missing dimension" in the present-day ecological program. "The Cross is our guiding symbol in the supreme sacrifice to which we are all called," he said. *"Without the Cross, without sacrifice, there can be no blessing and no cosmic transfiguration."*[30]

A third deep foundation for Patriarch Bartholomew's doctrine of personhood is his understanding of the "mysteries" or sacraments of the Church. Even if in the present volume he does write in detail about baptism and the Eucharist, he makes it clear at the end of Chapter 5 that these and the other "mysteries" express specifically the relational character of our personhood, its meaning as encounter and communion. The sacraments, furthermore, as matter transfigured by the Spirit, restore our wholeness and "intimacy" with the natural world. Any ecological theology, if it is to be genuinely Christian, has inevitably to be a sacramental theology.

Finally, if we are to share in the co-inherence of the Trinity, if we are to enter into the meaning of Christ's Cross and Resurrection, and if we are to live the sacramental life, this can only be through inner prayer. This is the fourth deep foundation. Here the Patriarch stresses the normative value of monastic spirituality for the vocation of every Christian. He draws attention to the immense contribution made to the Orthodox Church as a whole by Mount Athos, the chief center of Eastern Christian monasticism since the tenth century. There were tensions between the Patriarch and the Athonite monks around 1994–95 regarding the internal autonomy of Athos vis-à-vis the Patriarchate. But these disagreements do not in any way signify that Bartholomew undervalues the high ideals that Athonite monasticism embodies. On the contrary, he goes so far as to call Mount Athos "the spiritual heart of the Ecumenical Throne."

Bartholomew appeals in particular to the great collection of

Orthodox ascetic and mystical texts edited on the Holy Mountain under the title *The Philokalia*, meaning "Love of Beauty." He draws attention to the central "Philokalic" theme, the notion of *hesychia*, of silence or stillness. This is to be construed not in negative terms as a pause between words, as the cessation of speech, but affirmatively as an attitude of waiting upon God and *listening* to the Spirit. It is not an absence but a Presence. Thus "silence," like "prayer," is basically a "relationship" word. Here, as so often, the Patriarch is thinking in terms of encounter and communion. Equally the heart, a key concept in Orthodox ascetic theology, is understood by the Patriarch in a relational perspective: it is "the place where God, humanity, and world coincide in a harmonious . . . relationship." This is the best definition of the heart that I have ever come across!

"I NEVER DESPAIR"

In the course of this book Patriarch Bartholomew has sharp and challenging things to say, especially about the misuse of the environment and the injustice in our world. Yet at the same time he is definitely a prophet of hope, not of doom. It is hope that forms the theme of his Epilogue: "Hope is essential for life . . . And there is always hope." He is not afraid to call himself an optimist: "I never despair. I am always optimistic that a solution will be found."[31] He ends his discussion of ecology in Chapter 6 on a similarly sanguine note: "Curiously, I have never been overwhelmed by the ecological problems of our time. We are indeed facing an environmental crisis . . . Nevertheless, I have always considered in an optimistic way the fundamental goodness and positive intention of humanity."

Inspired by this hopefulness, the Patriarch does not speak with passive resignation, but consistently urges the need for action. "We cannot remain idle," he insists.[32] In the Common Declaration on

Environmental Ethics that he signed with the Pope at the conclusion of the 2002 Adriatic symposium, the two of them affirm: "God has not abandoned the world . . . It is not too late."[33] Patriarch Bartholomew looks to the future not with dejection but with expectation, and in this he is an example to all of us. It is no coincidence that in the last sentence of this book, he chooses to speak of "a new dawn . . . for the sake of our future generations."

+ KALLISTOS [WARE] OF DIOKLEIA

OXFORD, U.K.

ECUMENICAL PATRIARCH BARTHOLOMEW

BIOGRAPHICAL NOTE

I am but . . . a servant on a mission.

—SAINT BARSANUPHIUS OF GAZA (SIXTH CENTURY)

The current Ecumenical Patriarch, Bartholomew, was born and baptized Demetrios Archondonis on February 29, 1940, on the small island of Imvros (today known as Gökçeada) off the coast of Turkey. On the day of his election, October 22, 1991, he became 270th archbishop of the two-thousand-year-old Church founded by Saint Andrew, serving as Archbishop of Constantinople, New Rome, and Ecumenical Patriarch. Since then, His All Holiness Bartholomew presides among all Orthodox Primates as the spiritual leader of 300 million faithful. From his childhood years through his ecclesiastical tenure, Patriarch Bartholomew has exhibited a combination of authority and vulnerability alike.

The son of Christos Archondonis, the local café proprietor, who sometimes also served as a barber, the young Demetrios grew up in the humble village of Saints Theodores on the small mountainous Aegean island.[1] Christos and Merope had four children: the eldest was a girl; Demetrios was the second of three boys. His father was strict; his mother was gentle. Demetrios worked in the café during his summer vacations, acquiring social skills in the village center, where people gathered to chat, drink coffee, and click their worry beads as they discussed politics and the destiny of the world.

At the time, some eight thousand Orthodox Christians lived on Imvros. Today, although life has become peaceful once again, few inhabitants remain; much of the island's land has been confiscated; Greek schools have been closed; Saints Theodores is now called Village of the Olive Trees. The village chapel of St. George has been restored at the initiative of the present Patriarch, while the priest currently serving the chapel is the son of the Patriarch's former parish priest Father Asterios. Demetrios's family used to own some property with a small chapel dedicated to Saint Marina. To this day, an icon of the saint in his bedroom reminds Patriarch Bartholomew of his childhood years; he also preserves some soil taken from that chapel, which his family would tend.

EARLY YEARS AND EDUCATION

The young Demetrios was blessed with a spiritual father, the village pastor, Father Asterios, who called on him to assist in the altar both in the village at the central church dedicated to Saint George and whenever he traveled to the numerous remote, tiny white chapels that adorn the island's countryside. Father Asterios would walk for miles along narrow paths, through snow and rain, accompanied by a donkey carrying the young Demetrios and the sacred vessels for the services. Although no one was present but the two of them, Father Asterios would look at his pocket watch and ring the bell when it was time to start the service with Demetrios. Father Asterios was a faithful, elderly man with no formal education beyond the primary level; he would repeatedly make basic errors in reading the prayers and psalms. Yet Demetrios was early inspired by the Orthodox Church's liturgy and ritual as well as its spiritual practices and traditions. Father Asterios gave Demetrios the fabric for his first vestment as a deacon.

The then Church head of Imvros and Tenedos was Metropolitan Meliton (1913–89), a highly gifted and influential bishop in the hierarchy of Constantinople, who would surely have succeeded Patriarch Athenagoras (1886–1972) to the Ecumenical Throne had his name not been removed from the list of eligible candidates by the Turkish authorities.[2] Early recognizing the diverse talents of the future Patriarch, Meliton took Demetrios under his wing, supporting and directing him throughout his primary, secondary, and tertiary education, often at his own expense.

THE PATRIARCHAL THEOLOGICAL SCHOOL OF HALKI

After completing elementary studies in his native village of Saints Theodores, Demetrios traveled to the city of Constantinople (today, Istanbul, Turkey), where he attended the junior high school of the Zographeion Lyceum. He returned to Imvros for the first years of his secondary education, daily walking five kilometers each way to the closest town of Panagia. Some of his early essays and favorite poems, preserved in the original manuscript exercise books, have recently been published in Greece.[3] His senior secondary education and seminary formation took place at the prestigious Patriarchal Theological School of Halki, an island with two pine-covered hills among the "islands of the princes" on the Sea of Marmara.[4] In close proximity to Istanbul, which offers regular ferry service, Halki is a quaint island with no cars; people travel on foot or by carriage. There, numerous leaders of the (especially, but not only) Greek-speaking Orthodox world have been trained. There, also, aristocratic Greek families from Istanbul vacationed. The function of Halki has been diminished both as a secondary school and as a graduate seminary since the late 1950s, and it was officially closed by Turkish authorities in the early 1970s. The magnificent nineteenth-century building

contains a library of forty thousand books and historical manu-
scripts, classrooms filled with old wooden desks, and spacious reception and dormitory rooms. It is Bartholomew's dream and desire to
reopen the Patriarchal Theological School. He persistently underlines the 1923 Treaty of Lausanne and Turkey's obligation both to
recognize the legal status of the Patriarchate as being ecumenical in
scope and nature and to respect its right to educate its clergy and
leaders.[5]

POSTGRADUATE STUDIES AND TRAVELS

After completing his undergraduate studies at the Patriarchal Theological School of Halki in 1961, Bartholomew served as a reserve of-
ficer in the Turkish military in Gallipoli from 1961 to 1963. He was
ordained to the diaconate in 1961 and to the priesthood in 1969. It
was at the time of his ordination to the diaconate that Demetrios received the monastic name Bartholomew, in honor of an Imvrian
monk who had lived on Mount Athos and edited liturgical texts. Patriarch Bartholomew still recalls how his ordination was the fulfillment of all his dreams. The ordination to the diaconate was held at
the Cathedral of Imvros.

Between ordinations, he pursued graduate studies at the Pontif-
ical Oriental Institute, which is attached to the Gregorian University
in Rome. The institute was founded in 1917 by Benedict XV in the
hope that Roman Catholic and Orthodox students would study together. In Rome, Bartholomew mastered Italian, Latin, and French.
He was also exposed to the theology of Jean Daniélou (1905–74),
Henri de Lubac (1896–1991), and Yves Congar (1904–95). Moreover,
Bartholomew was in Rome during the sessions of the Second Vatican General Council (1962–65), the first time in centuries that any
Orthodox representative was present at a council of such magni-

tude. In Rome, Bartholomew completed his doctoral dissertation, *The Codification of the Holy Canons and the Canonical Constitution of the Orthodox Church*, subsequently published in 1970 by the Patriarchal Institute for Patristic Studies in Thessaloníki, Greece. Bartholomew later became a founding member of the Society of Canon Law of the Oriental Churches, serving also as its vice president for multiple terms.

After his studies in Rome, Bartholomew was sent on scholarship by Patriarch Athenagoras to the Ecumenical Institute in Bossey, Switzerland, an academic center affiliated with the World Council of Churches and directed at the time by the progressive Greek Orthodox theologian Professor Nikos Nissiotis (1925–86), who was also professor of the philosophy and psychology of religion at the University of Athens. Under Nissiotis, Bartholomew was introduced to the contemporary philosophy of existentialism and personalism, as well as to the understanding of theology in light of the mystery of the Holy Spirit. Finally, at the University of Munich, Bartholomew was able to learn German and be initiated into the writings of such theologians as Karl Rahner (1904–84) and the current Pope, Joseph Ratzinger (now Benedict XVI).

RETURN TO CONSTANTINOPLE

During this period of his life, Bartholomew became well acquainted and worked closely with Patriarch Athenagoras, the renowned and charismatic leader of the Orthodox Church at the time, who later promoted Bartholomew to the rank of archimandrite. Upon completion of his studies, Bartholomew returned to Constantinople in 1968, where he served as assistant dean at the Patriarchal Theological School of Halki until 1972. Patriarch Athenagoras died in 1972, whereupon Bartholomew served as personal secretary to his successor, Patriarch Demetrios (1914–91), whose side he never left. Bartholomew was elected Metropolitan of Philadelphia on Christmas Day 1973 and retained his position as director of the Private Patriarchal Office until 1990.

As personal and administrative assistant to the Ecumenical Patriarch, Bartholomew was largely responsible for many of the initiatives undertaken by the late Patriarch Demetrios. These included a commitment to ecumenical relations through bilateral dialogues, such as the theological dialogue between the Roman Catholic and the Orthodox churches, which officially opened in 1980. This "dialogue of truth" complemented and completed the "dialogue of love" previously initiated by Patriarch Athenagoras together with Popes John XXIII (1881–1963) and Paul VI (1897–1978). To date, this dialogue has produced three significant statements on the sacramental understanding of the Church (1982), on faith sacraments, and the unity of the Church (1987), and on the ordained ministry (1988); it also attempted to deal with the thorny problem of Uniatism (1993). After a hiatus, the dialogue resumed its commitment and work in 2006.

Moreover, through the inspiration and collaboration of Bartholomew, Patriarch Demetrios continued preparations for a forthcoming Great and Holy Council by convening three significant Pan-Orthodox conferences at the Orthodox Center of the Ecumenical Patriarchate in Chambésy, Switzerland. Finally, in 1989, the Ecumenical Patriarchate initiated its worldwide efforts for the protection of the natural environment with the publication of an encyclical letter to all Orthodox churches, establishing September 1—the first day of the ecclesiastical calendar—as a day of prayer for God's creation.

In 1990, Bartholomew (then Metropolitan of Philadelphia) was elected Metropolitan of Chalcedon, serving at a young age as the senior metropolitan on the Holy Synod and representing the

Ecumenical Patriarchate on the highest levels at various commissions of interchurch and interreligious relations, accompanying Patriarch Demetrios on numerous visits to Orthodox churches and nations, while also effecting official visits to the Pope of Rome, the Archbishop of Canterbury, and the World Council of Churches; in the latter, Bartholomew served as member of the Faith and Order Commission, as well as elected member of the executive and central committees.

ECUMENICAL PATRIARCH BARTHOLOMEW

When Patriarch Demetrios died in 1991, Bartholomew was unanimously elected and enthusiastically received as the Ecumenical Patriarch at the tender age of fifty-one. He was solemnly enthroned on November 2, 1991. From the outset, Patriarch Bartholomew has been profoundly conscious of his commitment to the ancient See that he has inherited as its Primate, as well as of the vision that shapes and directs his ministry. He serves at once as a son and a father of the Church, obligated simultaneously to adhere to and to advance its living tradition. He is a servant of the Church while at the same time being defined by his mission; in the words of Saint Barsanuphius the Great (d. 543), he is "but . . . a servant on a mission."[6]

His tenure has been characterized by inter-Orthodox cooperation, by inter-Christian and interreligious dialogue, as well as by formal trips to other Orthodox countries seldom previously visited. He has exchanged official visitations and accepted numerous invitations with ecclesiastical and state dignitaries. In his home city of Constantinople, Patriarch Bartholomew has restored all of the existing churches, monasteries, pilgrim sites, and charitable centers, which had formerly been either abandoned or dilapidated.

Patriarch Bartholomew is as comfortable preaching about the spiritual legacy of the Orthodox Church as he is promoting sociopolitical issues of his immediate cultural environment and praying for respect toward Islam or for global peace. He has traveled more widely than any other Orthodox Patriarch in history; he has also conducted liturgical services in historically significant places in Asia Minor, such as Cappadocia and Pergamon, where acts of worship would have been unthinkable even twenty-five years ago. He has also received sympathetic, albeit sometimes controversial, attention in the Turkish media and been invited to offer public lectures in Turkish on Christian-Muslim relations.

ECUMENICAL MISSION

As a citizen of Turkey, Bartholomew has acquired, through personal experience, a unique perspective on religious tolerance and interfaith dialogue. He has worked for reconciliation among Christian churches (through the World Council of Churches and significant bilateral dialogues) and has an international reputation for environmental awareness and protection.[7] He has worked to advance reconciliation among Catholic, Muslim, and Orthodox communities, such as in the former Yugoslavia, and is supportive of peace-building measures to defuse global conflict in the Balkans and ecclesiastical politics in Ukraine. He has also presided over the restoration of the Autocephalous Church of Albania and the Autonomous Church of Estonia, proving a constant source of spiritual and moral support to those traditionally Orthodox countries emerging from decades of wide-scale religious persecution behind the Iron Curtain.

The Ecumenical Patriarch's role as the primary spiritual leader of the Orthodox Christian world and transnational figure of global significance continues to grow increasingly vital. Patriarch

Bartholomew has co-sponsored international peace conferences, as well as meetings on the subjects of racism and fundamentalism, bringing together Christians, Muslims, and Jews for the purpose of generating greater cooperation and mutual understanding. He has been invited to address the European Parliament, UNESCO, and the World Economic Forum, as well as numerous national parliaments. His efforts to promote religious freedom and human rights, his initiatives to advance religious tolerance and mutual respect among the world's religions, and his work toward international peace and environmental protection earned him the Congressional Gold Medal of the U.S. Congress in 1997, during his first official visit to the United States. On the occasion of a dinner hosted at the White House, President Bill Clinton praised the Patriarch "as a great world leader who can inspire every American."

His initiatives for reconciliation include his efforts to raise environmental awareness throughout the world. He has organized annual educational seminars and institutes on the island of Halki (1994–98), which were co-sponsored by His Royal Highness Prince Philip of Edinburgh, as well as biennial international, interreligious, and interdisciplinary symposia (1995 to date) in the Mediterranean Sea, the Black Sea, the Danube River, the Adriatic Sea, the Baltic Sea, the Amazon River, and, most recently, the Arctic Ocean. These endeavors have earned Bartholomew the title "Green Patriarch" and several significant environmental prizes.

Ecumenical Patriarch Bartholomew holds numerous honorary doctorates, from institutions such as Athens and Thessaloníki (in Greece), Georgetown and Yale (in the United States), Flinders and Manila (in Australasia), London, Edinburgh, and Leuven, as well as Moscow and Bucharest (in Europe). Besides his native Greek and Turkish, he is fluent in English, Italian, German, French, and classical Greek and Latin.

THE PATRIARCH AS BRIDGE BUILDER

"To build a bridge between the East and West has long been a major concern for His All-Holiness," noted Dr. Joël Delobel of the Catholic University of Leuven, Belgium, in conferring an honorary doctorate on Patriarch Bartholomew in 1996. "The Patriarch's entire life has been one of preparation for the task of bridge builder."

The first of these bridges is one that reaches out to the various Orthodox churches . . . The second bridge is one which reaches out to Europe, a bridge which has been created from the Patriarch's vigorous pleas for the extension of the European Union to the East and the Southeast of Europe. In the midst of current hesitation concerning the future of the Union, his unremitting plea for a complete Union and his concern for the protection of the environment are guiding lights for both East and West. The third bridge is one that will facilitate the dialogue between all the Christian churches.

It is all the more important, then, that a church leader such as Patriarch Bartholomew travel all over the world to encourage mutual understanding, to face the problems and create solutions. There is no other way. Such bridge builders are desperately needed.

As early as 1993, Patriarch Bartholomew intensified his wide-ranging outreach to the non-Orthodox world by traveling to Brussels in order to meet with the president of the European Commission, Jacques Delors, making such a powerful and positive impression that he was invited to address a plenary session of the European Parliament the following year. In 1994, Patriarch Bartholomew also joined with the Appeal of Conscience Foundation to organize the international Conference on Peace and Tolerance held in Istanbul. The conference assembled Christians, Jews, and Muslims in an effort to reduce the friction between the various faiths and diminish the hostility that often results.

In 1995, during a visit to the Holy Land, Patriarch Bartholomew met not only with the Orthodox Patriarch of Jerusalem but also with the Israeli prime minister, Yitzhak Rabin, and the PLO chairman, Yasser Arafat. Later that same year, in addition to formal visits throughout the world in order to meet leaders and faithful in his own pastoral jurisdiction, he traveled to Norway to celebrate the one thousandth anniversary of Christianity in that country, to Paris to meet with President Jacques Chirac, to Lourdes to address a conference of Roman Catholic prelates, and to Japan and England to attend international summit conferences on the environment. These visits not only indicate the busy schedule of the Ecumenical Patriarch but also reflect the inner soul of an open-minded leader.

In 2003 the Patriarch continued his program of visits to Orthodox communities around the globe, and held the fifth of a series of meetings as part of a dialogue he helped initiate several years earlier between Orthodox Christians and Jews. The following year he made a bold effort to build a bridge to a corner of the world most hostile to religion, namely Cuba. Fidel Castro, whose government rebuilt a church belonging to the island's small Orthodox community as a gesture of respect for the Patriarch, personally welcomed the religious leader and praised him for his efforts to promote international understanding and environmental protection.

In early 2006 the Ecumenical Patriarch again visited the United States, where, after celebrating the Feast of the Epiphany (January 6) with Orthodox Christians, he flew to New Orleans in order to witness the destruction of Hurricane Katrina and comfort victims of the natural disaster. A photograph on the front page of the *New York Times* pictured him walking through the wreckage of the city.

Throughout his ministry, Patriarch Bartholomew has focused on the people most in need and on the most difficult issues facing humanity. His tireless efforts on behalf of religious freedom, human rights, and protection of the natural environment have justly earned him a special place among the world's global leaders and foremost apostles of love, peace, and reconciliation.

THE PATRIARCH AS PEACEMAKER

As mentioned, one of his favorite catchphrases has been: "War in the name of religion is war against religion."[8] The Patriarch has firsthand experience of suffering; he knows what it is like to be under constant siege, taunted by extremists who regularly demonstrate outside the walls of the Patriarchate, calling for its ouster from Turkey. His see, established in the fourth century and once boasting treasures as vast as the Vatican, has been reduced to a small, abandoned enclave in a decaying corner of Istanbul called "the Lighthouse" (or *Phanar*). Almost all of its property has been seized by Turkish governments over the twentieth century; its schools and churches have been either closed or else denied restoration. The Turkish government as a whole follows a policy that vehemently refuses to recognize his ancient ecumenical status as the spiritual leader of a major religious faith, stubbornly insisting he is only the head of the small Greek Orthodox community of Istanbul.

Yet none of the abuse that Ecumenical Patriarch Bartholomew has either experienced or witnessed has lessened his compassion and support for the Turkish people and his determination to serve as a bridge between Turkey and Europe. For instance, he has supported all international efforts to strengthen Turkey's economy and

democracy, to the point of inviting severe criticism from Greek con-
servatives. He has proved a fervant advocate of Turkey's efforts to
join the European Union, traveling widely throughout Europe to
speak out in favor of its admission. "The incorporation of Turkey
into the European Union," he has stated before Europeans in several
capitals, "may well provide a concrete example and powerful symbol of mutually beneficial cooperation between the Western and Islamic worlds, putting an end to talk of a clash of civilizations" (245).
The unqualified support of such an eminent and prominent Christian leader has substantially mitigated the opposition of many
skeptics in Europe who question the wisdom of admitting a
predominantly Muslim country of seventy million into the European Union, which opened negotiations with Turkey at the end of
2004.

At a time when hostility and misunderstanding between the
Christian West and the Muslim world have reached a dangerous impasse, Patriarch Bartholomew is initiating deliberate efforts to reach
out to Muslims throughout the Middle East. He is firmly convinced
that Orthodox Christianity has a unique vocation and special responsibility to assist in the process of rapprochement between East
and West. For, like the Turkish Republic, the Ecumenical Patriarchate is situated amid two continents, Europe and Asia, with a foot
in both worlds.

Moreover, grounding his efforts on a 550-year history of coexistence with Muslims in the Middle East, Patriarch Bartholomew has
organized a series of bilateral conversations and theological discussions with Muslim leaders throughout the region in what he calls "a
dialogue of loving truth." Indeed, in order to strengthen that dialogue, he has traveled extensively to Libya, Syria, Egypt, Iran, Jordan, Azerbaijan, Qatar, Kazakhstan, and Bahrain and met with
political and religious figures in those countries, which no other
Christian head-of-church has ever visited. As a result, the Patriarch

has earned greater credibility and achieved greater opportunity to create bridges between Christianity and Islam than any other prominent Christian leader.

Patriarch Bartholomew has focused the international respect he has gained both in the West as well as in the Muslim world on the creation of a joint forum among religious leaders against the use of violence and the threat of terrorism. Thus, during a conference that he organized in Brussels in the aftermath of September 11, together with the President of the European Commission, Romano Prodi, he addressed strong words to the attendees about religious extremists and terrorists, noting to *Time* magazine that "they may be the most wicked false prophets of all. When they bomb, shoot, and destroy, they steal more than life itself; they undermine faith, and faith is the only way to break the cycle of hatred and retribution." The Patriarch played a key role there in forging the Brussels Declaration that affirmed, echoing the Berne Declaration of 1992: "War in the name of religion is war against religion."

Over the past fifteen years, Ecumenical Patriarch Bartholomew has boldly addressed and assumed leadership on the most difficult issues facing the world—the increasingly deep mistrust between East and West, the ongoing ecological destruction of the natural environment, and the sharp divisions that characterize the major religious faiths and Christian confessions. Speaking from a tradition of centuries-long martyrdom and from the contemporary experience of persecution, the difficulty of the issues he grapples with does not daunt him. Instead, he remains determined to persevere and make a difference, recognizing that the journey toward unity and the struggle for unity define the supreme calling of a religious leader.

VISION OF A PATRIARCH

From the moment of his enthronement, Patriarch Bartholomew recognized that his tenure was part of a long line of historical figures. He is well aware that he sits on a throne honored in the past by such sacred personalities as Saint Gregory the Theologian (fourth century), Saint John Chrysostom (fourth century), John the Faster (sixth century), Photius the Great (ninth century), Philotheos Kokkinos (fourteenth century), Gennadios Scholarios (fifteenth century), Gregory V (nineteenth century), and Joachim III (twentieth century). Although the Patriarchal Throne was vacant for very brief periods of turmoil in 980–84, 1241–44, 1451–53, and 1918–21, Patriarch Bartholomew senses how integrally connected the past is with the present. "This church," he likes to say, "is diachronic; it extends to the ages."

From the moment, and indeed from the very address, of his enthronement, Patriarch Bartholomew outlined the dimensions of his leadership and vision within the Orthodox Church: vigilant education in matters of theology, liturgy, and spirituality; the strengthening of Orthodox unity and cooperation; the continuation of ecumenical engagements with other Christian churches and confessions; the intensification of interreligious dialogue for peaceful coexistence; and the initiation of discussion and action for the protection of the environment against ecological pollution and destruction.

Perhaps no other church leader in history has emphasized ecumenical dialogue and communication as a primary intention of his tenure. Certainly no other church leader in history has ever brought environmental issues to the foreground, indeed to the very center of personal and ecclesiastical attention. Patriarch Bartholomew has long placed the environment at the head of his Church's agenda, developing ecological programs, chairing Pan-Orthodox gatherings, organizing educational seminars, and initiating unique seaborne environmental symposia throughout the world over the last two decades.

To initiate readers into the world of the Orthodox Church, and particularly of the Ecumenical Patriarchate, I have selected passages from an unpublished address of the Patriarch:

The Ecumenical Patriarchate, over which our Modesty presides, is an institution with a history of sixteen centuries, during which it retained its See in Constantinople. It constitutes *par excellence* the center of all the local Orthodox churches. It heads these not by administering them, but by virtue of the primacy of its ministry of Pan-Orthodox unity and the coordination of the activity of all of Orthodoxy. Orthodox Christians on four continents, excluding Africa, that do not fall under the jurisdiction of autocephalous churches fall under the direct jurisdiction of the Ecumenical Patriarchate. The most important of these autocephalous churches are: the Patriarchates of Alexandria, Antioch, Jerusalem, Moscow, Serbia, Romania, Bulgaria, Georgia, and the Autocephalous Churches of Cyprus, Greece, Poland, Albania, and certain others. Consequently, the Orthodox churches of Europe, America, and the rest of Asia and Australia, which are not under the jurisdiction of the aforementioned autocephalous churches, fall under the Ecumenical Patriarchate.

The function of the Ecumenical Patriarchate in the life of the entire Orthodox Church emanates from its centuries-old ministry in the witness, protection, and spread of the Orthodox faith. The Ecumenical Patriarchate has a supranational and supra-regional character. From the lofty consciousness of this fact, but also from a sense of its spiritual responsibility for the development of the faith in Christ of all people, regardless of race and language, and especially in the context of the selfsame linguistic and other presuppositions were born the new regional churches of the East, from Caspia to the Baltics, and from the Balkans to Central Europe, where its missionary activity was extended. This activity already extends to the Far East, America, and Australia, where conditions allow, with absolute respect for the freedom of religious consciousness of all and without resorting to methods of proselytizing. Essentially, wherever there are Orthodox Christian immigrants or natives, a church is established and it constitutes a magnet only for those who come freely.

The Orthodox Church is distinguished from other Christian churches in that it has preserved unadulterated the first and most ancient ecclesiastical tradition and teaching, has avoided innovations and personal interpretations of the Holy Scriptures and dogmas of the faith, and is administered according to the ancient synodical system under local bishops in collaboration with the faithful and successive groups of both local and broader episcopal synods, of which the highest is the Ecumenical Synod, that of the Orthodox worldwide. The basic administrative canons, the details of which are regulated according to local needs, have been determined by the seven ecumenical synods. The Church is not managed by regional states in which it resides, although it collaborates in good works when asked to do so.

Within the entire Orthodox Church there is absolute cooperation in goodwill and mutual respect. Perchance minor human problems are addressed successfully through the application of the evangelical spirit. Furthermore, the Ecumenical Patriarchate coordinates ongoing dialogues between Orthodox and heterodox churches, many of which are evolving with propitious prospects while others move at a slower pace. The objective of these dialogues is the removal of obstacles to the union of all the divided churches.

As becomes clear from the above, all Orthodox feel that they are constituents of one essentially spiritual community. "When one member suffers, so do all." They feel that they commune in the suffering of their fellow Christians and participate in their joys. Only if one perceives the catholicity of union can one understand the expressions of the Orthodox, which refer to the suffering of the other Orthodox and of the whole world as if they were their own.[9]

PORTRAIT OF A PATRIARCH

It takes a mystic and poet to describe the Patriarch as a person. The following excerpts are reprinted, with the publisher's permission, from Olivier Clément's *Conversations with Ecumenical Patriarch Bartholomew I*:

As a person, the Patriarch is full of contrasts, complementary facets of a strong personality. He is frail, willful, kind and discreet on the one hand, active and enterprising on the other. Unassuming, almost timid, yet, when necessary, he can be domineering. He reveals a sharp sense of humor, but with a sober and determined sense of his mission. He is rigorous, attentive to detail, yet wisely visionary.

He is of medium height, with a clear face remarkable for its fine features, and particularly for the piercing blue eyes behind large glasses. Simultaneously young and old, he unites the modern culture which glorifies youth with a traditional culture whose ideal was the "noble old man." As patriarch, he grew a convincing, almost white beard. His hair has turned white—he must have been blond, or auburn, one cannot now say. His face is now crowned with white. What is striking is an extreme refinement—physical, as well as moral—such that, despite the kindness of the eyes and of the smile, one feels rather dull and awkward in his presence.

He loves art, poetry and nature. Whenever possible, he takes refuge on Halki, in refreshing solitude, to reflect and to work in peace. He detests ritualism, preferring brief and meaningful celebrations. He appreciates the virile sobriety of Byzantine music . . .

He loves children and knows how to speak with them, to amuse them, to offer them sweets or small change. "They preserve something of paradise," he says . . .

He works hard—in fact he is an indefatigable worker. He has an exceedingly strong sense of responsibility for Orthodoxy in the world of today and tomorrow. The unwieldiness and divisions of the Orthodox Church weigh heavily in his heart . . . He knows also that it is necessary to respect the entire human being, and therefore also the earth which humanity represents and to which it can communicate God's grace. These, he affirms, are the criteria for evaluating life and Christian conduct in the world, both for individuals and for churches.

Orthodoxy is a witness soiled by history, but nevertheless a witness of the undivided Church, a call to the undivided Church, both one and diverse, in the image of the Trinity.

The task is immense and, as he well knows, it is not without risk. Bartholomew stands "between glory and the abyss," a friend who admires him whispers . . . More exactly, he stands between the Cross and Resurrection.[10]

A LIFE IN THE DAY OF A PATRIARCH

Patriarch Bartholomew will often honor individuals with an invitation to accompany him on official visits overseas, or to diverse conferences and events that he is invited to attend. At other times, the Patriarch will invite visitors to his office, in response to requests for interviews or articles. The late Patriarch Athenagoras is said to have symbolically locked the problems of the day in a small drawer on his desk each night as he prepared for the evening Compline service prior to sleeping. Patriarch Bartholomew seems to lock them in his heart, caring for and responding to them in touching ways throughout the day and night. One of the icons in his office portrays Saint Hypomone (or "Patience"), a martyr of the early Church.

Nevertheless, one of the most moving experiences for me was spending a day simply observing him at work in the Phanar. I was there on official business, routinely assisting in the preparation of several texts for the Church through research in the archives. The Patriarch was in fact entirely unaware that I was also observing him for purposes of preparing this biographical description. What follows, then, is a spontaneous sketch of his program on that rainy winter day in January 2005.

It was a typical schedule for the hardworking Patriarch: nothing unusual; nothing extraordinary; nothing extreme; nothing "staged." Yet what became increasingly evident was the way in which the global is intimately connected to the local, the modest way in which the universal is vividly reflected in the parochial, and the way in which the ecumenical is unmistakably related to the pastoral in the ministry of Ecumenical Patriarch Bartholomew. This was how the day's events unfolded:

- The Patriarch attended morning services and the Divine Liturgy at the Patriarchal Cathedral of St. George. When in Constantinople, he is always present for morning prayers at 8:00.

- The Liturgy was followed by a reception of a group of visitors, students from the Balkans, whom the Patriarch formally addressed in the Hall of the Throne. Each of them wanted to greet him personally as he or she was introduced.

- The Patriarch then retired to his private office for deliberations and decisions, including visits by clergy and laity, as well as untold comings and goings by Patriarchal staff and secretaries for the dictation, preparation, revision, and signing of letters. The Patriarch personally reads every letter and text sent to, and prepared as a response by, his office. "It is the least," he says, "that my correspondents deserve."

- Lunch hardly allowed time for relaxation inasmuch as it, too, entailed visits by local bishops and one bishop from abroad, as well as certain lay dignitaries with appointments to speak with him. Some of these also later met with him privately.

- In the late afternoon, the Patriarch visited a home for the elderly, established and run by Roman Catholic Sisters of the Poor. After speaking with the nuns in French and English, the Patriarch spent most of his time addressing all of the residents, the greater majority of whom were Muslim, in Turkish. The residents are Turks, Armenians, Slavs, and Greeks. The resident Greeks always have personal requests to make: a message to be sent to a distant relative or a greeting to convey to a friend. That evening Patriarch Bartholomew was approached by an elderly woman who complained that she could not secure tickets to a local musical concert. The Patriarch asked for the cell phone of a bishop accompanying him in order to call another bishop, whom he asked to secure tickets and arrange for the elderly woman to be personally accompanied to the concert.

- On the way to his next appointment, the Patriarch stopped to pick up a journalist who had requested an interview on general Church-related matters as well as global issues, such as war and the environment, for a European publication.

• His next two stops were to an ill metropolitan, whom he regularly visits, and to a young, newly married Muslim employee of the Patriarchate celebrating his birthday. While the visits were brief, they were certainly not hurried.

• Whether at the offices of the Phanar (in the small chapel behind the administration) or in the privacy of his home, the Patriarch closes each day with evening prayer, or Compline.

At each of these scheduled appointments and visits, the Patriarch was generous with his time; none of the people at these appointments or visits received the impression that they were being hurried. How is it even possible for anyone to imagine the intensity of this daily routine, which did not include any programmed international conference, address to a political forum, or official visit to a foreign nation? Yet what is most impressive is not so much the ordinary business or daily schedule, which in itself is surely exceptional and extraordinary. Rather, it is the personal encounter with numerous individuals and the pastoral engagement with diverse groups that keep the Patriarch grounded in reality and even humility.

JOHN CHRYSSAVGIS

ENCOUNTERING THE MYSTERY

I.
HISTORICAL PERSPECTIVES

THE ORTHODOX CHURCH AND
THE ECUMENICAL PATRIARCHATE

*This is the faith of the Apostles; this faith has
established the universe.*

—SEVENTH ECUMENICAL COUNCIL (EIGHTH CENTURY)

I t will be helpful from the outset for readers to gain some insight into the world of the Orthodox Church with a general reflection on the history and teaching, as well as the spirituality and practice, of the Church through the centuries.[1] This will be followed by a brief survey of the history and role of the Ecumenical Patriarchate in order to present the broad scope and overall structure of the Church.

PROFILE OF THE ORTHODOX CHURCH

The Orthodox Church numbers some 300 million people worldwide. Geographically, its primary area of distribution lies along the coast of the (northeastern) Mediterranean, in Eastern and Northern Europe, and in the Middle East. Composed of several self-governing or Patriarchal churches, it constitutes a form of international federation within which each local church retains its independence while remaining committed to unity in faith and worship.

The Orthodox Church does not have a centralized authority or leadership, instead comprising a constellation of independent and equal national churches, among which the Ecumenical Patriarch is historically and traditionally honored as "first among equals." In this regard, the Ecumenical Patriarchate bears a primacy of honor and service; its authority lies not in administration but in coordination. Therefore, it serves as the primary focal point of unity, fostering consensus among the various Orthodox churches. In addition to the responsibility of facilitating Orthodoxy unity, the Ecumenical Patriarch has immediate jurisdiction over the Greek, Ukrainian, Carpatho-Russian, and Albanian Orthodox churches in the United States and Canada as well as all Greek Orthodox churches in Europe, South America, Australasia, and the areas of Greece freed from Turkish occupation after the Balkan wars, including Crete and Macedonia.

Although it is certainly of Eastern origin, the Orthodox Church nonetheless regards itself as the "one, holy, catholic and apostolic Church" and may be found today throughout the world, in countries such as America, Australia, Western Europe, Japan, and Asia.[2] It is defined not in relation or in contrast to Roman Catholicism or Protestantism, but rather as a seamless continuation and spiritual succession of the early Church of the Apostles, martyrs, confessors, monastics, great teachers, and saints.

The term "Orthodox" was first adopted in the early-fourth-century Christian Church by the Greek Fathers, namely by the great teachers and theologians of the early Church, in order to determine and distinguish the canonical faith from heterodox, or heretical, doctrines and deviations. Today, the term forms part of the official title of the Eastern Christian Church and those in communion with it. Also included in the title are certain other Eastern churches that were separated in the fifth century as a result of the Monophysite controversy, a theological dispute over the question of interpreting Christ's divine and human natures.

The title "Patriarch" is adopted for the head of various Orthodox churches. It was originally confined to the five ancient Churches of Rome, Constantinople, Alexandria, Antioch, and Jerusalem—the "Pentarchy," or five ruling churches, officially codified under the emperor Justinian (527–65). The title was later extended to the Metropolitan of Moscow in the sixteenth century, to the Archbishops of Serbia and Bulgaria in the early twentieth century, and to the head of the Romanian Church in the middle of the twentieth century.[3] The ancient Church of Georgia adopted the exceptional title "Catholicos" for their primate.

The hierarchy and administration of the Orthodox Church are based on the ancient orders of bishop, presbyter (or priest), and deacon. Each diocese has integrity as the full expression of the Church while maintaining full communion or unity of faith with every other diocese. Many people tend to think of the Church as a vast, worldwide institution. Nevertheless, the concept of universality, or catholicity, is understood as being expressed in the local community. This is a fundamental aspect of Orthodox theology and tradition, which recognize each local eucharistic gathering as related on the principle of identity and as reflecting the fullness of the Body of Christ.

Such is the general vision of the Church, or the overall structure of what is called ecclesiology. Within this vision, one may refer interchangeably to the "Orthodox Church" (collectively) as well as to the "Orthodox churches" (individually). For the Church is the "one Body of Christ," which comprises "many parts."

HISTORY OF THE ORTHODOX CHURCH

The Eastern Orthodox Church is characterized by its continuity with the apostolic tradition, adhering to the faith and practices defined by the ecumenical councils. However, the Orthodox Church is not only defined by this historical perspective. Like the god of antiquity Janus, the Orthodox Church looks both ways: backward toward the sources of the historical Church and forward—or upward—toward the heavenly kingdom. This is true not only historically, since Orthodoxy derives authority from the early Church Fathers and the lives of the saints in order to discern the spirits of the times in every age. It is also valid spiritually, inasmuch as Orthodoxy draws inspiration from the age to come in order to make sense of the present reality. The first aspect is summarized in the term "tradition." The second dimension is a worldview summarized in the word "eschatology."4

Therefore, in its very essence, Orthodoxy is a Church at once rooted in the past and looking toward the future. It is this dual nature that permits Orthodoxy to speak boldly about critical contemporary issues while at the same time firmly retaining its respect for doctrinal formulations and sacred practices of the early Church. It is, therefore, what we like to call a "living tradition." The vivid sense of continuity with the past and community with the future—with those who lived saintly lives on this earth, as well as with those who live in what is called the "Church triumphant"—shapes the way that Orthodox faithful think, feel, and live.

Moreover, the Orthodox Church has been deeply marked by a sense of *martyrdom* and suffering. Through the divine blood shed by Christ on the Cross, the Orthodox Church has learned that the very persecutions and troubles that beset the early Church became the seed for the growth of the Christian Church. Indeed, even in more recent centuries, especially in Asia Minor and in Russia, the story of the Orthodox Church has been marred by persecutions and divisions that have shaped the identity and defined the spirituality of the Orthodox themselves. Humility that results from suffering is a distinctively Orthodox virtue, which has accurately defined and profoundly shaped Orthodox theology and spirituality through the centuries.

Thus, anyone reading the history of the Orthodox Church must learn to appreciate and incorporate the darker moments within the more illumined moments and historical events. For instance, it is impossible to speak of the suffering of the early martyrs during the first three centuries without intimating the way in which "red martyrdom" gave way to a "white martyrdom" with the development of *monasticism* around the same period. Anthony of Egypt abandoned his ascetic discipline in the desert of Egypt to support his fellow Christian martyrs. Since he was not persecuted in Alexandria, he returned to his "inner desert," as he liked to call his more remote place of abode, and increased his ascetic labors—namely, the martyrdom of the spirit—as a way of substituting for the martyrdom of the flesh. The early monks lived on a daily basis as if they were prepared to die like the early martyrs; they are to be admired in their preparedness at all times to bear witness to the Word of God in their world.

Moreover, one cannot fully appreciate the way in which *theological doctrine* and *spiritual life* were perceived as two sides of the same coin by the early Christians, as well as by the Orthodox as their contemporary successors, unless one is able to appreciate the profound connection, intimate friendship, and mutual respect that developed between the likes of Anthony of Egypt (known as the "father of monasticism") and Athanasius of Alexandria (one of the early and staunch defenders of the orthodoxy of faith).

This is precisely why the Orthodox Church places such great

emphasis on the *accurate articulation of doctrinal formulations*. Not because this is how God is ultimately known or defined. For it is impossible either to comprehend or ever to contain the fullness of the divinity, whether in rational concepts or in written documents. Nevertheless, every word and every letter is critical inasmuch as it reflects the tested witness of a saint, even the blood of a martyr, who has experienced a glimpse of the divine energies. The seven great ecumenical councils, from the first held in 325 (at the time of Athanasius of Alexandria) through the seventh in 787 (in support of the veneration of sacred images),[5] are therefore careful to determine with meticulous precision the most appropriate words with which to describe the inexpressible and inexhaustible divine experience. It is no surprise, then, that Saint Athanasius of Alexandria was exiled five times for affirming the correctness of the term *homo-ousios* (or "of the same essence") rather than the term *homoi-ousios* (or "of similar essence") to describe the relationship between God the Father and God the Son in the Holy Trinity; one letter was a superfluous iota in the pursuit of theological precision. Thus, the eighth-century defender of sacred icons Saint John of Damascus (675–749) wrote:

We do not change the everlasting boundaries that our Fathers have set, but we keep the tradition, just as we have received it.[6]

For the Orthodox, it has always been crucial to preserve the invaluable treasure of the faith with care and respect, "neither adding anything, nor taking anything away."[7]

These discussions were by no means the monopoly of specialists; theology was never an esoteric or academic exercise. Ordinary Christians were all involved in theological debates: they would be divided on doctrinal issues; they would take sides in ecclesiastical controversies. Saint Gregory of Nyssa complained that, during the

Second Ecumenical Council (381), the city of Constantinople was alive with such unending discussions:

The whole city is full of it: the squares, the market places, the cross-roads, the alleyways; salesmen of old clothes, money changers, food sellers; they are all busy arguing. If you ask someone for change, he will philosophize about the begotten and the unbegotten nature of God; if you inquire about the price of bread, you are told by way of reply that the Father is greater than the Son; and if you ask the attendant whether your bath is ready, he will answer that the Son was made out of nothing.[8]

Throughout its history, the Orthodox Church is not only concerned with traditional consistency and purity; it also values the element of *historical continuity*. For example, in twentieth-century Istanbul (formerly Constantinople, and the See of the Ecumenical Patriarch), the Patriarchate is still known as "Rum Patrikhanesi" (namely, the Roman Patriarchate). Furthermore, the Greeks of the *polis* (namely, the capital "city" of the Byzantine Empire, as Constantinople is still known) continue to call themselves "Romaioi" or "Romioi" (namely, "Romans"). Behind these somewhat strange and seemingly anachronistic traditions, there lies a historical seed of great importance. Under the pressure of barbarian invasions, the Roman Empire in the West collapsed during the fifth century. As a result, the medieval society that eventually emerged there may well have retained certain links with, but at the same time fundamentally differed from, the immediate past. By contrast, however, the East knew no such sudden break in its history; there, the Roman Empire survived for over a thousand years until the middle of the fifteenth century. Despite numerous religious, economic, political, and social changes, as well as its tragic decline in size and resources, the Byzantine Empire remained—at least until the fall of Constantinople in

1453—essentially the same Roman Empire as that over which Augustus had ruled in the first century of the Christian era.

The period that ensued after the first millennium of undivided Christendom, often known as the "Byzantine era" proper (from the eleventh to the fifteenth centuries) or the "Church in captivity" (from the fifteenth to the nineteenth centuries), is marked by the progressively deteriorating relations between Eastern and Western churches, the rapid increase in missionary expansion, and a remarkable revival of theological writing, liturgical commentary, and spiritual experience.[9] Two efforts to heal the Great Schism between the Roman and the Orthodox churches, which occurred gradually over centuries but culminated especially in the middle of the eleventh century (1054), did not come to fruition: the Council of Lyons (1274) and the Council of Florence (1437–38). Moreover, the fourth Crusade left indelible scars in the memories of the Eastern Christians with regard to their Western brothers, especially after the fall of Antioch (1098) and Jerusalem (1100), together with the perverse and lawless sacking of Constantinople (1204).

Nevertheless, the same period is also characterized by the Christianization of the Slavs from the tenth century and the development of a rich spiritual teaching, based on the experience of the Hesychasts in the fourteenth century, whose theology was articulated in spiritual treatises by their spokesman Saint Gregory Palamas (1296–1359) and in liturgical treatises by Saint Nicholas Cabasilas (1322–90).[10] Even during the occupation of Byzantium by Islam from 1453 to 1821—a period of intense suffering and mere survival, as well as of unprecedented agony and anxiety for the Orthodox Church—the spiritual light of previous centuries was never completely lost. In the nineteenth century, for instance, an entire spiritual renewal was inspired by the writings of *The Philokalia*, with its emphasis on mystical "prayer of the heart." In addition, new national churches appeared and flourished in the Balkans and throughout Europe, although the Orthodox Church always insisted on refuting and condemning religious nationalism (or "ethnophyletism"). Finally, during the twentieth century, beyond a new wave of missionary activity throughout the world, especially in Africa and Asia, the Ecumenical Patriarchate insisted on fraternal collaboration among the various Orthodox churches and ecumenical conversation with other churches and religions.

THEOLOGY THROUGH THE CENTURIES

The Orthodox Church is characterized by a profound sense of continuity not only with the times but also with the teachings of the apostolic Church. With regard to its faith and practices, it adheres to the decisions of the first seven ecumenical councils. The word "Orthodox" signifies both "right believing" and "right worshipping," and so the Orthodox Church is recognized as the bearer of an uninterrupted living tradition of true faith lived out in worship.

In expressing its belief and worship, the Orthodox Church looks for consistency with Scripture and tradition. Indeed, the roots of the Church lie in Scripture and tradition, as these are manifested in the life of the Church and the early Fathers. However, external criteria of truth are not foremost; Orthodox Christianity seeks the living experience of truth accessible in the communion of saints, wherein the Mother of God, or Theotokos, holds a special place of honor. Venerated from the early cult of the martyrs, the saints in general are honored as witnesses to the fullness of the experience to which all baptized Christians are called and, as such, are considered intercessors for all Christians. In most Orthodox cultures, the faithful are baptized with the name of a saint, celebrating the feast day of that saint in the place of a birthday. In some Slavic Orthodox cultures, the entire family will honor a certain saint as its patron, passing this tradition on through generations.

For the Orthodox Church, the doctrine of the Holy Trinity—namely, the teaching about God as three distinct persons rather than as a monolithic deity—underlies all theology and spirituality. Salvation is always understood in personal terms; it implies personality and particularity. Yet salvation is also communal; it implies fellowship and sharing. It is on the teaching about the Holy Trinity, and not on any worldly concept of authority and power, that the entire conciliar and hierarchical structure of the Orthodox Church rests. Furthermore, the mystery of the Trinity is revealed in the supreme act of divine love expressed through the Incarnation of the Word of God that assumed flesh, embracing and healing all humanity, which is called to become deified by grace, as well as reconciling and sanctifying the entire creation, which is called to transfiguration by divine energy.

The members of the Church constitute the precious Body of Christ, within which the ultimate goal of the Christian life is participation in the deified humanity of Jesus Christ. Moreover, this salvation through participation is accomplished through the Holy Spirit in the sacramental life of the Church. The Orthodox Church experiences and expresses its theology in worship. This accounts for the survival of the Church in times of turmoil. It was this liturgical dimension of the Church that encouraged and educated Orthodox faithful during the four hundred years of Ottoman occupation of Byzantium (1453–1821), as well as more recently during persecutions in postrevolutionary Russia during the early to mid-twentieth century.

Orthodox worship and spirituality appeal to all the senses. Therefore, icons, or sacred images, reflect a sense of beauty and glory, providing perhaps the most striking and most widely appreciated aspect of the Orthodox Church. The distinctiveness and diversity of icons are the fruit of a long theological reflection unique to the Orthodox world. However, icons are honored and venerated; they are never idolized or worshipped. They are the faith depicted in color, simultaneously constituting part of the transfigured cosmos.[11] Since early Christian times, and particularly since the Seventh Ecumenical Council of 787, sacred icons have provided specific affirmation of the doctrine of divine Incarnation as well as general education in matters of faith. The end of a long controversy over icons in 843 is solemnly remembered each year on the first Sunday of Great Lent, also known as the Sunday of Orthodoxy.

Finally, the importance of apophatic (or negative) theology, underlining the mystery and transcendence of God even while affirming the divine presence and immanence, dictates a reluctance to define or pontificate on matters of ethical importance. The deeper conviction always is that truth can never be either objectivized or exhausted, while each human person is also uniquely created in the image of God, never able to be reduced to anything less than a mystery.

HISTORY OF THE ECUMENICAL PATRIARCHATE

The Church of Constantinople is traditionally regarded as being founded by Saint Andrew, the "first-called" of the Apostles and elder brother of Saint Peter. The first Bishop of Byzantium was Stachys (38–54), a disciple of the Apostle Andrew.

Following the establishment of Constantinople as the state capital of the Roman Empire in the early part of the fourth century,[12] a series of significant ecclesiastical events saw the status of the Bishop of New Rome, as the city was then called, rapidly elevated to its current position of esteem and privilege. In 330, the emperor

Constantine transferred the capital of the Roman Empire to Byzans (or Byzantium); the city was renamed Constantinople and New Rome, while its bishopric was elevated to an archbishopric. The Metropolitan of Heracleia, to whom Byzantium was formerly subject, now came under the jurisdiction of Constantinople and enjoyed the privileges of the latter's most senior See, followed by the dioceses of Ephesus and Caesarea.[13] The third canon of the Second Ecumenical Council held in Constantinople (381) conferred upon the bishop of this city second rank after the Bishop of Rome. Less than a century later, the twenty-eighth canon of the Fourth Ecumenical Council held in Chalcedon (451) offered Constantinople equal ranking to Rome and special responsibilities throughout the rest of the world, even expanding its jurisdiction to territories hitherto unclaimed.

As titles, "Ecumenical Patriarch" and "Ecumenical Patriarchate" date from the sixth century and belong exclusively to the Archbishop of Constantinople. Originally, the phrases signified the jurisdiction of the "bishop of the *oikoumene*"—or bishop, at least in theory, of the inhabited earth, but, in practice, of the Roman Empire. Thus, they do not imply any claim of jurisdiction in or over the Church of Rome. The two phrases were first adopted by Patriarch John IV (582–95), also known as Saint John the Faster, who recognized the wider pastoral responsibility of the Church of Constantinople and the supranational character of his church within the Byzantine commonwealth or federation of Orthodox churches.

The Great Schism of 1054—in fact, the culmination of a gradual estrangement over many centuries—resulted in formal separation between the churches of the East and the West, granting Constantinople sole authority and jurisdiction over the Orthodox churches throughout the world, as well as honorary primacy—serving as the "first among equals"—within the various autocephalous, or ecclesiastically independent, churches. Nevertheless, even after

1054, there continued to be many friendly contacts between Orthodoxy and Rome, indeed until the late seventeenth and early eighteenth centuries.

After the capture of Constantinople by the Latins during the
fourth Crusade (1204), the Ecumenical Patriarchate was temporarily transferred to Nicaea (1206), but the emperor Michael VIII
Palaeologos restored it to Constantinople when he recaptured the
city in 1261. When the city became the capital of the Ottoman Empire in 1453, the Ecumenical Patriarch (at the time, Gennadios II)
was recognized as Ethnarch of the Orthodox peoples, with increased authority over the Eastern patriarchates and the Balkan
churches, as well as farther afield.[14]

Following the Turkish conquest of Constantinople in 1453, the
influence of the Ecumenical Patriarchate diminished as most of its
property and churches, including the great Church of the Holy Wisdom built by Justinian in the sixth century, were seized and its leaders restricted. Nevertheless, it persevered and very soon reasserted
its reconciliatory role and spiritual impact on the world while sur-
viving within an often hostile environment. As the historian Sir
Steven Runciman liked to remark: "The great achievement of the
Patriarchate was that, in spite of humiliation and poverty and dis-
dain, the Orthodox Church endured and endures as a great spiritual
force."

From that time, the Ecumenical Patriarchate became a powerful
symbol of unity, rendering service and solidarity to the Eastern
churches. In difficult periods, the Ecumenical Patriarchate was con-
sulted for the resolution of problems. Frequently, especially during
periods of turmoil or persecution, patriarchs of other churches even
resided in Constantinople, which was the venue for meetings of the
Holy Synod that was chaired by the Ecumenical Patriarch.

The Ecumenical Patriarchate also sponsored missionary growth
through the centuries, the most notable of which was the conver-

sion of the Kievan Rus in the tenth century and the most recent of which was the missionary work in Southeast Asia in the last century. This pastoral role and missionary responsibility have earned the Ecumenical Patriarchate the reputation as the "golden beacon of Orthodoxy, preserving the unwaning brilliance of Christianity."

Currently, the Ecumenical Patriarchate is actively engaged in diverse ecclesiastical activities and ministries, some of which will be cited throughout this book. Furthermore, it has historically proved to be a dynamic leader in the ecumenical movement, fully participating in the World Council of Churches from its inception, as well as in local ecumenical bodies, instituting and chairing bilateral theological dialogues with non-Orthodox Christians as well as with other monotheistic faiths.

THE ROLE OF THE ECUMENICAL PATRIARCHATE

The Ecumenical Patriarchate is regarded as the highest See and holiest center of the Orthodox Christian Church throughout the world. It is an institution with a history spanning seventeen centuries, during which it retained its administrative offices in Constantinople. It constitutes the spiritual center of all the local or independent Orthodox churches, exercising its leadership among these not by administration but rather by virtue of its primacy in the ministry of Pan-Orthodox unity and the coordination of the activities within Orthodoxy as a whole. Raised in this atmosphere of openness and dialogue, particularly during the tenure of Patriarch Athenagoras, I learned from a tender age to breathe the air of the *oikoumene*, to recognize the breadth of theological discourse, and to embrace the universe of ecclesiastical reconciliation. In later years, I also learned to appreciate a similar connection between church and environment:

For us at the Ecumenical Patriarchate, the term ecumenical is more than a name: it is a worldview, and a way of life. The Lord intervenes and fills His creation with His divine presence in a continuous bond. Let us work together so that we may renew the harmony between heaven and earth, so that we may transform every detail and every element of life. Let us love one another. With love, let us share with others everything we know and especially that which is useful in order to educate godly persons so that they may sanctify God's creation for the glory of His holy name.[15]

The function of the Ecumenical Patriarchate as center *par excellence* of the life of the entire Orthodox world emanates from its centuries-old ministry in the witness, protection, and outreach of the Orthodox faith. This is precisely why the Ecumenical Patriarchate possesses a supranational and supra-regional character. From this lofty consciousness and responsibility for the people of Christ, regardless of race and language, were born the new regional churches of the East, from the Caspian to the Baltics, and from the Balkans to Central Europe. The breadth of this jurisdiction today extends to the Far East, to America, and to Australia.

Orthodox Christians on all continents that do not fall under the jurisdiction of the autocephalous (independent) or autonomous (semi-independent) churches fall under the direct jurisdiction of the Ecumenical Patriarchate. The most important of the autocephalous churches are the ancient Patriarchates of Alexandria, Antioch, and Jerusalem (as well as the ancient Archdiocese of Mount Sinai), the Patriarchates of Russia, Serbia, Romania, Bulgaria, and Georgia, and the churches of Cyprus, Greece, Poland, Albania, the Czech lands, and Slovakia. The autonomous churches include those of Finland and Estonia. Moreover, the Orthodox churches in Europe, America, Australia, and Britain, which do not lie within the jurisdiction of the aforementioned autocephalous churches, lie directly within the administrative responsibility of the Ecumenical Patriarchate. Nonetheless, all Orthodox churches feel that they are constituents of one essentially spiritual community, wherein "when one member suffers, so do all" (1 Cor. 12:26). It is a true sense of unity in diversity.

In order to provide a sketch of the immediate jurisdictional scope of the Ecumenical Patriarchate and offer readers an outline of its wide range of administrative responsibility, I here list the various churches that make up our administrative ecclesiastical responsibility:

- The Archdiocese of Constantinople (including the districts of Stavrodromion, Tataoula, the Bosphorus, Hypsomatheia, and the Phanar), together with the four Metropolitan Sees in Asia Minor, namely Chalcedon, Derkon, Imvros (with Tenedos), and the Princes Islands

- The thirty-six Metropolitanates of the "New Lands" in northern Greece,[16] which were temporarily transferred, for pastoral and practical reasons, to the jurisdiction of the Autocephalous Church of Greece in 1928

- The semiautonomous Archdiocese of Crete

- The five Metropolitanates of the Dodecanese islands[17]

- The Archdiocese of (North) America

- The Archdiocese of Australia

- The Archdiocese of Thyateira and Great Britain (with Western Europe, Malta, and Ireland)

- The Metropolitanate of France

- The Metropolitanate of Germany (and Central Europe)

- The Metropolitanate of Austria (with Hungary and mid-Europe)

- The Metropolitanate of Sweden and all Scandinavia

- The Metropolitanate of Belgium

- The Metropolitanate of New Zealand (and Japan)

- The Metropolitanate of Switzerland

- The Metropolitanate of Italy (and Southern Europe)

- The Metropolitanate of Toronto (and Canada)

  - The Ukrainian Diocese of Canada

- The Metropolitanate of Buenos Aires (Argentina and South America)

- The Metropolitanate of Panama (and Central America)

- The Metropolitanate of Hong Kong (with India, the Philippine Islands, Singapore, and Indonesia)

- The Metropolitanate of Spain and Portugal

- The Metropolitanate of Korea

  - The Patriarchal Exarchate of the Russian Orthodox parishes in Western Europe

- A number of Patriarchal and Stavropegic institutions, such as the monastery of St. John the Evangelist on the island of Patmos, the monastic republic of twenty communities and numerous hermitages on Mount Athos, and the historic monasteries of Vlatades and St. Anastasia in Thessaloníki

- A number of international Patriarchal institutes, such as the Patristic Institute in Thessaloníki, the Orthodox Center in Chambésy, and the Orthodox Academy in Crete

- A number of organizations worldwide, such as the Permanent Representative Office in the World Council of Churches, the Orthodox Liaison Office in the European Union, and the Patriarchal Representative Office in Athens

CONCLUSION: ORTHODOXY AS
THE HIDDEN TREASURE OF THE WEST

In many ways, while the Orthodox Church has Eastern roots and a formative presence in the West, its rich tradition and spirituality remain largely unknown to the world. Despite growing scholarly interest and increasing attention worldwide, the history and theology of the Byzantine Empire are still largely overlooked in literature and learning. Thus, with few exceptions, it is common to hear people speaking of the history of Christianity as beginning with Jesus Christ and the Apostles, continuing in the Western Empire and the Roman Catholic Church, and leading through the Protestant Reformation to the present times. For the most part, people still ignore the immense contribution and uninterrupted continuity of the Eastern Church from the earliest of apostolic times. Even scholars of both repute and credibility have communicated misconceptions about the Orthodox Church, which has been perceived as a quaint relic from an exotic past. Byzantium remains the best-kept secret in the West.

It is the Byzantine East that preserved the literary works of classical civilization and Roman law, making them available to the Western Renaissance. Plato and Aristotle would simply not have been known without Arabic translations of the high Middle Ages. It was the Byzantine East that Christianized the Slavic North and protected the European South from invasions by the Goths and Visigoths. The western part of the Roman Empire very quickly lost its power and prestige. Nevertheless, the silent presence of Byzantium is still more far-reaching. From the forks we use to dine to the hospitals we depend on for healing and to the universities where we pursue advanced knowledge, the legacy of Byzantium has proved a lasting and profound influence.

All of the earliest councils of the Church, which provided the definitive and formative doctrine of the Christian faith, were held in neither Italy nor Greece, but in Asia Minor. In fact, following the fifth-century collapse of the Western Empire, after which the West entered a period known as the Dark Ages, the eastern part of the empire continued to provide a source of wisdom and prove a center of culture for over a thousand years. Furthermore, the Byzantine currency, the gold solidus or bezant, held its value for seven centuries, making it the most stable currency in history. Even on a social level, the Byzantines were known for their hospitals and rehabilitation centers, dating back to as early as the fifth century; moreover, Byzantine laws forbade the use of torture in legal proceedings. Finally, while the Orthodox Church has had an enormous impact on Eastern Europe and the Mediterranean, it has also had a historic and vibrant presence in the West since at least the mid-eighteenth century.

The Orthodox Church remains the spiritual heir of Byzantium, to this day heralding the theological and mystical treasure of that civilization. More than any museum or library can ever preserve, the Orthodox Church is the eloquent expression of the early Church and the living spirit of Byzantium. In many ways, the West is yet to acknowledge the fullness of its debt to Byzantium and the Eastern Church.

II.
SONG AND SPACE

ART, ARCHITECTURE, AND LITURGY

Standing in the temple of Thy glory,
we think we are in heaven.
—ORTHODOX LENTEN HYMN

HEAVEN ON EARTH: LITURGY AND ICONS

There is a well-known legend, preserved in *The Russian Primary Chronicle*, about Prince Vladimir of Kiev, who once sent a group of envoys throughout the world in order to ascertain the most authentic religion. Based on the findings of his envoys, Vladimir was determined to espouse the faith of that people. His ambassadors traveled to the Bulgars, to Germany, and then to Rome, in each place learning about the religious practices and traditions. Finally, however, they journeyed to Constantinople, where they experienced liturgy in the Great Church of Christ, known as the Church of the Holy Wisdom (or St. Sophia). Upon their return, overwhelmed by the beauty they encountered, they were convinced that "in that place, God dwells among men." This is how they described their experience to the prince:

> We knew not whether we were on heaven or on earth, for surely there is no such splendor or beauty anywhere on earth. We can-

not describe it to you; only this we know, that God dwells there among people . . . We cannot forget that beauty.

It is a fact that in the ninth century, the liturgy of St. Sophia Cathedral would have been quite overwhelming by today's standards, reflecting all the splendor and grandeur of the Byzantine Empire. The sheer pomp of the ritual, together with the large numbers of clergy and the glory of the music, would have provided a memorable experience for any visitor. Moreover, the beauty of the icons and the glory of the architecture offered a splendid context for any occasion of worship.

Icons had already long been established in the city of Constantine. Nevertheless, this was not always the case. What many contemporary Orthodox Christians take for granted, when they venerate the icons at the entrance to a church as well as on the icon screen (or *iconostasis*) before the altar, is found in seed during earlier centuries, although it is more fully and more formally developed in later centuries, notwithstanding periods of turmoil and controversy.

Ecclesiastical writers of the formative Christian centuries were neither immediately nor spontaneously open to the notion of religious images. For they were influenced to a greater or lesser degree by ancient Hebraic traditions rather than by Hellenistic elements. And the Old Testament clearly expresses reservation with regard to images of the divine.[1] Moreover, the theological arguments of the opponents of icons (who came to be known as iconoclasts[2]) were derived not purely from Jewish sources but especially from a fear of pagan idolatry, and perhaps also from an unduly harsh criticism of Greek philosophical thought.

In fact, however, discoveries from archaeological excavations attest to the presence of religious images in the early Christian Church well before the fourth century. Didactic and decorative images, narrative and symbolic depictions, were introduced into Christian houses of worship and gathering places, as well as cemeteries and catacombs, from at least as early as the third century. These images included symbolic representations such as the "fish" or the "anchor," as well as more developed depictions of the "good shepherd" or "Daniel in the lion's den." For the most part, these images were recollections or interpretations of Scripture.

These primitive stages and early seeds of iconography proved as decisive as they did definitive for the development of images in later centuries. The theological implication and doctrinal conviction—later explicitly expressed by Saint John of Damascus, the eighth-century champion of sacred images—were that "God Himself was the first to paint and present icons."[3]

ICONS AND THEOLOGY

In recent years, with the generous support of the late Pope John Paul II (1978–2005), the relics of two renowned Ecumenical Patriarchs—Gregory the Theologian (329–89) and Saint John Chrysostom (347–407)—were returned to their proper home, namely Constantinople, where the men had served as archbishops in the late fourth and early fifth centuries. Both of these saints were deeply influential for the development of art and liturgy in the early Church.

Saint Gregory led the Church of Constantinople during the famous Second Ecumenical Council of 381. This gathering completed the Nicene-Constantinopolitan Creed, which is still recited by Orthodox Christians throughout the world both in Divine Liturgy and in personal prayer. The writings of Saint Gregory are noted for their particularly poetic and colorful tones, as well as for their emphasis on the principles of art. Indeed, he is considered one of only three Church Fathers who are known as theologians, precisely for the poetic and mystical dimension of their writing. Gregory connects human art and painting with the supreme art of divine creation described in the Book of Genesis. Indeed, he describes art as "a second creation."[4]

Saint John Chrysostom is acknowledged as perhaps the greatest of Christian preachers through the centuries, renowned throughout history for his emphasis on the pious and practical application of theological affirmations.[5] Saint John's sermons also underline the perspective of the heavenly kingdom, which is in turn reflected in human art and culture.[6] The spiritual thought of these great theologians echoes the pioneering and creative work of their predecessor Basil the Great (330–79), who was Archbishop of Caesarea in Asia Minor. For Saint Basil, the development of human art reveals the wonderful formation of the human soul.[7]

Thus, from the early centuries of the Church, Orthodox Christians have inherited more than simply the fundamental principles of the Christian faith. They have also derived an appreciation for the development of artistic and cultural values. Otherwise, how could one ever explain the effort of the gifted architects of the Church of the Holy Wisdom, Anthemius and Isidore, to surpass—within a period of only two centuries—their classical predecessors in ancient Greece in order for St. Sophia to succeed and even supersede the perfection of the Parthenon? Who would deny that this same Church of the Holy Wisdom represents theology spelled out in the grammar of magnificent domes, mosaics or frescoes, pillars, and light? Every word articulated in theology, like every stroke of an iconographer's paintbrush, every musical note chanted in psalmody, and every stone carved in a chapel or a cathedral, is an attempt to re-create the divine beauty that inspires every living being as well as everything that breathes to praise the Lord.

THE ECUMENICAL COUNCILS

Nevertheless, it was the ecumenical councils of the first eight centuries that finally determined the essential role and defined the theological importance of icons. These councils rooted their decisions in Scripture and established their theology on the doctrine of the divine Incarnation. According to Gregory the Theologian, the Incarnation of the divine Word of God, in the person of Jesus Christ of Nazareth, rendered the inconceivable conceivable in the Virgin Mother, the incomprehensible comprehensible in the human heart, and the uncircumscribable describable in created matter.[8]

These ecumenical councils retain their unique significance with regard to the formation and appreciation of doctrine in the Orthodox Church. The "great" or "ecumenical" councils, as they are variously known to and accepted by both Eastern and Western churches, were adopted by a large part of Christendom inasmuch as they defined and defended the fundamental doctrines of the Christian Church. All of them were held either in or near the city of Constantinople.

Thus, for example, the First Ecumenical Council (Nicaea, 325) underlined the divinity of Christ. It stressed that Jesus Christ of Nazareth, the incarnate Son of the living God, shares one and the same essence as the Father. The Second Ecumenical Council (Constantinople, 381) confirmed the earlier, Nicaean teaching about Jesus Christ, further expanding it to include the understanding of the Holy Spirit. It declared that the Spirit of God also proceeds from the same essence of the Father. The "Symbol of Faith," otherwise known in the Orthodox Church as the Creed, remains to this day the very same as that originally defined during these two early councils of the Church. It is recited in most of the sacraments, but especially during the baptism of every Orthodox Christian and each celebration of the Divine Liturgy.

The Third Ecumenical Council (Ephesus, 431) proceeded along the same path, proposing and affirming the fullness of the humanity of Jesus Christ. The person of Jesus Christ was understood as a union of two distinct natures. The Fourth Ecumenical Council (Chalcedon, 451) proclaimed that this union in the person of Christ was "without confusion, without change, without division, and without separation." Not only was Christ understood in terms of his consubstantiality (literally, as having one and the same essence) with the Father, but he was also understood to be consubstantial with humanity (namely, as having one and the same essence with each of us as human beings).

The fullness of the human nature in Jesus Christ was sealed with the teachings of the Fifth Ecumenical Council (Constantinople, 553) and the Sixth Ecumenical Council (Constantinople, 680–81), as well as the Quinisext Council (Constantinople, 692). Each of these councils insisted firmly on the humanity and reality of the will and soul of the incarnate Son of God. The point was that God was fully identified with every aspect of human nature, "in every respect tempted as we are, yet without sin" (cf. Heb. 4:15).

Finally, the Seventh Ecumenical Council (Nicaea, 787) affirmed the use of sacred images as genuine expressions of the Christian faith in the doctrine of the divine Incarnation. This final council was not simply the result of a debate or discussion on the importance of religious art. It was a continuation and confirmation of the earlier definitions on the fullness of the humanity of the Word of God. What is often considered the last of the great councils was not simply an afterthought to the intense theological debates of earlier centuries. It is intimately and inseparably connected to those discussions, serving as their fitting and final conclusion.

THE TEACHING ON ICONS

Therefore, since the earliest of Christian times, but especially since the Seventh Ecumenical Council of 787, sacred icons have provided a specific, visible, and public affirmation of the doctrine of divine Incarnation as well as a general education of Orthodox Christians in matters of faith. This truth, however, is not only celebrated formally in churches; it is embraced in every Orthodox home. The house where I was raised is now empty; but I recall ever so vividly the family living room, where in my mother's icon corner (or *ikonostasion*, in exactly the same way that the altar icon screen is called in church) there proudly stood an icon of Christ, as well as an icon depicting the Mother of God, John the Baptist, and Saint Joseph. The icon of Christ stood around ten inches tall and was contained within a large glass vase; as a child, I used to think it was a miracle that the icon could ever penetrate the small opening of the vase. The icon of Saint Joseph still lies above my bed; it was included because my mother's uncle was a monk named Joseph at Vatopedi Monastery on Mount Athos. My mother would with religious regularity burn incense every Saturday evening in preparation for Sunday and on major feast days.

The Orthodox tradition professes and proclaims that the Word of God, who is by nature inconceivable, was nevertheless conceived in the human womb of a virgin mother, Mary of Nazareth. Through Mary, the incomprehensible divinity of the heavenly Father is somehow mysteriously—not unlike the icon inside the vase in my living room—and mystically able to be comprehended and contained within the human heart. The uncircumscribable and inaccessible nature of the living God is rendered describable and accessible in human flesh and material creation.[9] This is why Saint John of Damascus (675–749) was able to remark:

I depict the invisible God not in His divine invisibility, but inasmuch as He became visible by sharing in our flesh and blood. I do not create an image of the invisible divinity, but I depict the visible flesh of the incarnate God.[10]

Now, when Orthodox Christians speak of icons, they refer to a broader range of religious expressions, including portable icons on wood, frescoes, or miniatures, as well as images on a variety of materials and vessels. The primary significance is not so much the particular kind of material on which the icon is depicted as the relationship of the depicted image to the heavenly prototype. This is what ultimately safeguards the Orthodox veneration of icons from any charge of idolatry. For the Orthodox Christian definitely reserves all worship and ultimate reference to the Creator alone. The creation is never seen as an end in itself. One is able to reach and worship the Creator through the spiritual life of the saints and the sacred beauty of creation itself.

What is said, then, about icons may also be understood in terms of the veneration of saintly relics (see 2 Kings 13:21), as well as in regard to the Orthodox approach to the natural environment. Like icons, relics are always accessible, constituting a central feature of Orthodox piety. Like the entire creation, relics are a call to transformation and holiness. They are a visible reminder of a heavenly vocation. They are pointers, signifying another, supreme reality. This is precisely why the wood of portable icons will often be carved inward, for the icon is an invitation to another, inner world. Moreover, frescoes on walls will often be painted at average human proportions of height and size, standing only a little higher than those praying inside the church. This is because frescoes express an invitation to rise higher than daily expectations, yet without any unrealistic sense of naïveté.

THE SPIRITUAL DEPTH OF THE ICON

In a word, icons are best understood in terms of encounter and relationships. In any case, by definition, icons are always an expression of a relational theology. Those who venerate sacred images are drawn into a relationship with the person or event that is depicted. Saint Basil clearly states that "the honor of the icon is transferred to the prototype."[11] In order to appreciate the spiritual depth of the icon, one must first enter and participate in the living community of the Church or communion of believers. This is why icons are intimately connected to prayer and worship. The Greek word for "beauty" or "goodness" is *kallos*, the same word used by the Greek translation (or Septuagint version) of the Hebrew Old Testament, which describes the response of God after the creation of the world. Goodness was the divine reaction to the beauty of the world:

And God saw that the light was good (Gen. 1:4) . . . it was good (Gen. 1:12, 18, 21, 25) . . . And it was so. God saw everything that he had made and, indeed, it was very good (Gen. 1:30–31).

This word *kallos* also contains—both etymologically and symbolically—the sense of call. Beauty is a call, beyond the here and now, to the original principle and purpose of the world.

Therefore, the spiritual way is never disconnected from the created and material world. It includes and involves every aspect and every detail of creation, to the last speck of dust just as "to the least of our brothers and sisters" (Matt. 25:40). The presence of icons in an Orthodox church as well as in an Orthodox home underlines this conviction. And the same truth is underlined in liturgy, with the use of bread, wine, water, oil, wheat, flowers, and wood. It is not only the soul but also the body and all of created matter that are sanctified and deified. All people and all things are created and called to become "good" and "beautiful." Ultimately, the recognition of this spiritual—or iconic—dimension in everyone and everything is an essential feature of Orthodox theology and spirituality.

Therefore, the "relative veneration and relative honor" that are attributed to creation serve to underline and can never undermine the absolute worship and glory that are reserved for the Creator.[12] It is a matter of proper relationships, which the saints have realized and preserved through the ages for our imitation. The saints are the ones who once knew how to pray while they were living on this earth; they are now the ones who know how to intercede for the life of the world from their heavenly abode.

LITURGY AS HOME OF THE ICON

My mother taught me from an early age the spiritual depth and meaning of icons. Each morning she would light a candle and burn incense before the icons in our home, kneeling in prayer for the safety and salvation of her household, which in her eyes and in her heart resembled a miniature church. Indeed, the icon corner of every Orthodox home is a place of spiritual reflection and veneration. It is where an Orthodox Christian feels at one with the company of saints in the comfort of his or her home. The simple faith of believers often retains the fullness of authentic doctrine, just as an oyster shell contains a precious pearl. This is "the pearl of great price" (Matt. 13:46), which no intellectual discourse or discussion can ever fully comprehend. It is a truth that is best painted in color and sung in notes, rather than articulated in concepts. This is why prayer and liturgy best conceal the full significance and expression of the icon.

Indeed, what icons do in terms of material space, liturgy achieves in terms of spiritual song. In other words, liturgy reveals the essential, not simply the secondary, significance of icons; for, in worship, icons are embraced for their spiritual, not simply their artistic, value. Unfortunately, icons are all too often viewed by outsiders as something distinctively Eastern, even exotic, or perhaps aesthetic. They are normally presented as portraying something of the "mystical" wealth or attractiveness in Orthodox spirituality, which is not an unfounded claim. Indeed, in the past, some Western thinkers have believed that icons represent an alienation of the Orthodox Church from the early Christian Church, an extension and influence of elements of classical Greek religion on the Church of the East. Nothing could be further from the truth.

Within the parameters of liturgy, icons express the potential for personal and mystical encounter with God. It is, as the old Christian adage goes, "the rule of prayer that determines the rule of faith" (*lex orandi lex est credendi*). Liturgy becomes the space and moment where God is properly worshipped in spirit (cf. John 4:23–24). We know that "no one has ever seen God, except the only-begotten Son, who is close to the Father's heart, who has made Him known" (John 1:18).[13]

This was certainly the experience that we gained at the Patriarchal Theological School of Halki, where the academy was integrally linked to the liturgy. The school was situated within a monastery; the dean was like the abbot of a community. There was a roster of daily and weekly liturgical services and roles for each student. Our understanding of theology was permanently bonded with the song of liturgy. Our studies literally had the aroma of incense. There were books and papers; there were teachers and administrators; there were classrooms and libraries. But there were also bread and oil and wax and incense and flowers. Our theological studies were part and parcel of a larger worldview, never unrelated to liturgy and never isolated from reality.

In liturgy, then, the communion of believers "hears with their ears" and "sees with their eyes" and "touches with their hands" the very word of life "that was with the Father and was revealed to us" (1 John 1:1–2). The phrase of Saint Gregory the Theologian, that "the unassumed is unhealed,"[14] is realized in all its fullness and richness during the Divine Liturgy, when all the various materials used in icons—such as wood, egg, and color—are adopted into the new vision of the world in the perspective of the kingdom. No person and nothing whatsoever are excluded from this experience. Everyone becomes a part of this encounter with God; everything assumes mystical or sacramental value.

And it is indeed a new perspective that icons offer "those who venerate their mystery in faith." Icons shatter the restricted vision of the intellectual—and even of the purely artistic—world. They disclose another worldview, the worldview of the age to come. In this way, however, icons also reveal the proper nature and full potential of the present age and world. When we learn how this life and this world are imbued by the sacredness and beauty of the divine life and kingdom, everything assumes new dimensions and new proportions. Everyday events and ordinary occurrences become extraordinarily significant and sacred. There is a moment during the morning prayers of Great Lent when Orthodox Christians chant in humble awe: "Standing in the temple of Thy glory, we think we are in heaven." That is how it feels! That is what we believe and profess! Indeed, that is precisely how it is!

Icons, then, are properly appreciated and fully comprehended only within their liturgical dimension, especially since the liturgy itself comprises an image of the divine plan for the salvation of the whole world. Indeed, the entire liturgical cycle—the recollection throughout the yearly calendar of the major events in the life of Jesus Christ—becomes a comprehensive commentary on this mystery of the divine economy. In liturgy, artistic elation becomes mystical encounter. It becomes a theophany—or showering epiphany—of the divine energies, before which one can only stand in awe and kneel in prayer. More than merely an inspiration, icons are an "inflammation"—as Saint Gregory the Theologian puts it—of the human soul, when it remembers and realizes the kingdom. The soul literally burns as it recalls its rightful place as a member of the communion of saints.

ICONS AND ARCHITECTURE

Furthermore, the architecture of the Church again articulates the same truth, surrounded as it is with sacred images. A traditional Orthodox church has three dimensions, often reflected by means of three distinct spatial areas. The basic structure of a traditional Orthodox church presents a synthesis of two classical elements of design: the dome (which was introduced as early as the fourth century) and the basilica (which is the earliest and simplest example of church architecture, originally built from available regional materials such as wood, stone, and brick).

Nevertheless, even beyond fundamental structural styles, an Orthodox church is integrally and spiritually three-dimensional. The church has three clearly defined spaces, three definite architectural zones. The dome is the first space and most prominent architectural feature, reserved for the image of Christ (or the Pantokrator, namely "the one who contains and holds all"). It is the central feature that embraces and enlightens the entire building. The dome is symbolic of the heavenly kingdom, where the Father together with the Son creates, saves, and judges. The second space is the church proper (the nave, or *naos*). This area is filled with images of the saints and martyrs, monks and married people alike, who appear almost to blend in with the congregation itself. Finally, in traditional Orthodox churches, the third space or zone—known as the apse—is dedicated to the Mother of God (or Theotokos, as Orthodox faithful refer to her). The image of the Theotokos in the apse is often called the Platytera (or "the one more spacious than all").

Space and geometry share the same language as icons and liturgy; they speak the language of theology. Wherever there is a dome, it is circular in shape, symbolic of the eternal and uncircumscribable divinity, a line without beginning or end.[15] Moreover, the floor plan of the church proper is rectangular, an image of the defined and limited nature of this world with its clear demarcations, beginnings, and ends. This rectangular shape is also representative of the world as our home (or *oikos*) and as receptive of divine economy (or *oiko-nomia*). Finally, the apse in the middle serves to hold together the upper and lower zones, belonging to both and yet pertaining to neither, uniting both the heavenly and the earthly realms, while at the same time inviting people to reconcile Creator and creation in their own bodies as well as in their surrounding world. The icon of the Mother of God, who is normally depicted in the apse, assumes both spherical and rectangular shape. She is the personification of this vocation and reconciliation. Thus, the apse reveals the sign and presence of God piercing history and entering time. In traditional churches, the absence of many pews further breaks down the separation between heaven and earth. Any subsidiary vaults and structural extensions assume the shape of a cross, the ultimate symbol of reconciliation and transfiguration (especially from the sixth-century reign of Justinian).

The same iconographic pattern is extended and applies to the Evangelists, or authors of the four Gospels, who are depicted above the four columns supporting the church's dome, as well as to Saint

John the Baptist, or Forerunner, who is portrayed on the icon screen, always turned toward and pointing to Jesus.

THE LITURGY AND THE WORLD

All that is joyfully celebrated in liturgy, solemnly chanted in hymns, and eloquently preached in sermons is also artistically preserved in icons and architecture. They mystery that holds everything together is the sacred relationship between God and the world; it is the sacramental encounter to which we are all called through prayer and worship. The same truth that is recalled in the home when Orthodox Christians burn incense before icons is also realized in church when Orthodox Christians light candles before icons as they enter the building. Upon entering a church building, every Orthodox Christian—laypersons as well as ordained clergy, including bishops and even patriarchs—will stop to light a candle before an icon, which stands as a heavenly image of the "cloud of witnesses." We are all a part of something much larger than our lives.

Each person is created "in the image of God" (Gen. 1:26). Yet this unique seal does not lead to exclusiveness or division; in fact, it results in a common bond and solidarity. So once the candle is lit at the entrance to the church, it is placed alongside all the other lit candles, a symbol of the fact that we are not disconnected individuals but instead constitute a community of believers, the living Body of Christ. It is only then—after lighting a candle and venerating an icon—that the faithful will enter the body of the church, where as a community they are rendered "a mystical image of Cherubim" in order to "chant the thrice-holy hymn to the life-giving Trinity."[16] That is the ultimate mystery, to which we are all called. That is, as a fourteenth-century commentator on the Divine Liturgy, Saint Nicholas Cabasilas (1322–90), noted, "the end and meaning of everything, beyond which it is not possible to go, and to which nothing can be added."[17] In liturgy, Orthodox Christians sense that they are a part not only of something larger than themselves. They are a part of a world that simultaneously transcends and contains this world; they are a part of no less than heaven.

Saint Nicholas Cabasilas remarks that "the life in Christ begins in this life and its seeds are planted from this world. Its completion is realized in the next life, since it is the age to come that we expect."[18] The light of the icons is precisely the light of the kingdom. It is this light that is experienced in liturgy. After Easter, for forty days, just as during every service of matins prior to the celebration of the liturgy, Orthodox Christians chant, "We have seen the Resurrection of Christ." And after Communion during each liturgy, they sing: "We have seen the true light." They do not claim first to believe the true faith or to proclaim the true Christ. Rather, they are convinced that they have experienced the illumination of Christ's divine grace.[19]

According to the Orthodox way in the spiritual life, everything derives its source and essence from its connection to and dependence on the Divine Liturgy. Even the administrative life of the Church does not reflect and should not imitate secular organizations and worldly structures. Rather, it should be a mirror image, an authentic icon, of the order and values encountered in liturgical worship. It is not by accident that the meal table in Orthodox monasteries is always an organic continuation—both architecturally and spiritually—of the altar table: the refectory is situated at the west end of the church building; on great feasts, there is a solemn procession from the church to the dining hall. The sanctification of the sacred gifts, the bread and wine, is supposed to spread to and pervade the whole of creation. Indeed, in the Orthodox Church, everything may be said to stem from that table of the holy altar: every ministry, every service, every office, every authority, every administrative jurisdiction. In this way, we can appreciate why Saint Maximus the Confessor (580–662) spoke of a "cosmic liturgy," which is offered by the entire world through the sacrificial Lamb of Revelation.

CONCLUSION: THE RECONCILIATION OF THE WORLD

I experienced this all-embracing significance of the Divine Liturgy with overwhelming vividness when I had the opportunity to offer the Eucharist in the magnificent church of San Apollinare in Ravenna. The event was part of the fourth international environmental symposium organized in the Adriatic Sea by the Religious and Scientific Committee of the Ecumenical Patriarchate during the summer of 2002. The sixth-century mosaics of the church provide a unique symbol of the cosmic celebration that occurs during the liturgy, depicting as they do all of creation and the natural environment in prayerful worship. It was a historic occasion because this was the first time that Orthodox worship was taking place in this church for almost a thousand years. Therefore, the liturgy itself seemed to be not only reconciling the world but also bridging the past with the present; the silence of ten centuries was only an intermission in the prayer of the world.

Each evening, as I shut the door to my office, I do not leave behind the people and the issues I have faced during that day. I bring them with me and within my heart to the small Patriarchal Chapel, where they are all offered in prayer during the Compline service that closes the day. The chapel is a small refuge from the daily deluge of problems, a splendid occasion to meditate on the wonders of God, who loves us as we are. What more could I ever ask for? What more could I ever do?

III.
THE GIFT OF THEOLOGY

BASIC PRINCIPLES AND PERSPECTIVES

God is a mystery, unable to be grasped.
Otherwise, God would not be God.
—EVAGRIUS OF PONTUS (FOURTH CENTURY)

THE WAY OF THE FATHERS

This chapter aims at describing, in very broad strokes, the key features of Orthodox theology. From the outset, however, it should be noted that in the Orthodox Church, theology is considered a gift. It is not something acquired through mere study or scholarly research. It is not some complicated system of intellectual discourse, the monopoly of a few specialists whose lifetimes are spent in libraries. It is not taught; rather, it is caught. Moreover, by the same token, it is not some arbitrary expression or personal opinion. Indeed, it cannot be articulated outside the living continuity of tradition. Nor again is it simply the result of some authoritative declaration, publicly professed or dogmatically imposed by the institutional church. Rather, it is the fruit of a communal conscience and consensus. Theology can never be understood as some infallible proclamation by a single or even a collective source. It always derives from, is produced by, and is interpreted within the experience of the total community. Therefore, instead of reflecting personally on the subject of theology, I consider it more appropriate to offer readers a brief exposition on the gift of theology from an Orthodox perspective by quoting directly from the experience and teachings of the Church Fathers.

Theological and spiritual insights clearly form the basis of each of the chapters in this book. However, in this chapter I shall survey some of the leading representatives and classic writers of the Eastern Orthodox spiritual tradition, especially from the fourth through the fourteenth centuries, some of whom are even my direct predecessors and forefathers on the Ecumenical Throne. The very idea of theology, at least in the mind of the Orthodox Church, emerges out of the study of the Church Fathers. The foundation of Orthodox theology rests firmly on the tradition of the Church Fathers, namely on those whose inspiration and instruction have formed the conscience of the Church through the ages. This is not easy to appreciate in an age like ours, when innovation and independence shape society and culture. The emphasis throughout this chapter is on tradition and continuity through personal experience, the inspiration from the All-Holy Spirit, through which every living being receives divine life and light. Furthermore, I shall consider some liturgical as well as more contemporary sources in an effort to explore the fundamental characteristics and criteria of traditional theology and draw out certain implications for the modern world.

THE SEAMLESS GARMENT OF TRADITION

Sometimes when one listens to exponents of the Christian faith, it is easy to gain the impression that God stopped speaking to the Church and to the world around two thousand years ago, or at least somewhere between that time and the present. According to this view, there have been certain "golden ages" in history when God was freely and profusely revealed. Yet outside of these periods, God somehow unfortunately withdrew, leaving the world in the "dark ages." Of course, while there was indeed a remarkable and creative working of the Holy Spirit in the early years of Christianity, this should be regarded only as the beginning of a tradition and not as the end. After all, to claim that there are no living embodiments of the Spirit today—that there are no Church Fathers or even Mothers—is tantamount to denying the living presence of the Spirit of God. In the Orthodox Church, we believe that we remember the flames and not the ashes of the early Church Fathers.

According to the Orthodox theological perspective, therefore, the authority of the Fathers depends less on antiquity; it is not related to their *historical* proximity to the early Church and Christ, namely to the age of the Apostles and martyrs. Their authority is grounded, rather, on the quality of their testimony; it is related to their closeness to the *faith*—and not simply to the times—of the Apostles. This is why the tenth-century mystic Saint Symeon the New Theologian (949–1022) can be described by his contemporary biographer and closest disciple, Niketas Stethatos (1005–90), as someone "entirely possessed by the Spirit—his thought being equal to that of the Apostles—for the divine Spirit inspired his every movement."[1]

It is truly regrettable, then, that the prevailing tendency among many historians and theologians today is to concentrate on the period of the primitive Church and then to leap over centuries to the period of particular denominational, academic, or even personal interest. The result is always a reduction—whether for reasons of preference or, what is worse, of prejudice—of the vision and scope of theology. The life and practice of the Orthodox Church know no such interruption in the age of the Church Fathers. The overall structure of the liturgical cycle in the Orthodox Church, like its general pattern of spirituality, still follows the way of the Fathers. No one can ever deny the unique theological brilliance of Church

Fathers in the fourth and fifth centuries, but to denigrate the significance of later writers would surely result in a distorted and myopic theological vision. Saint Maximus the Confessor (580–662), Saint Symeon the New Theologian (949–1022), and Saint Gregory Palamas (1296–1359) would be unthinkable, even unintelligible, without their Cappadocian predecessors of the fourth century, namely Saint Basil the Great (330–79), Saint Gregory the Theologian (329–89), and Saint John Chrysostom (347–407). They are not merely "appendices" to the earlier Fathers.

Even phrases or formulas, which Orthodox themselves are prone to using for the sake of convenience—such as "the Church of the Seven Councils" and "the Byzantine Church"—prove more restrictive than descriptive in the end. It is the conviction of the saints that the Church has by no means ceased to think and live creatively since the Seventh Ecumenical Council (787). Thus *The Philokalia* of Nikodemos of Mount Athos (1749–1809) includes writings from the early age of Saint Anthony of Egypt (250–356) in the third century up to the Hesychasts of the fourteenth century. Indeed, its compiler, Saint Nikodemos, would himself be counted among the Fathers of the Church. All of the communion of saints—both men and women, known and unknown, erudite and unlettered, mystical and ascetic, clergy and laity alike—are included, at least for purposes of the Orthodox understanding of theology and spirituality, within the scope of the phrase "Church Fathers."

THE WAY OF THE SPIRIT

This of course implies a dynamic, even charismatic understanding of the Church. Inspired by the living Spirit of God, the living body of the Church can never be reduced to a static reality or mere institution. As Symeon the New Theologian wrote in the tenth century,

it would be considered heresy and a subversion of Scripture to claim
that later generations do not have access to the Holy Spirit or cannot acquire the same vision of God as given to the early Apostles,
Fathers, and saints:

> Those of whom I speak and whom I call heretics are those who
> say that there is no one in our times and in our midst who is able
> to keep the Gospel commandments and become like the holy
> Fathers . . . Now those who say that this is impossible have not
> fallen into one particular heresy, but rather into all of them, if
> I may say so, since this one surpasses and covers them all in
> impiety and abundance of blasphemy. One who makes this
> claim subverts all the divine Scriptures. I think (that by making
> this claim) such a person states that the Holy Gospel is now re-
> cited in vain, that the writings of Basil the Great and of our
> other priests and holy Fathers are irrelevant or have even been
> frivolously written. If, then, it is impossible for us to carry out in
> action and observe without fail all the things that God says, and
> all that the saints after first practicing them have left in writing
> for our instruction, why did they at that time trouble to write
> them down and why do we read them in Church? Those who
> make these claims shut up the heaven that Christ opened for us,
> and cut off the way to it that he inaugurated for us. God who is
> above all, stands, as it were, at the gate of heaven and peers out
> of it so that the faithful see him, and through his Holy Gospel
> cries out and says, "Come to me, all who labor and are heavy
> laden and I will give you rest" (Mt. 11:28). But these opponents
> of God or, rather, antichrists say, "It is impossible, impossible!"[2]

Staretz Silouan of Mount Athos (1866–1938), a more recent
saint—whom the Ecumenical Patriarchate recognized as recently as
1988, on the occasion of the millennial celebration of the Christian-

ization of Russia (988–1988)—expresses the conscience of the Orthodox Church with regard to the gift of theology when he claims: "It is one thing to speak of God; it is quite another thing to know God."[3] This critical statement by the popular twentieth-century elder will serve as the springboard over the next pages for a more detailed account of the gift of theology, in accordance with the ages-long tradition of the Orthodox Church.

WHO IS A THEOLOGIAN?

From the outset, it must be reiterated that the title "theologian" has, to date, been reserved for only three saintly personalities of the Church, namely the divine Apostle and Evangelist John, our predecessor Gregory the Theologian, and the greatest among mystics, Symeon the New Theologian. This sparing use of the title "theologian" reveals the sacred awe with which the Church approaches matters relating to God and reminds us of a hymn descriptive of the Mother of God, which might serve as the starting point for all those undertaking the task of theology: "Let all approach as before the sacred covenant; let none approach with uninitiate hands."[4] These words echo the ominous circumstances of Uzzah in the Old Testament (1 Chron. 13), who touches the shaking ark of the covenant with profane hands and meets with instantaneous death.

To perceive God as "consuming fire" and consequently to admit our innate inability to comprehend the divine nature is at the same time to underline our utter speechlessness and complete silence as finite human beings before the Creator of all beings and all things. We are unable to define God intellectually; and we are unable even to describe God adequately. Therefore, all theology is made possible exclusively through the gift of the Holy Spirit. It is the divine Spirit that allows us to approach and encounter the mystery of theology in a manner that is worthy of God.

The *Life of Maximos Kafsokalyvites*, a biographical treatise on the great fourteenth-century Athonite ascetic (1270–1365), contains a conversation on the question of contemplative prayer, which is sometimes called "the prayer of the intellect [*nous*]" in Orthodox spirituality. The conversation takes place between the saint and his contemporary ascetic and mentor in the way of prayer, namely Saint Gregory of Sinai (ca. 1255–ca. 1337). Saint Maximos observes:

> The gift of sacred theology is the most supreme and sublime of all gifts of the Holy Spirit. Therefore, it embraces them all, just as a hen broods over its offspring. This is the reason why, more so than the other gifts, it attracts and inspires the human heart with divine love and passion. For just as God, as the subject of theology, is above all and beyond all, being described as supremely and extremely passionate, theology too is more valuable and more beautiful than anything else.[5]

In a similar vein, the thirteenth-century monk Saint Joseph Vryennios endeavors to define with accuracy the content and essence of theology when he writes: "Theology is the art of arts and the science of all sciences, whose sole source and subject and conclusion is God."[6] According to the tradition of the early Church Fathers and ecclesiastical writers, theology is the study of God; indeed, more precisely, it is the study of the Holy Trinity. It is, however, never simply the accumulation of knowledge about the divine nature; it should be the source of an authentic and good life. In this regard, theology is an encounter with the living, personal God: Father, Son, and Holy Spirit. The Orthodox Church claims that it represents not so much the sum total of teachings or traditions inherited from the past. The

Orthodox faith is primarily a personal encounter of love and a personal relationship of trust in the personal God, with whom we are able to converse "as a man talks to a friend" (Exod. 33:11). In the fourth century, Saint Athanasius the Great (ca. 296–373) claimed:

> Theology is perfected in the Trinity, which alone is the true and unique way of piety, constituting goodness and truth alike. This is eternally the case because goodness and truth neither develop nor grow, while the fullness of theology can never exist as a matter of addition.[7]

Consequently, theologians are the ones who have spoken and written about God as Trinity through personal experience, particularly as the Trinitarian God is revealed in the sacred Scriptures. The same Athanasius underlines the element of continuity in the succession of such teachers: "Those Scriptures were addressed in word and writing to theologians. We have, therefore, received them from those who were inspired as teachers, who also became witnesses of the divinity of Christ. Just as we have received them, so do we transmit them."[8] And elsewhere he remarks: "I am not speaking of my own accord, but in accordance with what I have learned from theologians who have taught me, one of whom is Paul."[9] Thus, theology is always received; it is never merely repeated. It is an act of the Church; it is never whimsical, even if impressively articulated. This is what ultimately safeguards the humility of those who teach theology.

SAINT JOHN THE DIVINE: SOURCE OF THEOLOGY

The Orthodox Church describes with vividness the way in which this gift is received from above—being taught from above and caught by the saints, from as early as the Gospel of Saint John the

Divine. It is no wonder that the Gospel of John is the central evangelical text of the Orthodox Church: its emphasis on light and resurrection, together with its theological eloquence and poetic expressiveness, renders it natural for the entire yearly cycle of biblical readings in the Orthodox Church to begin with this Gospel from Easter Sunday. Indeed, the hermeneutical tradition of the Church considers the moment when Saint John reclined upon the breast of our Lord Jesus Christ during the Last Supper as the starting point of the theological journey. It is from this event that the gift of theology is derived and drawn, as if from a life-giving spring and source.

The hymns for the feast of this Evangelist and Apostle (commemorated on May 24 in the Orthodox calendar) claim that "he was filled with love, and thus also fulfilled in theology," since "God is love" (1 John 4:8). Saint John was the clearest voice and greatest herald of divine love. In the words of Didymus the Blind of Alexandria (310–95): "He was the greatest among theologians, having received the gift of theology from the source; that is to say directly from his beloved and gracious Savior."[10] Therefore, theology is never merely some abstract, theoretical teaching about God. It is always "a power, glory, and force that is able to transform the world and perform great wonders."[11]

Two other renowned theologians—who nonetheless did not receive this title as a formal appellation—were granted the gift of divine knowledge through the intervention of Mary, the Mother of God, together with Saint John the Divine. The first of these is Saint Gregory of Neocaesarea (213–70), the great illuminator of the region of Pontus, who is also known as Gregory Thaumaturgus (or Wonderworker). His biography, written by Saint Gregory of Nyssa (330–95), describes the crowning moment of divine theophany:

Having received ordination (namely to the office of bishop), Gregory was sleepless for many days, entreating the Lord to re-

veal to him clearly the mystery of piety (namely theology) in order to avoid error and heresy. For, during that period, there were
numerous false teachings, and Gregory desired to find the genuine truth. While praying, then, he was granted the vision of a
priestly and gracious elder, whose dignified composure he admired. [This elder was in fact Saint John the Evangelist and Theologian.] So he inquired of the elder his identity and the reason for
which he had come. The elder replied: "The Lord sent me to dispel every doubt that you have and to reveal for you the exact definition of pious faith." Upon hearing these words of the elder with
great elation, Gregory also saw a brilliant woman standing beside
him. A very bright light shone through her and lit up the room,
which was extremely dark, and she spoke the following words to
the elder: "John, genuine friend of my Son and God, make manifest to this young man the mystery of truth." In obedience to the
command of the most holy Theotokos, the evangelist then wrote
down this teaching about the mystery of the Holy Trinity and af-
terward handed it to Gregory:

There is one God, the Father of the living Word, source of all
wisdom and energy, eternal in essence. Light from Light, perfect
begetter of the perfect Son, Father of the only-begotten Son.

Moreover, there is one Lord, only begotten of the only Father,
God from God, the very likeness and image of divinity. This Son
is Word in action, wisdom constitutive and comprehensive of
all, creative force of all things. True Son of the true Father, invisible of invisible, incorruptible of incorruptible, immortal of immortal, eternal of eternal.

And, finally, there is one Holy Spirit, whose existence proceeds
from God and comes to all people through the Son. This Spirit
is the perfect image of the perfect Son and life-source of all that
lives. Sacred source of holiness, bestowing all sanctification.

In the Spirit, God the Father is revealed, the One who is above all things and within all things. The Son, too, is God, through whom all things are made . . . Immutable and unchangeable, the same Trinity forevermore.[12]

A similar appearance of the Evangelist John is mentioned also by the biographer of Saint John Chrysostom, our predecessor on the Ecumenical Throne. When he was still a young man, John lived as an ascetic in the desert near Antioch. There, an elderly and godly ascetic named Hesychius witnessed the following vision while praying:

A man dressed in white and awesome in countenance appeared to be descending from heaven, finally standing before Chrysostom while the latter was praying; this man [who was John the Evangelist and Theologian] was holding a rolled-up manuscript. When the saint saw him, he fell on his face out of fear, but the man raised him and said: "Do not be afraid; take courage." So Chrysostom asked him who he was. The man responded: "I have been sent by God to you; simply receive what I am giving you." It appeared, then, that this man was granting the rolled-up manuscript to John Chrysostom, saying to him: "I am the theologian and evangelist John; receive this manuscript that I am offering you. Henceforth your intellect will be opened in order to understand the meaning of all sacred Scripture." Chrysostom replied: "I am unworthy of such a grace." However, the man made the sign of the cross, embraced him to give him courage, and ascended to heaven.[13]

BYZANTINE THEOLOGIANS AND MYSTICS

Several centuries later, Saint Symeon the New Theologian was living as a monk in the renowned Studite monastery of Constantinople and, later, as abbot of the Monastery of St. Mamas in the same city. His experience upon receiving the gift of theology from above is equally as powerful as the previous examples. It was recorded for posterity by his closest disciple and biographer, Niketas Stethatos, during the eleventh century:

> [S]uddenly, a boundless light shone down upon him from heaven and seemed to tear open the roof above his room. It filled his soul again with inexpressible joy and pleasure, as if everything else seemed dark by comparison with that infinite brilliance and radiant light—for it was night. And behold, a voice was heard from within that divine light, saying: "From the apostle and disciple of Christ, the mediator and intercessor for us before God." When, beyond any expectation, Symeon heard these things, his intellect was in ecstasy and his senses in fear. For he swore to the God that had appeared to him that he was entirely filled with that divine light, shedding "valleys" of tears as a result, until he felt another hand comforting him, encouraging him to write, and directing him.[14]

Another predecessor of ours on the Throne of Constantinople, Saint Philotheos Kokkinos (ca. 1300–79), who was of one soul and shared the same struggle as the renowned defender of the Hesychasts in the fourteenth century, Saint Gregory Palamas, describes two events that reveal the heavenly gift of theology granted by the great illuminator of the divine light. In his affectionate biography of Gregory, Philotheos writes:

One day, as Gregory was resting alone and had turned his thoughts within and toward God, at a time when he was awake and not asleep, suddenly there appeared before his eyes a dignified and venerable man. It was John, the exceptional Disciple and friend of Christ. The latter looked upon Gregory with bright eyes and said: "Behold, Gregory, my child, you see that I have come because I have been sent by the most holy queen of all in order to ask you why it is that, each night and day and almost each hour, you never cease crying out 'Enlighten my darkness; enlighten my darkness.' " Upon hearing this, Gregory replied: "As a passionate and sinful man, what else could I ask from God? It is necessary and proper for me to ask this in my prayer in order that I might be forgiven and enlightened . . ." Then, the beloved Disciple and holy Evangelist . . . filled his heart with ineffable joy and exultation through the gifts of theology.[15]

The life of Saint Gregory Palamas describes another vision about the gift of theology. This vision was relayed directly by Saint Gregory to his disciple Dorotheos, who was among the founding fathers of the historic Patriarchal Monastery of Vlatades in Thessaloníki, which to this day lies within the jurisdiction of the Ecumenical Patriarchate. The saint experienced this vision at the skete of Saint Savva, which is situated immediately above the tenth-century Holy Monastery of the Great Lavra on Mount Athos. It underlines the importance of theology as encounter and communion; theology is a divine gift to be shared with everyone:

While Gregory had his intellect focused upon God through sacred silence and prayer, it seemed as if he was overtaken by light sleep; it was then that he experienced this vision: He saw that he was holding a jar filled with milk, which suddenly began to rise, as if from a well, pouring out and over the top of the jar. Then, it appeared as if the milk was transformed into the most beautiful and most fragrant wine, pouring over his hands and onto his clothes, so that they were drenched and filled with the fragrance . . . After this, he heard a luminous voice saying: "Why, Gregory do you not also share this wonderful drink with others, especially since it is pouring out so generously? Why do you let it waste in vain? Do you not know that this is a gift from God and that it will never stop flowing? You have to share it. And as for what results come of it for those who receive it, you must leave this to the Master."

All of these charismatic experiences of theology by saints, who receive the revelation of theology from above—whether directly from God, or through the Mother of God, or again through the theologian-saint John the Divine—are especially significant in light of the Orthodox understanding of theology. For, according to Orthodox tradition and practice, these kinds of mystical experiences— whether in the form of dreams or ecstatic raptures—are quite exceptional, at least by comparison with the same in the Western churches. The Eastern Church is normally very reserved about expressing or endorsing individual experiences, preferring instead to ground all experience in the life of the community, within which alone does it assume purpose. Therefore, the emphasis on these particular examples of mystical experience through the centuries renders still more evident the conviction of Orthodox tradition that all theology is a gift from God. If one speaks theologically, then one always does so within the context of an intimate relationship with God, who is the source of all theology. Moreover, if one articulates theology within the context of prayer, then one also realizes that the most appropriate method of theology is the way of silence before the awesome divine mystery that can never be fully grasped or described.

APOPHATIC THEOLOGY

The final word, then, of theology is silence; its essence lies in the absence of words. For if it is difficult, as Saint Gregory the Theologian claims, to conceive God, it is impossible to define God. Theology is best not said; it is most authentic when it is expressed in silence. This is why icons of Saint John the Evangelist or Theologian will depict him with his fingers across his sealed mouth, as if to underline the importance and mystery of silence. So the way of Orthodox theology and spirituality cannot be properly understood without an appreciation of its negative or apophatic dimension.

Apophaticism is usually associated with the mystical writings of Saint Dionysius the Areopagite, who flourished toward the end of the fifth century, although this form of theology is not an innovation of Saint Dionysius.[16] Already in Scripture there are many allusions to the apophatic element of theology,[17] while it is fully developed from as early as the fourth century with the Cappodocian Fathers, particularly in their treatises against their contemporary Eunomius, who claimed that the human intellect could know the very essence of God. Saint Gregory of Nyssa expresses the paradox or mystery of theology in the following way:

> The true knowledge and vision of God consists in this—in seeing that God is invisible, because what we see lies beyond all knowledge, being wholly separated by the darkness of incomprehensibility . . . What is the significance of the fact that Moses went right into the darkness and saw God there? (cf. Exodus

20:21) At first sight, the account of this vision of God seems to contradict the earlier one (cf. Exodus 3). For, whereas on that occasion the divine was actually seen in light, this time the divine is seen in darkness. But we should not regard this as reflecting any inconsistency, at least on the level of the mystical meaning, which concerns us here. Through it the Word is teaching us that, in the initial stages, religious knowledge comes to people as illumination. So what we recognize as contrary to religion is darkness, and escape from that darkness is achieved through participation in the light. From there the mind moves forward; and, by its ever-increasing and more perfect attention, it forms an idea of the apprehension of reality. The closer it approaches the vision of God, the more it recognizes the invisible character of the divine nature.[18]

Through the apophatic approach, then, Orthodox theology affirms the absolute transcendence of God while at the same time underlining the abiding immanence of God. For God is both beyond us and with us; God is both above us and within us. The ascent of the human intellect toward God may be described as a creative process of elimination resembling the soul's *katharsis* and discarding all forms of idolatry. This inaccessibility of God is due not simply to the fallen nature of the human person—as it is perhaps in the classical philosophers, who emphasize the divine nature of the human mind—but rather to an ontological gap between created and Creator. This gap ultimately secures a sense of humility for the student of theology, who at times recognizes the limitations of the human intellect. The gap between created and Creator is sometimes blurred in certain modern schools of thought, but it is a fundamental principle in the theology of the early Church Fathers. The impact that this way of theologizing has on the understanding of the natural environment has been questioned by some, who wonder if the inaccessibility of God undermines the presence of God in the world. Yet the apophatic approach of the Fathers is to be taken more in the sense of "God-talk" than of "world-talk."

Negative theology as such is not of course unknown to Neoplatonist thought, and the *via negativa* is also characteristic of Scholasticism in later centuries. In fact, all religions adopt—to one degree or another—a fundamentally negative approach with respect to God, inasmuch as they are aware of the awesome and mysterious divine transcendence.[19] However, apophatic theology is not simply another intellectual method of approaching the mystery of God. It is not a better or even a more effective way of knowing God. Theology always remains the knowledge beyond all knowledge; ultimately, it is a form of divine "ignorance."[20]

Even the doctrines of the Church do not presume to exhaust or define the fullness of truth. They are pointers that delineate the guidelines and borders beyond which it is risky to proceed. They are symbols which indicate that we only catch glimpses of the divine light. We do not simply believe in the Resurrection; rather, as the Orthodox liturgy proclaims: "We have seen the Resurrection; we have seen the true light."[21] Indeed, even the summary of Christian faith, sometimes—though wrongly—known as the Creed, is more properly termed the "Symbol of Faith."[22] For no list of affirmations can ever encapsulate the faith that we hold.

Therefore, theology transcends all formulation and definition, being identified rather with personal encounter and a loving relationship with God in the communion of prayer. In such a union, the desire always remains insatiable and unending: it is the love of the bride in the Song of Songs, who forever stretches out her hands toward the one that cannot be grasped, who ever reaches for the one that cannot be attained.[23]

Negative theology, therefore, is not merely a corrective or corresponding way to the affirmative approach. It is the only way to God;

and it is certainly the only way proposed by the Church Fathers. The Church Fathers are not mere philosophers speculating about abstract divine concepts; they are heralds of a theology that is in its very essence a mystery. They are the ones who have personally experienced communion with the living God as both encounter and mystery.

The apophatic attitude gave to the Fathers of the Church that freedom and liberality with which they employed philosophical terms without running the risk of being misunderstood or of falling into a "theology of concepts" . . . The apophatic way does not lead to an absence, to an utter emptiness; for the unknowable God of the Christians is not the impersonal God of the philosophers. It is to the Holy Trinity "superessential, more than divine, and more than good" . . . that the author of the Mystical Theology commends himself in entering upon the way, which is to bring him to a presence and a fullness, which are without measure.[24]

CONCLUSION: THEOLOGY TODAY

In our age and in our world, where everything seems to be evaluated and negotiated on the basis of rational thinking, apophatic theology conveys the true meaning and experience of Orthodox life and tradition. For theology is a suprarational mystery into which one is initiated only through unwavering faith, which alone permits us to approach the living God, before whom everything is subjected. The late Father Sophrony Sakharov (1896–1993), the spiritual elder of a monastic brotherhood located just outside of London, writes;

It often happens that, after experiencing a certain measure of grace, man does not grow in grace but loses it. And then his religious life concentrates in his brain, as an abstract conception. In this state he frequently imagines himself possessed of spiritual knowledge, not perceiving that this sort of abstract understanding, though it may follow a certain experience of grace, is a peculiar perversion of the Divine word, and the Holy Scriptures in essence remain for him "a book . . . sealed with seven seals" (Rev. 5:1).[25]

Perhaps his wise words will also explain why, although there are plenty of theologians, so few experience God as the one who shapes the journey of their lives and not simply the concepts of their minds.

The Church Fathers mentioned in this chapter—only a small number among the endless multitude of known and unknown theologians of the Orthodox Church—experienced the learning of theology directly from God. They received the grace of theology in a moment of living prayer and in a context of intense vigilance, fully conscious of their unworthiness to participate in the sacred mysteries of theology. In their understanding, the prevailing principle was the doctrine of The Philokalia, according to which, "If you are a theologian, then you will pray; and if you pray truly, then you are a theologian."[26]

Perhaps this principle offers some insights into why theology provides little if any challenge or even direction in the contemporary world. It gives us a clue as to why theology remains a lifeless and spineless human creation. If theology fails to recover its connection to vigilance and prayer, as well as to the received prayer and liturgy of the Church, then it will have no reason to continue in the future history of humanity as a dry and rationalistic exercise alongside the many other theoretical sciences. It will simply fill up our libraries with intellectual dissertations, which may be excellently argued but hardly able to inspire the human soul toward the life-giving and lifesaving love of God. Authentic theology, however, can sustain the world; it nourishes the entire community. This was certainly the way that the Church Fathers understood theology. In the aftermath of the long controversy over sacred iconography, which lasted some 150 years from the early eighth to the mid-ninth centuries, the Seventh Ecumenical Council (787) defined Orthodoxy with this proclamation:

As the prophets have seen, as the apostles have taught, as the church has received, as the teachers have formulated in doctrine, as the world has understood, as grace has shone, as truth has been received, and as wisdom has freely spoken . . . so we speak, so we proclaim: This is the faith of the apostles; this is the faith of the fathers; this is the faith of the Orthodox; this faith has established the universe.[27]

IV.
VOCATION OF LOVE

MONASTICISM AS CHOICE AND CALLING

*The most important thing that happens between
God and the world is learning to love and be loved.*
—KALLISTOS KATAPHYGIOTIS (FOURTEENTH CENTURY)

CELIBACY AND FREEDOM

The priesthood has always been an important part of my life, both
in my childhood and throughout my formation. I still recall the
clergy that played a key role in my early years on the island of
Imvros. These were priests, for the most part celibate, and hierarchs,
who are always celibate in the Orthodox tradition. In the Orthodox
Church, a deacon and a priest may choose to exercise their ministry
as married clergy. Ordination does not require celibacy. A bishop,
however, must remain celibate. Yet it never occurred to me that
celibacy was isolated from freedom. The choice of a celibate priesthood never felt like an imposition or a mandate. It is a choice as well
as a calling.

The notion of freedom is critical in Orthodox faith and life.[1]
Freedom is as much a part of the ministry in the Orthodox way as
it is of baptism in the Christian life. Indeed, for Saint Basil the
Great, the celibate way of the monastic is nothing more than "the
life according to the Gospel."[2] All people are invited to respond to
the calling of Christ. All Christians aspire to "the formation of

Christ within" (Gal. 4:19). Monastics simply realize this goal in a different way; they realize it in silence. Their struggle is not so much to become preachers through words or activists through actions; rather, it is "a letter, inscribed in the heart, known and read by all" (2 Cor. 2–3). While the circumstances of the response to the Christian calling may vary, the way is effectively one and the same. In the Orthodox spiritual life, there is no sharp distinction between monastics and non-monastics. People often forget this, espousing some exclusivist or isolationist understanding of monasticism. However, this is far from the truth.

THE GOAL OF MONASTICISM

Just as monasticism is the voluntary submission to God's will, it can never contradict society or destroy the body. Although centuries of dualistic heresies and tendencies have left a marked impression on monasticism as escaping human society or crushing the human body, in fact monasticism seeks to reconcile the individual with society and to control the desires of the body by recalling the ultimate transformation of the body in the kingdom to come. This attitude toward the world and the body, known in theological terminology as "eschatological," underlines the positive significance of both in light of the final resurrection and restoration of all. In the final analysis, excessive abstinence in the ascetic way may be far more serious a vice than excessive overindulgence.

This is why classical Patristic texts of the Orthodox Church underline the joyful dimension of ascetic discipline. In the title to the seventh step of his renowned *Ladder of Divine Ascent*, Saint John Climacus (579–649) even coins the term "joyful sorrow" (*charmolype*)[3] to denote this reality of an ascetic rigor that looks to joy and love (cf. Rom. 13:10). In Orthodox monasticism, as in the

Orthodox spiritual life, passions are not something to be conquered; they are only overcome and transformed by greater passions. "And the greatest of these is love" (1 Cor. 13:13). According to a hymn chanted each year on the feast day of Saint Anthony of Egypt (January 17), we are exhorted to: "Love Christ, and to prefer nothing to love for Him." Moreover, the Orthodox Service for the Tonsure of a Monk encourages the novice with the following words:

> Walk your way with dignity; abandon all vain attachments; resist every desire that attracts you downward; transfer all of your yearning toward heaven.

Heavenly contemplation, or the vision of the divine light, is the goal of every Orthodox monastic. This goal was variously defined through the centuries by the Church Fathers, who articulated the theological and spiritual depth of the vision of God. This is precisely why the Church Fathers supported and defended those who practiced silence and stillness, from the earliest inhabitants of the desert in the fourth century through the Hesychasts of the fourteenth century to the monks and nuns throughout the world today. In the fourteenth century, however, this way of life came to a particular prominence with Saint Gregory Palamas (1296–1359), who became the chief spokesman for its evangelical and traditional roots. Indeed, Saint Gregory himself, who was born in Constantinople, was attracted to Mount Athos at a young age, seeking to learn and embrace the mystical knowledge of the Hesychast elders. As we have already seen, his persistent prayer was: "Lord Jesus Christ, enlighten my darkness!"[4]

EARLY MONASTICISM

The historical roots of monasticism lie in Scripture. Among the Prophets of the Old Testament, Elijah serves as the monastic prototype. In the New Testament, John the Baptist is the preeminent model of ascetic life. Moreover, Saint Paul stands as one of the first theological exponents of celibacy. The many and diverse expressions of monastic life were developed in Egypt and Syria during the third and fourth centuries, in Palestine and the West during the fifth and sixth centuries, in Asia Minor and Sinai during the seventh through ninth centuries, and on Mount Athos from the tenth century. From these places, monasticism was transferred to almost everywhere that Orthodox missions expanded through the centuries, with unique and popular expressions developing in the Slavic lands from the fourteenth through the twentieth centuries.

Eastern Christian monasticism began around the year 270, when Saint Anthony of Egypt (250–356) stood in the small church of a local village and heard the Gospel words: "If you want to be perfect, go sell your possessions and give to the poor . . . Then, come follow me" (Matt. 19:21).[5] On hearing these words, Anthony decided to pursue a life of complete poverty and radical solitude. The results were rapid and nothing short of miraculous. By the time of his death, "the desert had become a city."[6] The desert of Egypt was literally filled with monastics—both men and women—who practiced one of three lifestyles:

1. The hermit life,
2. The communal life, or
3. The middle way, known as the way of the skete.

These three ways are still found and, indeed, continue to flourish on Mount Athos, an entire peninsula in northern Greece dedicated to monasticism for the last millennium. Twenty monasteries and numerous sketes and cells adorn the spectacular Athonite mountainside and coast. On Mount Athos, also known as the Holy Mountain, many—both known and unknown—have lived holy lives.

MY VISIT TO MOUNT ATHOS

One year after my election and installation as Ecumenical Patriarch, I made a journey, in November 1992, to Mount Athos, which I consider the spiritual heart of the Ecumenical Throne. It was not the first time I was seeing Athos. I recall being able to see Mount Athos from my native Imvros on a clear day. Athos was always in people's conversations, either because of visiting monks or simply because of the weather. Older folks used to say: "If the Mountain looks red, then the northern wind will blow." I was even named Bartholomew after a monk from Koutloumousi Monastery on the Holy Mountain; he was from my island and had opened the first school on Imvros.

So I wanted this pilgrimage to be the solemn beginning of my pastoral and missionary trips throughout the world. It was also my way of honoring as Patriarch the dedication and commitment of those who have laid aside everything earthly to inherit the heavenly kingdom and to pray for the life of the world. Just as, in classical mythology, the son of Poseidon and Gaia, Antaeus, needed from time to time to touch the maternal body of the earth in order to renew his resources, I chose to begin my Patriarchal ministry with a journey to the Holy Mountain. Just as an Orthodox priest will begin the Divine Liturgy by formally "taking time" in the morning service to venerate the holy icons, it was appropriate for me to "take time out" in order to venerate the holy relics treasured on Mount Athos.

In a personal note during that time, I recall observing: "Mount Athos is an epic poem of the spiritual life!" During that visit, I spoke to various monastic communities and addressed the priority that monks ought to give to freedom in their lives through the discipline of obedience and humility. Obedience safeguards human nature from its tendency toward individualism and isolationism. Humility protects human beings from the heresy of fanaticism and extremism. And freedom is the invaluable spiritual goal to which we all aspire as created "in the image and likeness" of God (cf. Gen. 1:26). It is what, more than anything else, renders us godlike.

This freedom of choice is precisely what defines the respect with which Orthodox Christians have, through the centuries, regarded monasticism. When Saint Athanasius of Athos (920–1003) established the first monastery there in 963, known as the Great Lavra and sponsored by the Church and imperial authorities of the time, he institutionalized the words of Christ to Martha (a symbol of the active life in the world) about Mary (a symbol of the contemplative life in monasteries): "She has chosen the better part, which will not be taken away from her" (Luke 10:42). After all, as Christ declared elsewhere: "What will it profit anyone if they gain the whole world but forfeit their life?" (Matt. 16:26). It is hardly surprising to me that the Book of Revelation designates a special place even in the kingdom of heaven for those who have chosen the way of celibacy (Rev. 14:4).

WOMEN'S MONASTICISM

Mount Athos is an exclusively male community. Nevertheless, monasticism is not an exclusively male prerogative. Women's monasticism has always played a key role in the formation of the souls of our faithful. From the earliest times, even during the life of Anthony the Great, monastic communities have existed for women; historically, in fact, it appears that celibacy existed first among women.

The Orthodox Church has never differentiated between the value of the ascetic life for men and women. The Orthodox perception of the doctrine of creation is that the image and likeness of God, sealed in the creation of Adam, implied a distinction as well as a relation between the two genders: "God created man according to His own image; male and female He created them" (Gen. 1:27). As early as the fourth century, Saint Gregory the Theologian (329–89) recognized that "human laws have discriminated between men and women because the law-makers are men." However, as he added: "There is only one Creator of both men and women; one and the same dust covers them; one image adorns them; one law binds them; one death, just as one resurrection, defines them."[7]

In some ways, even during periods when male monasticism either wavered or even waned for various reasons, female monasticism continued to survive and even thrive. In the monastic way, there is an affirmation that through baptism in Christ, "there is no longer male or female; for all of you are one in Christ" (Gal. 3:28). Monasticism reminds us that we are—all of us—called to a higher dignity. None is excluded; there can be no discrimination. The Christian way is a narrow path; and the monastic way is equally a way of trials. Saint John Climacus, the seventh-century Abbot of Mount Sinai, where Moses once beheld God's presence and where to this day there stands the Orthodox Monastery of St. Catherine, observed: "Monasticism incarnates the ongoing force against our fallen nature."[8]

CENTERS OF PRAYER AND SPIRITUAL DIRECTION

Male and female monasteries have traditionally been places of intense prayer and spiritual direction. When people have dedicated their entire lives to the way of prayer, then they may also be trusted to offer a word of advice. In fourth-century Constantinople, a monastery was established, which came to be known as the brotherhood of the "sleepless ones" (or *Akoimetoi*), since liturgical worship and contemplative prayer continued without interruption all day and night as monks prayed ceaselessly in shifts for the life of the world. People have always visited such places in order to discover men and women of prayer and holiness. Monasteries in the Eastern Church are not normally places of scholarship—although numerous monks and nuns through the centuries were renowned intellectuals and teachers, as well as healers of body, mind, and soul. Furthermore, monasteries are not traditionally places of missionary activity—although, in the eighteenth century, Saint Kosmas the Aitolos (1714–79) received the formal blessing of his community on Mount Athos to evangelize. He traveled throughout Greece as an itinerant preacher, carrying only a cross that he held and a stool on which he stood.

Monasteries, then, have traditionally functioned as centers of spiritual renewal and refreshment. "In a dry and weary land, where there is no water" (Ps. 63:1), monasteries continue to offer hospitality and charity to those who are "tired out by the journey and the midday heat" (cf. John 4:6). They do so, however, predominantly through the silence of prayer, which is the seed of all spiritual life and the source of all virtue—perhaps far nobler than almsgiving and any other ascetic exercise.[9] They do so in particular through spiritual counsel and sacramental confession.

According to Orthodox practice, we cannot come to know our

deeper passions or console the inner heart without the presence of another person. A spiritual guide, an elder or confessor, is mandatory for the nurturing of the virtues and the development of the soul. There is simply no other way. This elder can take your soul into his soul and lighten the burden that you carry. We all need such an adviser, a confessor, before whom we can share our inner thoughts and reveal our deepest concerns. For spiritual direction is not some oriental status or eccentric luxury. While people sometimes identify the spiritual director with the role of a "guru," it is not exactly the same, because the spiritual elder is part of a larger tradition and community in the Church. In the Orthodox Church, spiritual direction is a fundamental necessity for spiritual balance and health. It is required not only of lay aspirants to the treasures of the heart but of every person—male and female, young and old, lay and ordained, deacon and priest and bishop alike. This means that while the monks and the abbots of the Holy Mountain sought to hear a word of advice from me, I, too, was and am—like every Orthodox priest and bishop—obliged in turn to seek a word of comfort from a spiritual father.

One of these elders was Father Paisios (1924–94), a simple yet profound monk. Born of pious parents in Cappadocia of Asia Minor, Father Paisios was one of those responsible for the rebirth of monasticism on Mount Athos, which was clearly waning—perhaps not spiritually, but certainly from the standpoint of physical resources and monastic population—when we celebrated its millennial anniversary in 1963. After a period of retreat on Mount Sinai, Father Paisios returned to the Holy Mountain, from where he directed numerous souls throughout the world. He would visit my predecessor, Patriarch Demetrios, when I served as his personal secretary; I was most impressed by his silence.

Anyone blessed to meet a living saint knows the unique sense of stillness that characterizes such a person; a saint appears to live at once in this world and in the age to come. What was most surprising about Father Paisios was that he was utterly human, filled with spontaneity and far from any pretense. God's light seemed to shine through the veil of his soul in a splendor, which made his visitor feel totally at ease and warmly welcomed. Later, I recall visiting him in his cell, just as so many others have done over the years. He would offer spiritual counsel as he shared an apple or orange that he had peeled. He was a genuine professor and missionary of the desert. What a paradox! An unordained monk hearing the inner life of an Ecumenical Patriarch! And he did so without the least self-consciousness. Spontaneity and sincerity are, sometimes, the humble context within which the Church functions most authentically.

THE WAY OF ASCESIS

When we think of asceticism or discipline, we imagine such things as fasting, vigils, and rigorous practices. In the words of Abba Isaac the Syrian (ca. 700): "No one ascends to heaven with comfort."[10] There can be no ascent without ascesis. That is indeed part of what is involved; but it is not the whole story. Ascesis implies a display of what in *The Philokalia* and other classics of the Orthodox spiritual life is called frugality or self-restraint (*enkrateia*). We are to exercise a form of voluntary self-limitation in order to overcome self-sufficiency in our lifestyle, making the crucial distinction between what we *want* and what we in fact *need*. Only through self-denial, through a willingness to forgo and say "no" or "enough," will we be able to rediscover what it means to be truly human. Ultimately, the spirit of ascesis is less a judgment on the material goods of the world than a way of liberation from the stress and anguish that result from the desire to "have more." It is the key to freedom from the gridlock of consumerism (cf. 1 Tim. 6:9–10).

The need for an ascetic spirit today may be summed up in a single word: "sacrifice." This is the missing dimension in our relationships with one another and also with the natural creation. I am thinking here of a sacrifice that is not cheap but costly: "I will not offer burnt offerings to the Lord my God that cost me nothing" (2 Sam. 24:24). There will be an effective, transformative change in our world only when we are prepared to make sacrifices that are radical, painful, and genuinely unselfish. If we sacrifice little or nothing, we shall achieve little or nothing. Needless to say, with regard to both nations and individuals, so much more is demanded from the rich than from the poor. Nevertheless, all of us are asked to sacrifice something for the sake of our fellow human beings and the creation itself.

Sacrifice is more a profound spiritual matter than a purely economic issue. I am referring here to sacrifice as an ethical rather than merely a technological value. Unselfishness implies generosity, rendering the world transparent and transforming it into the mystery of communion and sharing between created beings, between human beings, and between earth and heaven.

Speaking about sacrifice is unfashionable, even unpopular in the modern world. But if the idea of sacrifice is unpopular, it is because it is misunderstood. Many people have a false notion of what sacrifice actually means. They imagine that sacrifice involves loss or death. They regard sacrifice as somber or gloomy. Undoubtedly, this is the result of centuries of misconceptions with regard to renunciation and abstinence. The misunderstanding may also have been caused by centuries of religious abuse, reflected in distinctions between those who have and those who have not.

Nevertheless, the Israelites of the Old Testament had a very different view of sacrifice. To them, sacrifice meant not loss but gain, not death but life. Sacrifice was indeed costly, but it brought about not diminution but fulfillment. It was a change not for the worse but for the better. Above all, for the Jews of the Old Covenant, sacrifice signified not primarily giving up but simply giving. In its essence, sacrifice is a gift, a voluntary offering that symbolized sharing. Therefore, the sacrifices and fasting were reflections of worship and feasting, "seasons of joy and gladness, cheerful festivals" (Zech. 8:19).

Monasticism is intimately identified with the notion of sacrifice because, like monasticism, sacrifice implies an offering in freedom. Only what we offer in freedom and in love can be considered a true sacrifice. When we surrender something willingly and lovingly, we gain. Christ proclaimed this seemingly contradictory mystery when He taught: "Those who want to save their life will lose it" (Matt. 16:25). When we sacrifice our life and our belongings, we gain life in abundance and enrich the entire world. Such is the deeper experience of sacrifice: voluntary self-emptying brings self-fulfillment.

Moreover, in the Orthodox way, ascesis is not an end in itself but a means toward a goal. In this spiritual vision of sacrifice, at least for the Christian, the Cross becomes our guiding symbol. Without the Cross, there can be no sacrifice; without the Cross, there can be no transfiguration; without the Cross, there can be no resurrection. This is why ascesis is closely connected to spiritual freedom, constituting an expression and example of our free cooperation with God's divine will. There are of course limitations even to ascesis in the Orthodox Church. Yet even the rules that govern ascetic practices serve to underline this element of freedom. No one simply decides individually and in isolation how much to cut off or what to resist. Ascesis is bound by the contours of spiritual laws, ecclesiastical canons, and traditional practices. It is never at whim or at will.

MONASTICISM AND MARRIAGE

In comparing monasticism to a vocation of freedom and love, the Orthodox Church closely relates it to the sacrament of marriage. Celibacy and marriage are not contrasted with each other; instead, both are compared to and directed to the love of God. In this respect, monasticism is regarded as correlative and complementary to marriage. After all, the power of love can never be quenched; it can only be fulfilled. Thus, monastic chastity is completed in love, just as the sacrament of marriage is consummated in love. It is, therefore, unfortunate that centuries of negative connotations ascribed to the monastic way have contributed to a devaluation of marriage, as if the celibate life were somehow more pleasing to God or more spiritually fulfilling than marriage.

For the Church Fathers, love cannot be achieved without abstinence; chastity is impossible without charity.[11] Human "passions must be raised heavenward" by means of spiritual discipline and ascesis.[12] Even the most passionate love becomes "divine and blessed."[13] There is no aspect of human life and no quality of human nature that cannot be transformed and redirected, through prayer and ascesis, into a divine purpose and toward a spiritual goal.

In this regard, monasticism is a way of love, which is no less and no more than the way of the Christian Gospel, no different from or better than the way of marriage. Human beings are made to love; they are created in the image and likeness of God, who is communion. Indeed, human beings become truly human only in relation to others. This is as true of a monk as it is of a person living in the world. Monastic withdrawal should never be an abdication of social responsibility. Basically, like marriage, monasticism is a sacrament of love; yet it is the sacrament of mystical love, directed toward the fulfillment of the biblical command to love God and one's neighbor.[14] It is love that is greater than any human achievement or spiritual virtue. The living experience of love advances us to spiritual maturity, much more so than the severest ascetic discipline. The flame of love is what preserves the world alive. A single person burning with love can bring about the reconciliation of the whole world with God (see Gen. 18). This is why the Eastern Christian mystics speak of divine Eros, which consumes and directs one's entire being toward divine love. Encountering the mystery of love is the goal of the spiritual life, for the monk and the married person alike.

Thus, for the Orthodox Church, whether one is married or whether one is celibate, one is called to struggle to transform one's environment through love. Marriage is not idealized, and monasticism is not idolized. Both can be perceived in idolatrous ways if constituting ends in themselves. Both marriage and monasticism are powerful symbolic ways of straining toward the ultimate goal of love, whether through relationships in a family and society or through prayer in one's cell or community. The Church discerns, both through the immediate environment and within one's own context, the love of God in the eyes of every human being and in the sacredness of the natural environment. Whether speaking of marriage or monasticism, the Orthodox Church prefers to describe it as a way of learning how to live and how to love. Marriage and monasticism matter because people matter, because love matters, and because the welfare of human beings far surpasses any legal code or spiritual ambition. This is what provides both of them with the quality of a mystical sacrament.

THE PLACE OF MONASTICISM IN THE CHURCH

Through prayer, spiritual direction, and ascesis, monasticism assumes its rightful and proper place within the body of the Church, organically serving and preserving the unity of its members. Although monastics have sometimes resisted ecumenical ventures toward unity in the wider Church, they have consistently prayed "for the unity of all" within the Body of Christ. A passionate concern for doctrinal integrity has been a characteristic of Orthodox monasticism through the ages. Once again, this has been the case from the time of Anthony the Great (250–356), who supported his friend and bishop Athanasius of Alexandria (ca. 296–373) against the wave of doctrinal aberrations that caused turmoil in the Church of the fourth century. By promoting and practicing "the unity of the faith" within themselves,[15] expressed as union of body and soul through prayer, monastics strive to contribute toward the reconciliation of the whole world in Christ, who "gathers up all things in Him, things in heaven and things on earth" (Eph. 1:10).

After all, the Orthodox Church has never confined theological dialogue and ecumenical relations to academic discussions by experts in the history of religious thought. This would reduce the concept of reconciliation to an intellectualistic enterprise. Alongside the theological dialogue of truth, there is the essential communication and communion through prayer, which is the primary role and function of monastics. Their prayer of the heart keeps alive the whole world, as well as any hope for reconciliation in a world marked by division and turmoil. Their prayer also safeguards theological dialogue from becoming vain talk and babbling. Prayer reminds us of the goal of dialogue, which is the desire and command of Christ that "all may be one" (John 17:21).

PROPHETS OF THE KINGDOM IN THE WORLD

Perhaps the greatest contribution of the monastic way in our contemporary world is its prophetic presence in an age of confusion or ignorance, when people tend to overlook the spiritual dimension of the world. "A little yeast leavens the whole batch of dough" (Gal. 5:9). By purifying their own souls, monastics seek to purify the soul of every person as well as the soul of the world. The prayer of monastics sustains the whole world (Gen. 18:23–33). Their primarily spiritual importance, therefore, becomes social, moral, and even environmental. In the fourth century, Evagrius of Pontus defined the monk as "the one who is separated from all and at the same time united to all."[16] He was right.

By restoring the divine image within their own bodies and souls, monastics aspire to refresh the divine image within all people and to renew the face of God on the face of the whole world. Thus, a genuine monastery is "an icon of the church," says the great visionary Saint Basil (330–79).[17] Indeed, a genuine monastery might be said to constitute an icon of the entire world. It is an example and prototype of a healthy community. Within this context, a genuine monastic does not evade social responsibility; he or she seeks a deeper response to the meaning of life, in the re-creation and reformation, the transfiguration and transformation of the entire fallen world, by silently changing water into wine through Christ (cf. John 2:1–11).

Monasticism proposes a different way of perceiving and doing things in the world. In our age, we have become accustomed to seeing things in a particular way. Indeed, we are constantly bombarded by numerous images, both visual and aural, that determine our ways of responding and reacting. Monasticism provides us with a different set of values, an alternative way of living without compromising. Monasticism seeks to change the world with silence and humility, rather than through power and imposition. It changes the world from within, internally, and not from the outside, externally. In many ways, authentic monasticism proposes a revolutionary worldview, especially in a world where so many people are stuck in established ways that have proved destructive. The silence of the monks is a way of waiting on the grace of God, an earnest expectation of the kingdom.

By maintaining the spirit of the Gospel, monasticism is said to constitute the sinews of the Church (Saint Theodore the Studite, 759–826) and the lungs of the entire world. When it functions properly—and, like any other human institution, it does not always function smoothly—monasticism transmits clean air that sustains all people, all animals, and all creation. In many ways, then, the silent prayer of monastics bears greater influence and impact on the natural environment than numerous visible and loud actions that catch our attention. Saints cleanse their surroundings by spilling into them the grace of God that permeates and fulfills everything. It is no wonder that so many Orthodox saints had a natural and friendly relationship with animals that lived near them.

CONCLUSION: THE WORLD OF THE HEART

The role of monasticism and of Mount Athos today, in my humble opinion, is the preservation of the living tradition of silence and stillness, in accordance with the spirit of the great mystics, such as Saint John Climacus in the seventh century, Saint Symeon the New Theologian in the tenth century, and Saint Gregory Palamas in the fourteenth century. They must also retain alive the memory of the Athonite saints, such as Peter in the ninth century and Athanasios in the tenth century, or Maximos and Niphon in the fourteenth century, as well as that of numerous other saints, both known and unknown. Clergy and laity alike in the world are often consumed by the manifold concerns of this life, easily and sometimes understandably neglecting the goal of the spiritual life. Monastics are called to remember their vocation to cultivate the ground of the heart and to remind us all of the mysteries of the heart.

When I visited the Holy Mountain as Patriarch for the second time in October 2006, I reminded the monks of the holy peninsula that they bore the unique responsibility and privilege of maintaining the grandeur of silence. Their prayer is supposed to assume the burdens of those living in the world; their life ought to provide a moral compass for those in society, who are called to preserve a balance between what *actually* is and what *ought* to be. In this way, then, the silence of those who live in prayer serves for the world as "a haven of salvation."[18]

V.
SPIRITUALITY AND SACRAMENTS

PRAYER AND THE SPIRITUAL LIFE

If you [know how to] pray truly,
then you are a theologian.
—EVAGRIUS OF PONTUS (FOURTH CENTURY)

THE WAY OF PRAYER

The prayer of Orthodox Christians was primarily formed in the liturgy of the community rather than inside the walls of monasteries or in the hearts of individual saints. It is the liturgy that provided the regular expression and rhythmical pattern for adoration and intercession. Liturgy is not identical to prayer, even though it is the source and an essential part of prayer. Prayer accompanies every aspect of life and liturgy. The cycle of weekly services, the daily routine of morning prayer and evening song, and the unceasing invocation of the name of Jesus are as intimately connected and as integrally life-giving for the individual at prayer as blood cells are to a body. In this way, liturgy spills over and into the daily life of Orthodox Christians.

Prayer is the touchstone of a person's spiritual life. It discloses the true stature and authentic condition of one's life. Prayer is what ultimately reveals who we are in relation to God and other people. If we can pray, then we can talk to others; if we know how to pray, then we also know how to relate to others. Prayer is a mirror of the inner life. This applies equally to those who have chosen to consume their lives entirely in prayer and to laypersons, both men and women, whose life ought to be infused with prayer. Prayer is not the privilege of the few but the vocation of all. Prayer may be what monastics are preeminently designed to do, but it also constitutes the fundamental expression of the human relationship to God and to other people as well as to God's natural creation. As such, prayer is truly universal.

There are many different ways of praying. Yet prayer cannot be experienced by means of a detached perception or external connection, in the way that objects are experienced. Prayer must be personally lived or "touched," as Saint John Climacus (579–649) would prefer to say in his *Ladder of Divine Ascent*. We do not learn to pray from manuals or prayer books. Prayer cannot even exist in itself: it exists—as the English term denotes—only as the activity of someone at prayer. Simply put, a "pray-er" is a praying person. It is not a text, but a living human being; not a book, but a burning heart. "Prayer" is a relationship word; it can never be thought of in abstraction, isolated from others or from God. Prayer presupposes and aims at mystical connection or sacramental encounter. Unless this is clearly understood, all talk about prayer tends to falsify what is at stake.

This means that prayer must be inclusive of others, of all, and of the entire world. However, it is especially inclusive of God as the divine "Other." Saint John Climacus observes that faith in God is prayer's wing, proof, and self-verification. It is this openness to others that informs prayer at all times. Prayer is always a dialogue. When it involves silence, it is not a mute or sterile silence, but rather one that begets God. "Be still, and know that I am God" (Ps. 45:11). Silence implies a keen sense of listening, of expectancy, of anticipation. Prayer implies concern for what is going on inside us and around us. To quote once again from Saint John of the Ladder, "Silence exposes those who are truly able to love."[1]

The dialogical character of prayer means that God is able to speak, and the human heart is able to hear, through everyone and in everything. Prayer can never presume; prayer can never demonstrate or result in prejudice. To presume or exclude is the denial of prayer. On the one hand, God speaks unpredictably inasmuch as He surprises us with what matters in life, things that normally lie far beyond our petty interests and needs. On the other hand, God's voice is quite predictable, as we know well that responding "to the least of our brothers and sisters" (Matt. 25:40) is tantamount to responding to God.

How unfortunate it is that we have reduced prayer to a private act, an occasion for selfish complaint. In prayer, our concerns ought to be the concerns of others, of the world, and especially of those who cannot protect themselves. Otherwise, prayer becomes more than exclusive; it becomes divisive, which is the literal meaning of the term "diabolical." Authentic prayer reveals a sense of togetherness, not as a comfortable feeling of self-complacency but rather as an experience of at-one-ment or reconciliation with all humanity and all of God's creation. The *Macarian Homilies*, a late fourth-century spiritual classic, states that "those who pray truly and in silence, edify everybody everywhere." The cosmic significance of prayer and its universal force in the world have important qualifications, not least for the understanding of the role of believers in our age. For there can never be love for one person or group of people and not another. As the Christian Gospel puts it, to say that we love God when we do not love our neighbor is to be proved liars (cf. 1 John 4:20). This mutual interdependence of all humankind, as of all creation, is crucial in appreciating the wide-reaching effects of our thoughts, feelings, beliefs, and actions.

The foremost purpose of prayer is self-purification. "First of all," claims Evagrius of Pontus (346–99) in his masterpiece *On Prayer*, "pray to be purified from your passions." Unpurified, prayer becomes false piety, or quite simply false prayer. Self-regarding prayer is sinful prayer; or, more precisely, it is not prayer at all. In fact, the Desert Fathers and Mothers insist that not only is purity a prerequisite for prayer; purity actually is prayer. They speak of stripping ourselves of all that is unnecessary or superfluous, of all that prevents or delays us from connecting with our Creator, with our inner world, and with the rest of the world.

This is why the sequence of prayer recommended by the Church Fathers is: thanksgiving, confession, and petition. It is a suggestion that serves to underline the priority of looking outward toward others rather than focusing inwardly on ourselves:

> Before all else, let us first list sincere thanksgiving on the scroll of our prayer. On the second line, we should place confession and heartfelt contrition of the soul. Finally, let us present our petition to God. This has been shown to be the best way of prayer, revealed to someone by an angel.[2]

Although the author of *The Ladder of Divine Ascent* refers to this sequence as being revealed "by an angel," in fact it is not unprecedented in the spiritual classics, including Evagrius of Pontus in the fourth century, Abba Isaiah of Scetis in the fifth century, Barsanuphius and John in the sixth century, and Isaac the Syrian in the seventh century. Our concerns and preoccupations should not take center stage at the time of prayer. We should first allow a period of silence, when our personal interests and anxieties settle somewhat from the intensity of our daily routine, and then allow space for the needs of the world to rise to the surface of our hearts. Just as love arises from prayer, so, too, does prayer derive from silence.

Moreover, in the Orthodox tradition, prayer does not constitute a stage—whether preliminary or ultimate—in the spiritual life; rather, it is a pervasive activity that permeates all stages and all aspects of life. Prayer presupposes a life that is fully integrated with the life of the world rather than something that happens at a particular point in our daily or weekly routine. Our aim in reciting prayers on given occasions, and retiring for prayers at particular moments, is to advance from the stage of saying prayers to the point of becoming prayer. To adopt the words of an early theologian, Origen of Alexandria (175–254), "The entire life of a saint is one great, unbroken prayer." Our goal is to become fiery flames of prayer, living prayers, comforting those in despair and warming those in need.

THE JESUS PRAYER

The whole teaching about prayer and the entire discipline of prayer may be condensed into a short formula, commonly known as the Jesus Prayer. It is a prayer that was solemnized in the classic writings of *The Philokalia*[3] and popularized through more contemporary works, such as *The Way of a Pilgrim*,[4] the anonymous nineteenth-century story of a Russian wanderer in search of "unceasing prayer," and J. D. Salinger's 1955 and 1957 stories from the *New Yorker*, published separately under the title *Franny and Zooey*,[5] where members of the Glass family discuss the importance of education and the role of contemplative prayer.

The words of this brief prayer—"Lord Jesus Christ, Son of God, have mercy on me"[6]—are sometimes simply reduced to "Lord, have mercy." It is a perfectly simple prayer and should not be turned into an unduly complicated exercise. In this respect, the Jesus Prayer can be used by anyone inasmuch as it is a concise arrow-prayer that leads directly from our heart to the heart of God via the heart of the world. Due to its brevity, it provides a practical means of concentration and freedom from distraction. Consequently, it enables one to repeat the name of God spontaneously at all times and in all places, thereby actualizing the living presence of the divine person, who is named and thereby invoked. It is a way of taking seriously Saint Paul's admonition to "pray without ceasing" (1 Thess. 5:17).

While the roots of the Jesus Prayer may be traced back to Scripture (Exod. 3:14 and Phil. 2:9–11), its sources are already adumbrated in the fourth-century desert tradition. However, it assumes particular importance in the sixth and seventh centuries with the Palestinian and Sinaite schools of spirituality. The formula itself is first found in the tenth century but is established in the fourteenth century with the tradition of Hesychasm;[7] at that time, it is brought from Mount Sinai by Saint Gregory of Sinai (ca. 1255–ca. 1337) to Mount Athos, where it is symbolically preserved to this day for the whole world. Nevertheless, while the Jesus Prayer has been nurtured and cradled in monastic circles through the centuries, it has always been regarded not as a privilege of the monks but rather as the treasure of all those who wish to experience the fruit of prayer.

The Jesus Prayer is one way—albeit a powerful and tested way— of preserving the power of silence in prayer. Learning to be silent is far more difficult and far more important than learning to recite prayers. Silence is not the absence of noise but the gift or skill to discern between quiet and stillness. It is the power of learning to listen and the wisdom of learning to know. Silence is a way of being fully involved and active, of being fully alive and compassionate. In prayer, when words end in silence, we awaken to a new awareness and watchfulness. Silence shocks us out of numbness to the world and its needs; it sharpens our vision from the dullness of complacency and selfishness by focusing on the heart of all that matters. Silence is a way of noticing more clearly, of paying attention, and of responding more effectively.

Then, through silence and prayer, we no longer ignore what is going on around us; and we are no longer stuck in what merely concerns us. Then we can commit to a countercultural way, whereby we are no longer victims of our society's ways and norms, passively accepting or obsessively pursuing what is either fashionable or acceptable. This is because we recognize that we are all intimately interconnected and mutually interdependent. We come to know that nothing is self-contained, that there is no autonomy in our world. We appreciate that there can only be a distinction between a sense of responsibility and a lack thereof. Through the Jesus Prayer, one develops a greater sense of awareness and attentiveness to the world within and around.

THE WAY OF FASTING

Together with prayer, fasting is a critical form of ascetic discipline in the spiritual life. Physical practices of abstinence assist in breaking forceful habits that accrue within and harden the heart over years and even over generations. However, like the phenomenon of monasticism, which we explored in the previous chapter, the aim of fasting is not to denigrate or destroy the body, which is always respected as "a temple of God" (1 Cor. 3:16). Rather, it is to refine the whole person, to render the faculties more subtle and sensitive to the outside world as well as to "the inner kingdom."[8]

Fasting is another way of rejecting the split between heaven and earth. It is a way of recognizing the catastrophic results when reality is bifurcated by false spirituality. The early ascetics deeply valued fasting. So, too, do contemporary monastics. Indeed, even lay Orthodox Christians endeavor to meet the requirements of fasting, by abstaining from dairy and meat products almost half of the entire year. Perhaps this in itself is an unconscious effort to reconcile one half of the year with the other, secular time with the sacred time of eternity.

The whole notion of fasting or abstinence has lost its significance, or at least its positive connotation, over the centuries. Nowa-
days, it is used in a negative sense to imply the opposite of a healthy
diet or balanced engagement with the world. Those who fast are eccentric or extreme in their protest against the world; they are not
seen as expressing a sense of integration with the world. Yet the early
Christian and monastic interpretation of the word could not be
more different. In the early Church, fasting signified not allowing
worldly values or self-centeredness to distract us from what is most
essential in our relationship with God, with others, and with the
world.

Fasting implies a sense of freedom. Fasting is a way of not wanting, of wanting less, and of recognizing the wants of others. By abstaining from certain foods, we are not punishing ourselves but
instead able to reserve proper value for all foods. Moreover, fasting
implies alertness. By paying close attention to what we do, to the in-
take of food and the quantity of our possessions, we better appreciate the reality of suffering and the value of sharing. Fasting involves
the process of absorbing pain and transforming it into renewed
hope. It ultimately implies focusing on what really matters, priori-
tizing what one values, and acquiring an attitude of responsiveness
and responsibility.

Indeed, fasting underlines the dignity and value of everything
and everyone. The spiritual senses are gradually and increasingly refined in such a way as to understand where one's heart ought to be.
Fasting begins as a form of detachment; however, when we learn
what to let go of, we recognize what we should hold on to. Fasting
is a way not of renouncing the world but of embracing the entire
world, a way of looking at the world from another, a different, a
mystical or sacramental perspective. It is an expression of love and
compassion. The same discipline of fasting ought to characterize
our words (in silence), our actions (in charity), and our relation-

ships (in purity). Sacrifice and service coincide in the spiritual life. Fasting leads to one goal: namely, the goal of encounter or mystery. The wise inhabitants of the early desert of Egypt understood this truth well:

Abba Poemen (d. 449) said: "If three people meet, of whom the first fully preserves interior peace, the second gives thanks to God in illness, and the third serves with a pure mind, these three are doing the same work."9

In this way, prayer and fasting are never separated in the spiritual life from work and action. Instead, they liberate us in order to serve others more freely. We are no longer burdened by necessity or conditioning, but are prepared for the surprise of divine grace. Furthermore, this discipline through prayer and fasting leads to an attitude of humility, where the focus shifts from placing oneself at the center of the world to becoming involved in the service of others. A person of prayer and fasting can never tolerate creating miserable poverty for the sake of accumulating exorbitant wealth. The moral crisis of our global economic injustice is deeply spiritual, signaling that something is terribly amiss in our relationship with God, people, and material things. Most of us—at least those of us who live in societies shaped by Western concerns—remain insulated from and ignorant of this injustice created by current global trade and investment regimes. Fasting sensitizes us to awareness and knowledge.

Fasting means walking the way of the humble, assuming the power of prayer, and regaining a sense of wonder. It is recognizing God in all people and in all things; and it is valuing all people and all things in the light of God. It is a critical alternative to our consumer lifestyle in Western society, which does not permit us to notice the impact and effect of our customs and actions. Thus the spiritual world—conditioned by prayer and fasting—is anything but disconnected from the "real" world; by the same token, the "real" world is informed by the spiritual world. We are no longer disengaged from the injustice in our world. Our vision grows wider, our interest is enlarged, and our action becomes far-reaching. We cease to narrow life to our petty concerns and instead accept our vocation to transform the entire world.

Fasting does not deny the world but affirms the entire material creation. It recalls the hunger of others in a symbolic effort to identify with—or at least bring to mind—the suffering of the world in order to yearn for healing. Through fasting, the act of eating becomes the mystery of sharing, the recollection that "it is not good for man to be alone upon this earth" (Gen. 2:18) and that "man shall not live by bread alone" (Matt. 4:4). To fast, then, is to fast with and for others; ultimately, the goal of such fasting is to promote and celebrate a sense of fairness in what we have received. As is the case with every ascetic discipline in the spiritual life, one never fasts alone in the Orthodox Church; we always fast together, and we fast at set times. Fasting is a solemn reminder that everything we do relates to either the well-being or the wounding of others.

Thus, through fasting, we acknowledge that "the earth is the Lord's" (Ps. 24:1) and not ours to own or exploit, to consume or control. It is always to be shared in communion with others and returned in thanks to God. Fasting is learning to give, and not simply to give up; it is learning to connect, and not to disconnect; it is breaking down barriers of ignorance and indifference with my neighbor and with my world. It is restoring the primal vision of the world, as God intended it, and discerning the beauty of the world, as God created it. It offers a sense of liberation from greed and compulsion. Indeed, it offers a powerful corrective to our culture of selfish want and careless waste.

CONCLUSION: THE WORLD OF THE SACRAMENTS

We have already seen how community is brought to bear in prayer and fasting. The sacraments provide yet another way of relating to God and to the world, whereby everything is received and shared as gifts of encounter and communion. Unfortunately, the sacraments have themselves often been reduced to ritual observance, rather than being understood as a way of active engagement. Yet the notion of communion is much more than a way of pious inspiration or individual reward. It is an imperative for sharing. It is a powerful and privileged experience of encounter with God.

We have been accustomed to seeing the sacraments narrowly as community rituals or spiritual requirements. It is crucial, however, that we recall the sacramental or mystical principle of the whole world, recognizing that nothing in life is ultimately profane or secular. Everything is created by God, embraced by God, and reconciled by God. By the same token, everything bears the unique seal of God, the seed of God, and the very traces of God. This may be very difficult to see when people perceive the world in a mechanistic way, giving priority to their greedy desires rather than to the godly mystery. Such a worldview is far removed from the iconic or mystical dimension of the world, which envisages God as organically embodied and involved in the entire creation. In the concluding prayer to the Ninth Hour, recited each evening prior to Vespers, Orthodox Christians remember the role of humanity to discover and uncover the presence of God "at every hour and every moment, both in heaven and on earth, indeed in all places of his dominion" (Ps. 103:22). Such is the power of mystery in a sacramental view of the world.

The sacraments are the Church's way of restoring the intimacy between God and the world, which was lost through sin and evil. They are gifts from God, given in order to appropriate wholeness through transformation. Orthodox Christians in fact prefer to speak of "mystery" rather than "sacrament." The latter tends to imply acquisition of divine grace as something "objective"; the former signifies the radical otherness of God as "subject," even in the very existence of divine grace. In this respect, every aspect of this world and life is mysterious; and every aspect of divine life is sacramental. Mystery is that sacred space or moment when humanity and creation encounter the transcendent God.

Traditionally, it is said that there are seven sacraments. Yet this categorization is neither completely true nor always helpful. The Orthodox Church has in fact never limited itself to seven sacraments, preferring to speak of every aspect, moment, and stage of life as being sacramental or constituting a mystery—from birth to death. In fact, the funeral service was once classified as a mystery or sacrament in the Orthodox liturgical practice. The sacraments do not work in some magical manner; rather, they function "mystically," namely in a silent manner, permeating the hearts and lives of those who choose to be open to the possibility of encounter with God.

In the sacramental way, *baptism* becomes more than merely a formal initiation to an exclusive or closed community. Baptism is a re-creation of humanity and the world in the light of Christ. Through the water of baptism, we are immersed in the death and Resurrection of Christ (Rom. 14:8), being "planted together" (Rom. 6:5) forever with Christ. In a world where water is so carelessly wasted and polluted, the sacrament of baptism highlights the profound connection between the Spirit of God brooding over "the face of the world," as in the first moments of Genesis, and the entire universe. The living water of the living God is in this way able to renew and sanctify all of creation.

The sacrament of *chrismation*, known in other confessions as confirmation, is more than a confirmation of our personal invitation to discern Christ. It recognizes "the seal of the gift of the Holy

Spirit" in all human beings, in all corners of the world, and in all elements of the universe. We are called to recognize the face of God in the face of each person as well as in the face of the natural world. The word "chrismation" derives from the Greek *chrisma*, which means "anointing"; the "anointed one" is the "Christ," or the "Messiah" (in Hebrew). Our purpose, then, is to be "in Christ"[10] and Christlike, anointing and healing the world with our presence.

The sacrament of the *Eucharist* is pregnant with endless possibilities and opportunities for deepening our awareness of communion. In the Christian practice, it is an invitation to conform to the Body of Christ. The Eucharist is not a spiritual reward for rigorous discipline. It challenges individuals and communities to work for a just society, where basic food and water are plentiful for all and where everyone has enough.

The sacrament of *confession*—or reconciliation, as it is sometimes known—provides more than simply an occasion for the expression of remorse, the removal of guilt, or the assurance of forgiveness. Forgiveness provides occasion "for giving," for sharing and reconciling. It focuses attention on others and on God's creation—not only on ourselves or on our possessions. In the Christian Church, it is a way of reintegration into the Body of Christ. It is also a reintegration into the body of society and the world.

In the sacrament of *marriage*, a couple is invited to experience and celebrate oneness together, beyond the pain of separation or isolation. How unfortunate it is that this sacrament has been conveniently reduced to a form of social contract, somehow implying the urban lifestyle of Western society. In its spiritual sense, marriage is primarily an expression of the profound unity that exists between Creator and creation, between God and humanity, between body and soul, matter and spirit, time and eternity, heaven and earth.

The sacrament of *holy unction*—or healing, as it is termed in other churches—is not simply the final rites on a dying human being. In the Orthodox practice, it is adopted throughout life as the outpouring of "the oil of gladness" on the scars of the soul and the wounds of the world. It aims at healing the breach or brokenness between body and soul, mending the shattered parts of the heart and the earth, while reconciling heaven with all of God's creation.

Finally, the sacrament of *ordination* is not a declaration of the exclusive rights granted to the priesthood and hierarchy. Priesthood is in fact the royal vocation of all people. Through ordination, the Body of Christ receives a new expression and renewed vitality. The whole world is a sacred cathedral; no person is unordained for the kingdom, and no place is unhallowed in this world. When we can discern the presence of God in everyone and in every place, we can rejoice and celebrate the fullness of life.

It is tragic that Christians have become so alienated from the way of the sacraments. Our very notion of sacramental mystery is no longer associated with the meaning of life. Yet sacraments are what render life vital. They reconnect us to God, to other people, and to the natural world. Writers of the early Christian Church believed that Christ's flesh was a sacrament (Ignatius of Antioch, d. ca. 115); this should serve to underline the sacredness of all that involves the human flesh. Later mystics were convinced that our own flesh was a sacrament (Symeon the New Theologian, 949–1022) and that the whole world was a sacrament (Maximus the Confessor, 580–662).

VI.
THE WONDER OF CREATION

RELIGION AND ECOLOGY

My book is the nature of creation; therein,
I read the works of God.

—SAINT ANTHONY OF EGYPT (THIRD THROUGH FOURTH CENTURIES)

THE BEAUTY OF THE WORLD

My appreciation for the natural environment is directly related to the sacramental dimension of life and the world. I have always regarded the natural environment from the perspective of Orthodox spirituality. I have respected it as a place of encounter and communion with the Creator. As a young boy, accompanying the priest of my local village to services in remote chapels on my native island of Imvros, I connected the beauty of the mountainside to the splendor of the liturgy. The natural environment seems to provide me with a broader, panoramic vision of the world. I believe that in general nature's beauty leads us to a more open view of life and the created world, somewhat resembling a wide-angle focus from a camera, which ultimately prevents us human beings from selfishly using or even abusing its natural resources. It is through the spiritual lens of Orthodox theology that I can better appreciate the broader aspects of such problems as the threat to ocean fisheries, the disappearance of wetlands, the damage to coral reefs, or the destruction of animal and plant life.

The spiritual life demands an appropriate veneration—though not an absolute worship—of God's creation. The way we relate to material things directly reflects the way we relate to God. The sensitivity with which we handle worldly things clearly mirrors the sacredness that we reserve for heavenly things. And this is not simply a matter that concerns us as individuals. As we shall see in later chapters, it also concerns us as communities and as a society. We need to treat nature with the same awe and wonder that we show when we treasure a classical work of beauty and art.

In order, however, to reach this point of maturity and dignity toward the natural environment, we must take the time to listen to the voice of creation. And to do this, we must first be silent. As we have already seen, silence is a fundamental element of the ascetic way, which has already been outlined in previous chapters. Silence and ascesis, however, are critical also in developing a balanced environmental ethos as an alternative to the ways that we currently relate to the earth and deplete its natural resources. Sometimes, it takes effort to change our patterns and habits. *The Sayings of the Desert Fathers* relate of Abba Chaeremon that in the fourth century he deliberately constructed his cell "forty miles from the church and ten miles from the water" so that he might struggle a little to do his daily chores.[1] In Greece today, the island of Hydra still forbids the construction of roads and the traffic of cars. The same is true on the Princes Islands in Turkey.

So the ascetic way informs us of the critical importance of silence. For "the heavens declare the glory of God, and the firmament proclaims the creation of His hands" (Ps. 19:1). The ancient Liturgy of Saint James is celebrated only twice a year in Orthodox churches. However, in that service, there is a prayer that affirms the same conviction:

The heavens declare the glory of the Creator; the earth proclaims the sovereignty of God; the sea heralds the authority of the Lord; and every material and spiritual creature preaches the magnificence of God at all times.

When God spoke to Moses in the burning bush, communication occurred through a silent voice, as Saint Gregory of Nyssa informs us in his mystical classic, *The Life of Moses*. Nature is a book, opened wide for all to read and to learn. Each plant, each animal, and each microorganism tells a story, unfolds a mystery, relates an extraordinary harmony and balance, which are interdependent and complementary. Everything points to the same encounter and mystery.

The same dialogue of communication and mystery of communion is detected in the galaxies, where the countless stars betray the same mystical beauty and mathematical interconnectedness. We do not need this perspective in order to believe in God or to prove His existence. We need it to breathe; we need it for us simply to be. The coexistence and correlation between the boundlessly infinite and the most insignificantly finite things articulate a concelebration of joy and love. This is precisely what, in the seventh century, Saint Maximus the Confessor (580–662) called a "cosmic liturgy." There are "words" (or *logoi*) in creation that can be discerned with proper attentiveness. They are what the Church Fathers called "the word (or *logos*) of things," "the word (or *logos*) of beings," and "the word (or *logos*) of existence itself."

It is unfortunate when we lead our lives without even noticing the environmental concert that is playing out before our eyes and ears. In this orchestra, each minute detail plays a critical role, and every trivial aspect participates in an essential way. No single member—human or otherwise—can be removed without the entire picture being deeply affected. No single tree or animal can be removed without the entire picture being profoundly distorted, if not destroyed. When will we stop to hear the music of this harmony? It is an ongoing rhythm, even if we are not aware of it. When will we learn the alphabet of this divine language, so mysteriously concealed in nature? It is so clearly revealed in the created world around us. When will we learn to embrace the awesome beauty of the divine presence on the body of the world? Its contours are so markedly visible.

ORTHODOX THEOLOGY AND
THE NATURAL ENVIRONMENT

In its foremost and traditional symbol and declaration of faith, the Orthodox Church confesses "one God, maker of heaven and earth, and of all things visible and invisible." An Orthodox Christian perspective on the natural environment derives from the fundamental belief that the world was created by a loving God. The Judeo-Christian Scriptures state, in the Book of Genesis, that "God saw everything that was created and, indeed, it was very good" (Gen. 1:31). So the entire world contains seeds and traces of the living God. Moreover, the material and natural creation was granted by God to humanity as a gift, with the command to "serve and preserve the earth" (Gen. 2:15).

If the earth is sacred, then our relationship with the natural environment is mystical or sacramental; that is to say, it contains the seed and trace of God. In many ways, the "sin of Adam" is precisely his refusal to receive the world as a gift of encounter and communion with God and with the rest of creation. Saint Paul's Letter to the Romans emphasizes the consequences of sin: the fact that "from the beginning till now, the entire creation, which as we know has been groaning in pain" (Rom. 8:22), "awaits with eager longing this revelation by the children of God" (Rom. 8:19).

From this fundamental belief in the sacredness and beauty of all creation, the Orthodox Church articulates its crucial concept of cosmic transfiguration. This emphasis of Orthodox theology on personal and cosmic transfiguration is especially apparent in its liturgical feasts. The Feast of Christ's Transfiguration, celebrated on August 6, highlights the sacredness of all creation, which receives and offers a foretaste of the final resurrection and restoration of all things in the age to come. The *Macarian Homilies* underline the connection between the Transfiguration of Christ and the sanctification of human nature:

Just as the Lord's body was glorified, when he went up the [Tabor] mountain and was transfigured into glory and into infinite light . . . so, too, our human nature is transformed into the power of God, being kindled into fire and light.[2]

Yet the hymns of the day extend this divine light and transformative power to the whole world:

Today, on Mt. Tabor, in the manifestation of your light, O Lord, You were unaltered from the light of the unbegotten Father. We have seen the Father as light, and the Spirit as light, guiding with light the entire creation.

Moreover, the Feast of the Baptism of Jesus Christ on January 6 is known as the Theophany (meaning "the revelation of God") because it manifests the perfect obedience of Christ to the original command of Genesis and restores the purpose of the world as it was created and intended by God. The hymns of that day proclaim:

The nature of waters is sanctified, the earth is blessed, and the heavens are enlightened . . . so that by the elements of creation, and by the angels, and by human beings, by things both visible and invisible, God's most holy name may be glorified.

The breadth and depth, therefore, of the Orthodox cosmic vision imply that humanity is a part of this theophany, which is always greater than any one individual. Of course, the human race plays a unique role and has a unique responsibility; but it nevertheless constitutes *a part of* the universe that cannot be considered or conceived *apart from* the universe. In this way, the natural environment ceases to be something that we observe objectively and exploit selfishly and becomes a part of the "cosmic liturgy" or celebration of the essential interconnection and interdependence of all things.

In light of this, another seventh-century mystic, Saint Isaac the Syrian, claims that the aim of the spiritual life is therefore to acquire "a merciful heart, one which burns with love for the whole of creation . . . for all of God's creatures." This is echoed in the nineteenth century by the exhortation of Fyodor Dostoyevsky (1821–81) in *The Brothers Karamazov*:

Love all God's creation, the whole of it and every grain of sand. Love every leaf, every ray of God's light. Love the animals, love the plants, love everything. If you love everything, you will perceive the divine mystery in things.

Orthodox theology takes a further step and recognizes the natural creation as inseparable from the identity and destiny of humanity, because every human action leaves a lasting imprint on the body of the earth. Human attitudes and behavior toward creation directly impact on and reflect human attitudes and behavior toward other people. Ecology is inevitably related in both its etymology and its meaning to economy; our global economy is simply outgrowing the capacity of our planet to support it. At stake is not just our ability to live in a sustainable way but our very survival. Scientists estimate that those most hurt by global warming in years to come will be those who can least afford it. Therefore, the ecological problem of pollution is invariably connected to the social problem of poverty; and so all ecological activity is ultimately measured and properly judged by its impact and effect upon the poor (see Matt. 25).

It is clear that only a cooperative and collective response—by religious leaders, scientists, political authorities, and financial corporations—will appropriately and effectively address these critical issues of our time. For this reason, on September 1, 1989, Ecumenical Patriarch Demetrios (1914–91) issued an encyclical letter—the first of a series of annual messages since that time—to all Orthodox churches throughout the world, establishing that day, which is also the first day of the ecclesiastical year, as a day of prayer for the protection and preservation of the natural environment. This dedication was later embraced by the Conference of European Churches and, in turn, the World Council of Churches. As his successor to the Ecumenical Throne of Constantinople, I have encouraged the same sense of urgent concern over the environment in order to raise popular awareness and render international consciousness more sensitive to the irreversible destruction that threatens the planet today. The diverse initiatives of our Church include the creation of the Religious and Scientific Committee in 1995 and the organization of several interdisciplinary Religion, Science, and the Environment symposia to this day.[3] In this way, the Ecumenical Patriarchate is able to contribute to the preservation of the world around us.

ORTHODOX SPIRITUALITY AND
THE NATURAL ENVIRONMENT

"Around us" is of course precisely what the word "environment" means. We are always surrounded as human beings, from the moment of our birth to the time of our death. We grow and are nurtured, we learn and mature, within an environment. While this environment may be material or spiritual, it remains a constant and defining factor in our lives. We are shaped by family and friends, influenced by teachings and trends, just as we are surrounded by land and air, by sun and sea, by flora and fauna. In the fourth century, Saint Gregory the Theologian (329–89) observed that this is precisely how the Creator God intended human beings to be in relation to their natural environment.

The Word of God wanted to reveal that humanity participates in both worlds, namely in invisible as well as in visible nature. This is why Adam [that is to say, humanity] was created. From earthly matter, which was already created, God formed the human body; from the spiritual world, God breathed life into the soul of Adam, which we call the image of God. Therefore, Adam was placed on this earth as a second world, a large world within a small world, like an angel that worships God while participating in the spiritual and material worlds alike. Adam was created to protect and preserve the visible world, while at the same time being initiated into the spiritual world. Adam was destined to serve as a royal [from: *basileus*] steward [from: *oikonomos*] over creation—royalty, yet at the same time subject to a heavenly king; earthly, yet at the same time heavenly; temporary, yet at the same time immortal; visible by virtue of the body, yet at the same time invisible by virtue of the soul. Adam was between dignity and humility. Adam was called to glorify the divine benefactor on high, while at the same time suffering lowly humiliation. The purpose and end of the human mystery of creation is deification. So Adam is called to become god by divine grace, and to look solely toward God.

This is where the depth of Orthodox spirituality may differ somewhat from contemporary deep ecology. The difference lies not so much in the level of desire to preserve and to protect the natural resources of the world, which should be the priority of all human beings—from political leaders to individual citizens. It lies primarily in the worldview that is espoused. The difference may be detected less in the way we perceive the end result, which must certainly be sought and achieved by everyone and for the sake of everyone. Rather, it is discerned as the starting point of our attitudes and actions. Orthodox theology regards humanity as possessing a royal, but not a tyrannical, dimension. Belief in the stewardship and ministry of humanity within creation is marked by a profound sense of justice and also moderation.

We can be neither prideful in our authority nor falsely humble in our self-limitations. We are called to preserve creation by serving its Creator. Preservation and celebration are intimately connected. This is the interpretation that Orthodox theology and liturgy provide for the scriptural command "to till and to keep the earth" (Gen. 2:15), which might quite as easily be translated as the mandate "to serve and preserve the earth." We are to act as "faithful and prudent stewards" of this world (Luke 12:42), "like good stewards of the manifold grace of God" (1 Pet. 4:10). We can never act in isolation from God; we must always act in humble acknowledgment of God as Creator. All authority to regulate and minister comes from God and through God; and it is always directed to God for the glory of God (cf. Prov. 8:15).

The entire world was created by God for the privilege of all and for preservation by all.[4] The entire world is, therefore, the concern of the Church, which prays earnestly "for things in the world and for things above the world."[5] By the same token, the entire world should constitute the object of our prayer to God:

Remember, Lord, favorable winds, peaceful rains, beneficial freshness, the abundance of fruits, perfect ends, glorious years. For the eyes of all look in hope toward Thee. And Thou grantest them their timely nourishment. Thou openest Thy hand and fill all living things with good will.[6]

Send down rains to those places and people that so need them. Raise the rivers in their proper measure and according to Thy grace. Increase the fruits of the earth for their timely sowing and crop. We pray for good winds and for the earth's fruits; we pray for the balanced rise of river waters; and we pray for beneficial rains and fruitful crops.[7]

This means that the whole of material creation is properly perceived and preserved through the eyes of the liturgy.

ORTHODOX LITURGY AND
THE NATURAL ENVIRONMENT

In the Orthodox liturgical perspective, creation is received and conceived as a gift from God. The notion of creation-as-gift defines our Orthodox theological understanding of the environmental question in a concise and clear manner while at the same time determining the human response to that gift through the responsible and proper use of the created world. Each believer is called to celebrate life in a way that reflects the words of the Divine Liturgy: "Thine own from Thine own we offer to Thee, in all and for all."

Thus the Eastern Orthodox Church proposes a liturgical worldview. It proclaims a world richly imbued by God and a God profoundly involved in this world. Our "original sin," so it might be said, does not lie in any legalistic transgression of religious commands that might incur divine wrath or human guilt. Instead, it lies in our stubborn refusal as human beings to receive the world as a gift of encounter and reconciliation with our planet and to regard the world as the mystery of communion with the rest of humanity.

This is why the Ecumenical Patriarchate has initiated and organized a number of international and interdisciplinary symposia over the last decade: in the Aegean Sea (1995) and the Black Sea (1997), along the Danube River (1999) and in the Adriatic Sea (2002), in the Baltic Sea (2003), on the Amazon River (2006), and, most recently, in the Arctic Ocean (2007). For, like the air we breathe, water is the very source of life; if it is defiled or despoiled, the element and essence of our existence are threatened. Put simply: environmental degradation and destruction are tantamount to suicide. We appear to be inexorably trapped within lifestyles and systems that repeatedly ignore the constraints of nature, which are neither deniable nor negotiable. It looks all too likely that we will learn some things about our planet's capacity for survival only when things are beyond the point of no return.

One of the hymns of the Orthodox Church, chanted on the day of Christ's baptism in the Jordan River, a feast of renewal and regeneration for the entire world, articulates this tragedy: "I have become . . . the defilement of the air and the land and the water." At a time when we have polluted the air we breathe and the water we drink, we are called to restore within ourselves a sense of awe and delight, to respond to matter as to a mystery of ever-increasing connectedness and sacramental dimensions.

As a gift from God to humanity, creation becomes our companion, given to us for the sake of living in harmony with it and in communion with others. We are to use its resources in moderation and frugality, to cultivate it in love and humility, and to preserve it in accordance with the scriptural command to serve and preserve (cf. Gen. 2:15). Within the unimpaired natural environment, humanity discovers deep spiritual peace and rest; and in humanity that is spiritually cultivated by the peaceful grace of God, nature recognizes its harmonious and rightful place.

Nevertheless, the first-created human being misused the gift of freedom, instead preferring alienation from God-the-Giver and attachment to God's gift. Consequently, the double relationship of humanity to God and creation was distorted, and humanity became preoccupied with using and consuming the earth's resources. In this way, the human blessedness that flows from the love between God and humanity ceased to exist, and humanity sought to fill this void by drawing from creation itself—instead of from its Creator—the blessedness that was lacking. From grateful user, then, the human person became greedy abuser. In order to remedy this situation, human beings are called to return to a "eucharistic" and "ascetic" way of life, namely to be thankful by offering glory to God for the gift of creation while at the same time being respectful by practicing responsibility within the web of creation.

EUCHARISTIC AND ASCETIC BEINGS

Let me reflect further on these two critical words: "eucharistic" and "ascetic." The implications of the first word are quite easily appreciated. The term derives from the Greek word *eucharistia*, meaning "thanks," and is, in the Orthodox Church, understood also as the deeper significance of liturgy. In calling for a "eucharistic spirit," the Orthodox Church is reminding us that the created world is not simply our possession but a gift—a gift from God the Creator, a healing gift, a gift of wonder and beauty. Therefore, the proper response, upon receiving such a gift, is to accept and embrace it with gratitude and thanksgiving.

Thanksgiving underlines the sacramental worldview of the Orthodox Church. From the very moment of creation, this world was offered by God as a gift to be transformed and returned in gratitude. This is precisely how the Orthodox spiritual way avoids the problem of the world's domination by humanity. For if this world is a sacred mystery, then this in itself precludes any attempt at mastery by human beings. Indeed, the mastery or exploitative control of the world's resources is identified more with Adam's "original sin" than with God's wonderful gift. It is the result of selfishness and greed, which arise from alienation from God and the abandonment of a sacramental worldview. Sin separated the sacred from the secular, dismissing the latter to the domain of evil and surrendering it as prey to exploitation.

Thanksgiving, then, is a distinctive and definitive characteristic of human beings. A human is not merely a logical or political being. Above all, human beings are eucharistic creatures, capable of gratitude and endowed with the power to bless God for the gift of creation. Again, the Greek word for "blessing" (*eulogia*) implies having a good word to say about something or someone; it is the opposite of cursing the world. Other animals express their gratefulness simply by being themselves, by living in the world through their own instinctive manner. Yet we human beings possess a sense of self-awareness in an intuitive manner, and so consciously and by deliberate choice we can thank God for the world with eucharistic joy. Without such thanksgiving, we are not truly human.

A eucharistic spirit also implies using the earth's natural resources with a spirit of thankfulness, offering them back to God; indeed, we are to offer not only the earth's resources but ourselves. In the sacrament of the Eucharist, we return to God what is His own: namely, the bread and the wine, together with and through the entire community, which itself is offered in humble thanks to the Creator. As a result, God transforms the bread and wine, namely the world, into a mystery of encounter. All of us and all things represent the fruits of creation, which are no longer imprisoned by a fallen world but returned as liberated, purified from their fallen state, and capable of receiving the divine presence within themselves.

Whoever, then, gives thanks also experiences the joy that comes from appreciating that for which he or she is thankful. Conversely, whoever does not feel the need to be thankful for the wonder and beauty of the world, but instead demonstrates only selfishness or indifference, can never experience a deeper, divine joy, but only sullen sorrow and unquenched satisfaction. Such a person not only curses the world but experiences the world as curse. This is why people with so much can be so bitter, while others with so little can be so grateful.

The second term is "ascetic," which derives from the Greek verb *askeo* and implies a working of raw material with training or skill. Thus, we have the "ascetic ethos" of Orthodoxy that involves fasting and other similar spiritual disciplines. These make us recognize that everything we take for granted in fact comprises God's gifts, which are provided in order to satisfy our needs as they are shared fairly among all people. However, they are not ours to abuse and waste simply because we have the desire to consume them or the ability to pay for them.

The ascetic ethos is the intention and disciplined effort to protect the gift of creation and to preserve nature intact. It is the struggle for self-restraint and self-control, whereby we no longer willfully consume every fruit but instead manifest a sense of frugality and abstinence from certain fruits. Both the protection and the self-restraint are expressions of love for all of humanity and for the entire natural creation. Such love alone can protect the world from unnecessary waste and inevitable destruction. After all, just as the true nature of "God is love" (1 John 4:8), so, too, humanity is originally and innately endowed with the purpose of loving.

Our purpose is thus conjoined to the priest's prayer in the Divine Liturgy: "In offering to Thee, Thine own from Thine own, in all and for all—we praise Thee, we bless Thee, and we give thanks to Thee, O Lord." Then we are able to embrace all people and all things—not with fear or necessity, but with love and joy. Then we learn to care for the plants and for the animals, for the trees and for the rivers, for the mountains and for the seas, for all human beings and for the whole natural environment. Then we discover joy—rather than inflicting sorrow—in our life and in our world. As a result, we create and promote instruments of peace and life, not tools of violence and death. Then creation on the one hand and humanity on the other hand—the one that encompasses and the one that is encompassed—correspond fully and cooperate with each other. For they are no longer in contradiction or in conflict or in competition. Then, just as humanity offers creation in an act of priestly service and sacrifice, returning it to God, so also does creation offer itself in return as a gift to humanity for all generations that are to follow. Then everything becomes a form of exchange, the fruit of abundance, and a fulfillment of love. Then everything assumes its original vision and purpose, as God intended it from the moment of creation.

THE THIRD DAY OF CREATION

The brief yet powerful statement found in Genesis 1:11 corresponds to the majesty of this aspect of creation:

> Then God said: "Let the earth bring forth vegetation: plants yielding seed, and fruit trees of every kind on earth that bear fruit with the seed in it." And it was so . . . And God saw that it was good. And there was evening and there was morning, the third day.

We all know the healing and nourishing essence of plants; we all appreciate their manifold creative and cosmetic usefulness:

> Consider the lilies, how they grow: they neither toil nor spin; yet I tell you, even Solomon in all his glory was not clothed like one of these. (Luke 12:27)

Even the humblest and lowliest manifestations of God's created world comprise the most fundamental elements of life and the most precious aspects of natural beauty.

Nevertheless, by overgrazing or deforestation, we tend to disturb the balance of the plant world. Whether by excessive irrigation or urban construction, we interrupt the magnificent epic of the natural world. Our selfish ways have led us to ignore plants, or else to undervalue their importance. Our understanding of plants is sparse and selective. Our outlook is greed-oriented and profit-centered.

Yet plants are the center and source of life. Plants permit us to breathe and to dream. Plants provide the basis of spiritual and cultural life. A world without plants is a world without a sense of beauty. Indeed, a world without plants and vegetation is inconceivable and unimaginable. It would be a contradiction of life itself, tantamount to death. There is no such thing as a world where unsustainable development continues without critical reflection and self-control; there is no such thing as a planet that thoughtlessly and blindly proceeds along the present route of global warming. There is only wasteland and destruction. To adopt any other excuse or pretext is to deny the reality of land, water, and air pollution.

Plants are also the wisest of teachers and the best of models. For they turn toward light. They yearn for water. They cherish clean air. Their roots dig deep, while their reach is high. They are satisfied and sustained with so little. They transform and multiply everything that they draw from nature, including some things that appear wasteful or useless. They adapt spontaneously and produce abundantly—whether for the nourishment or admiration of others. They enjoy a microcosm of their own while contributing to the macrocosm around them.

THE FIFTH AND SIXTH DAYS OF CREATION

On the fifth and sixth days of creation, God is said to have made the variety of animals, as well as created man and woman in the divine image and likeness (Gen. 1:26). What most people seem to overlook is that the sixth day of creation is not entirely dedicated to the forming of Adam out of the earth. That sixth day was in fact shared with the creation of numerous "living creatures of every kind; cattle and creeping things and wild animals of the earth of every kind" (Gen. 1:24). This close connection between humanity and the rest of creation, from the very moment of genesis, is surely an important and powerful reminder of the intimate relationship that we share as human beings with the animal kingdom. While there is undoubtedly something unique about human creation in the divine image, there is more that unites us than separates us, not only as human beings but also with the created universe. It is a lesson we have learned in recent decades; but it is a lesson that we learned the hard way.

The saints of the early Eastern Church taught this same lesson long ago. The Desert Fathers knew that a person with a pure heart was able to sense the connection with the rest of creation, and especially with the animal world.[8] This is surely a reality that finds parallels in both Eastern and Western Christianity: one may recall Seraphim of Sarov (1759–1833) feeding the bear in the forest of the north, or Francis of Assisi (1181–1226) addressing the elements of the universe. This connection is not merely emotional; it is profoundly spiritual in its motive and content. It gives a sense of continuity and community with all of creation while providing an expression of identity and compassion with it—a recognition that, as Saint Paul put it, all things were created in Christ and in Christ all things hold together (Col. 1:15–17). This is why Abba Isaac of Nineveh can write from the desert of Syria in the seventh century:

What is a merciful heart? It is a heart, which is burning with love for the whole of creation: for human beings, for birds, for beasts, for demons—for all of God's creatures. When such persons recall or regard these creatures, their eyes are filled with tears. An overwhelming compassion makes their heart grow small and weak, and they cannot endure to hear or see any kind of suffering, even the smallest pain, inflicted upon any creature. Therefore, these persons never cease to pray with tears even for the irrational animals, for the enemies of truth, as well as for those who do them evil, asking that these may be protected and receive God's mercy. They even pray for the reptiles with such great compassion, which rises endlessly in their heart until they shine again and are glorious like God.[9]

Thus, love for God, love for human beings, and love for animals cannot be separated sharply. There may be a hierarchy of priority, but it is not a sharp distinction of comparison. The truth is that we are all one family—human beings and the living world alike—and all of us look to God the Creator: "These all look to you to give them ... When you open your hand, they are filled with good things. When you hide your face, they are dismayed. When you take away their breath, they die and return to their dust" (Ps. 104:27–29).

Precisely because of our faith as Orthodox Christians in the creation of the world by a loving God, and in the loving re-creation of the world by the divine Word at the Incarnation of God's Son, we cannot but be convinced environmentalists and firm believers in the sanctity of the material world. We await not simply a new heaven but also a new earth. We work toward that reality of a renewed and restored heaven and earth, where "the wolf shall feed with the lamb and the leopard shall lie down with the goat" (Isa. 11:6). This is not a utopian dream; for us as Orthodox Christians, this reality begins now. It is a pledge that we make to God that we shall embrace all of creation. It is what Orthodox theologians call an "inaugurated eschatology," or the final state already established and being realized in the present. "Behold, the kingdom of God is among [us]" (Luke 17:21). The transformation of the created world is a living reality for those who desire it and work toward the fullness of communion and the fairness of community among people throughout the world.

POVERTY AND INEQUALITY

The issue of environmental pollution and degradation cannot be isolated for the purpose of understanding or resolution. The environment is the home that surrounds the human species and constitutes the human habitat. Therefore, the environment cannot be appreciated or assessed alone, without a direct connection to the unique creatures that it surrounds, namely humans. Concern for the environment implies also concern for human problems of poverty, thirst, and hunger. This connection is detailed in a stark manner in the parable of the Last Judgment, where the Lord says: "I was hungry and you gave me food; I was thirsty and you gave me something to drink" (Matt. 25:35).

In earlier chapters, I referred to the importance of silence as waiting and depending on God's grace, and of fasting as not wanting or wanting less. In a sense, then, both silence and fasting anticipate the problems of poverty and hunger inasmuch as they encourage us not to waste. *Waiting* leads to not *wanting*, which in turn leads to not *wasting*. Prayer prepares us for abstinence and moderation, which render us more alert to the problems related to poverty and justice. These virtues are critical in a culture that is indifferent to waste and that stresses the need to hurry and the priority of individual wants over the needs of others.

Concern, then, for ecological issues is directly related to concern for issues of social justice, and particularly of world hunger. A Church that neglects to pray for the natural environment is a Church that refuses to offer food and drink to a suffering humanity. At the same time, a society that ignores the mandate to care for all human beings is a society that mistreats the very creation of God, including the natural environment. It is tantamount to blasphemy.

The terms "ecology" and "economy" share the same etymological root. Their common prefix "eco-" derives from the Greek word *oikos*, which signifies "home" or "dwelling." It is unfortunate and selfish, however, that we have restricted the application of this word to ourselves, as if we are the only inhabitants of this world. The fact is that no economic system—no matter how technologically or socially advanced—can survive the collapse of the environmental systems that support it. This planet is indeed our home; yet it is also the home of everyone, as it is the home of every animal creature, as well as of every form of life created by God. It is a sign of arrogance to presume that we human beings alone inhabit this world. Indeed, by the same token, it is a sign of arrogance to imagine that only the present generation inhabits this earth.

Ecology, then, is the *logos* or study of this world as the home of everyone and everything, while economy is the *nomos* or regulation, as the stewardship of our world as our home. How we understand creation will also determine how we treat the natural environment. Will we continue to use it in inappropriate and unsustainable ways? Or will we treat it as our home and the home of all humanity as well as the home of all living creatures? Will we, with the psalmist, remember that "everything that breathes praises God" (Ps. 150:6)?

As one of the more serious ethical, social, and political problems, poverty is directly and deeply connected to the ecological crisis. A poor farmer in Asia, in Africa, or in North America will daily face the reality of poverty. For farmers there, the misuse of technology or the eradication of trees is not merely harmful to the environment or destructive of nature; rather, it practically and profoundly affects the very survival of their families. Terminology such as "ecology," "deforestation," or "overfishing" is entirely absent from their daily conversation or concern. The "developed" world cannot demand from the "developing" poor an intellectual understanding with regard to the protection of the few earthly paradises that remain, especially in light of the fact that less than 10 percent of the world's population consumes over 90 percent of the earth's natural resources. However, with proper education, the "developing" world would be far more willing than the "developed" world to cooperate for the protection of creation.

Closely related to the problem of poverty is the problem of unemployment, which plagues societies throughout the world. It is abundantly clear that neither the moral counsel of religious leaders nor fragmented measures by socioeconomic strategists or political policy makers can curb this growing tragedy. The problem of unemployment compels us to reexamine the priorities of affluent societies in the West, and especially the unrestricted advance of development, which is considered only in positive economic terms. We appear to be trapped in the tyrannical cycle created by a need for constant productivity rises and increases in the supply of consumer goods. However, placing these two "necessities" on an equal footing imposes on society a relentless need for unending perfection and growth while restricting power over production to fewer and fewer. Concurrently, real or imaginary consumer needs constantly increase and rapidly expand. Thus the economy assumes a life of its own, a vicious cycle that becomes independent of human need or human concern. What is needed is a radical change in politics and economics, one that underlines the unique and primary value of the human person, thereby placing a human face on the concepts of employment and productivity.

The present situation reminds me of the poor widow in the Gospel who made her small offering in the treasury; this contribution was the equivalent of her entire possessions. "For all of them have contributed out of their abundance; but she out of her poverty has put in everything that she had, all that she had to live on" (Mark 12:44). We are not justified in demanding that the poorer nations make huge sacrifices, especially when some of them may contribute far less than the "developed" nations to the environmental crisis and to socioeconomic injustice. Of course, the situation in China and India highlights the alarming danger of such generalizations based solely on economic factors. Nevertheless, people in Western societies—as well as those that proclaim Western principles—ought to assume greater personal responsibility. They should contribute to the solution of the environmental crisis in accordance with their capacity in order not simply to assist the poor but to help wipe out poverty itself.

ENVIRONMENT, POVERTY, AND PEACE

Over the last decade, as already mentioned, it has been a privilege of our Ecumenical Patriarchate to initiate waterborne symposia on themes relating to the preservation of rivers and seas, organized by the Religious and Scientific Committee. Moreover, prior to and alongside these symposia, in five summer seminars held on the island of Halki in Turkey, we focused on the importance of ecological education and environmental awareness, exploring such issues as religious education (1994), ethics (1995), society (1996), justice (1997), and poverty (1998). All of these symposia and seminars have been characterized by an ecumenical, indeed interreligious and interdisciplinary, approach.

We have learned, therefore, that our efforts to protect the natural environment must be interdisciplinary. No single discipline or group can assume full responsibility for either the damage wrought on created nature or the vision of a sustainable future. Theologians and scientists must collaborate with economists and politicians if the desired results are to be effective. Moreover, we have learned that environmental action cannot be separated from human relations— whether in the form of international politics, human rights, or peace. The way we respond to the natural environment is clearly reflected in the way we treat human beings. The willingness to exploit the environment is directly revealed in the willingness to permit or promote human suffering.

It is evident, then, that all of our ecological activity is ultimately measured by its effect on people, especially the poor. There are two examples that come to mind in this regard from the history of the Ecumenical Patriarchate and from the traditions of the Orthodox Church. I have always carried in my heart a name with which the Ecumenical Patriarchate has been associated through the centuries; it has traditionally been called "The Church of the Poor of Christ."[10] This has been a constant reminder throughout my environmental listening and learning. Extending our concern and care to nature implies and involves changing our attitudes and practices toward human beings. The entire world is a gift from God, offered to us for the purpose of sharing. It exists not for us to appropriate but rather for us to preserve. If encounter is the consequence of our ecological concern, then ignoring the social dimensions of environmental justice is ultimately not beneficial even to the material creation itself.

The second example is taken from the annual celebration of the Feast of Saint Basil (on January 1), who was renowned as a "lover of the poor" (or *philoptochos*). Each year, Orthodox Christians cut the traditional *vassilopitta* ("bread of the kings"). It is a way of sharing the joy of the incoming new year while at the same time recalling our immediate responsibility for those in poverty. A coin is placed inside the sweet bread in memory of Saint Basil, who used to distribute money anonymously to the poor of Caesarea in Cappadocia. The first portion—after separating those of God the Trinity, as the supreme symbol of encounter and communion, and all the holy people in the communion of saints—is known as the "poor man's portion." The poor are a part of our world; we should invite them to share our bread. And this, of course, means the bread that we eat, but also the goods that we enjoy and the equality that we demand for ourselves.

The image of sharing in the Orthodox Church is the icon of the Holy Trinity, which traditionally represents the hospitality of Abraham and Sarah welcoming three strangers in the Palestinian desert. The story is related in Genesis 18 of Abraham sitting under the oak trees of Mamre:

> The Lord appeared to Abraham by the oaks of Mamre, as he sat at the entrance of his tent in the heat of the day. (Gen. 18:1)

Not only do the oaks provide refreshing shade for the Patriarch of Israel, but they are the circumstance for the revelation of God. By analogy, then, not only do the trees of the world provide nurture for humankind in diverse ways, but they also reflect the very presence of the Creator. Cutting them down almost implies eliminating the presence of the divine from our lives. Indeed, the Hebrew interpretation of this text insinuates that the oak trees themselves—like the visitors who appear at the same time—are involved in the revelation of God. For it is not until Abraham recognizes the presence of God in the trees (namely in creation, or the *adamah*) that he is also able to recognize God in his visitors (namely in human beings, or the *adam*). Creation, just like the human beings who appeared in the form of angels, is itself a manifestation of God in the world. We should always make this spiritual connection when we breathe in the oxygen that the trees breathe out; just as, in Christian circles, we recognize the breathing of the divine Spirit, who breathes where it wills (cf. John 3:8)—like the rustling of leaves in a forest. It is the Spirit that blows through creation that we worship whenever we share our resources with other human beings. It is the entire world that we sustain when we preserve the earth and offer food to our neighbor.[11]

In our efforts, then, for the preservation of the natural environment, how prepared are we to sacrifice some of our greedy lifestyles? When will we learn to say "Enough!"? When will we learn that treating all people, including the poor, in a just manner is more beneficial than charitable acts of goodwill? Will we direct our focus away from what we want to what the world needs? We may offer bread to the hungry—indeed, we may feel a sense of self-gratification in so doing—but when will we work toward a world that has no hunger? Moreover, do we endeavor to leave as light a footprint as possible on this planet for the sake of future generations? There are no excuses today for our lack of involvement. We have detailed information; the alarming statistics are readily available. We must choose to care. Otherwise, we do not really care. Otherwise, we become aggressors, betraying our inherent prerogatives as human beings, and violate the rights of others.

"Blessed are the peacemakers; for they shall be called children of God" (Matt. 5:9). To become children of God is to be fully committed to the will of God. This implies moving away from what we want to what God wants, just as Jesus Christ was revealed to be the Son of God when he said: "Yet, not what I want, but what you want" (Matt. 26:39). To be children of God means to be faithful to God's purpose and intent for creation, despite the social pressures that may contradict peace and justice. In order to be peacemakers and children of God, we must move away from what serves our own interests and focus on what respects and dignifies the rights of others. We must recognize that all human beings—and not only a few— deserve to share the resources of this world.

"Making peace" is certainly painstaking and slow work. Yet it is our only hope for the restoration of a broken world. By working to remove obstacles to peace, by working to heal human suffering, by working to preserve the natural environment, we can be assured that "God is with us" (Matt. 1:23 and Isa. 7:14). Then we are assured that we are never alone, and shall inherit both this world and the kingdom of heaven. Then we shall be worthy to hear the words of Christ on the day of truth and judgment: "Come, you who are blessed by my Father. Inherit the kingdom that was prepared for you from the creation of the world" (Matt. 25:34).

THE FAULT OF THE WEST

It is an easy, perhaps escapist option to criticize the West for the failures and ills of our world. Western civilization is certainly responsible for philosophical worldviews and practical developments that have negatively affected our minds and behavior. It has unreservedly promoted a barren sense of *intellectualism*, which has ruptured any balanced sense of spirituality. It has also introduced an unrestrained sense of *individualism*, which has shattered any healthy sense of community. Moreover, it has persistently encouraged the exploitation and abuse of nature through greedy market *consumerism*, which has destroyed the planet's ecosystems and depleted its resources. And it has uncritically espoused the extremes of economic *globalization* (at the expense of human beings) and exclusive *nationalism* (at the cost of human lives).

Yet the real fault ultimately lies within human nature itself, which is called to a renewed understanding of repentance. It would be more appropriate and beneficial if we were to consider our own responsibility within Western society, rather than seeking to blame particular cultures or structures. Not that the latter are insignificant; but the most political statement can sometimes be the most personal statement. What others do is usually what we are also guilty of as individuals. Paying closer attention to the way in which our wasteful ways stem from our propensity toward sin may be the simplest and most successful way of addressing the environmental crisis.

Far too long have we focused—as churches and religious communities—on the notion of sin as a rupture in individual relations either with each other or between humanity and God. The environmental crisis that we are facing reminds us of the cosmic proportions and consequences of sin, which are more than merely social or narrowly spiritual. It is my conviction that every act of pollution or destruction of the natural environment is an offense against God as Creator.

We are, as human beings, responsible for creation; but we have behaved as if we own creation. The problem of the environment is primarily neither an ethical nor a moral issue. It is an ontological issue, demanding a new way of being as well as a new way of behaving. Repentance implies precisely a radical change of ways, a new outlook and vision. The Greek word for "repentance" is *metanoia*, which signifies an inner transformation that inevitably involves a change in one's entire worldview. We repent not simply for things we feel that we do wrongly against God. Furthermore, we repent not simply for things that make us guilty in our relations with other people. Rather, we repent for the way we regard the world and, therefore, invariably treat—in fact, mistreat—the world around us.

In this respect, the concept of sin must be broadened to include all human beings and all of created nature. Religions must become sensitized to the seriousness and implications of this kind of sin if they are to encourage the right values and inspire the necessary virtues to protect God's creation in its human, animal, and natural expressions. During international negotiations that took place at the Hague in 2000, I strongly emphasized the threat to our planet's fragile ecosystems posed by global warming, as well as the urgent need for all religions to underline a renewed repentance in our attitude toward nature.

CONCLUSION: A NEW WORLDVIEW

Curiously, I have never been overwhelmed by the ecological problems of our time. We are indeed facing an environmental crisis, which can never be overlooked by politicians or overstated by scientists. Nevertheless, I have always considered in an optimistic way the fundamental goodness and positive intention of humanity "created in the image and likeness of God" (Gen. 1:26). There is a maturity and knowledge in humanity that accounts for this basic hopefulness. If I was not convinced of this, then I would be betraying my Orthodox conviction and firm belief that even the present age—like every age and place—conceals the presence of living saints. Our age is faced with a unique challenge. Never before, in the long history of our planet, has humanity found itself so "developed" that it faces the possible destruction of its own environment and species. Never before in the long history of this earth have the earth's ecosystems faced almost irreversible damage. It may be that future generations will one day view the senseless eradication of the magnificent repositories of genetic information and biodiversity in our age in much the same way as we view, in retrospect, the burning of the library in Alexandria in 48 B.C.E.[12] Therefore, our responsibility lies in accepting the need to respond in a unique way in order to meet our obligations to the generations that follow.

At the same time, I have also learned that the crisis we are facing in our world is not primarily ecological. It is a crisis concerning the way we envisage or imagine the world. We are treating our planet in an inhuman, godless manner precisely because we fail to see it as a gift inherited from above; it is our obligation to receive, respect, and in turn hand on this gift to future generations. Therefore, before we can effectively deal with problems of our environment, we must change the way we perceive the world. Otherwise, we are simply dealing with symptoms, not with their causes. We require a new worldview if we are to desire "a new earth" (Rev. 21:1).

So let us acquire a "eucharistic spirit" and an "ascetic ethos," bearing in mind that everything in the natural world, whether great or small, has its importance *within the universe and for the life of the world*; nothing whatsoever is useless or contemptible. Let us regard ourselves as responsible before God for every living creature and for the whole of natural creation. Let us treat everything with proper love and utmost care. Only in this way shall we secure a physical environment where life for the coming generations of humankind will be healthy and happy. Otherwise, the unquenchable greed of our generation will constitute a mortal sin resulting in destruction and death. This greed in turn will lead to the deprivation of our children's generation, despite our desire and claim to bequeath to them a better future. Ultimately, it is for our children that we must perceive our every action in the world as having a direct effect upon the future of the environment.

This is the source of my optimism. As we declared some years ago in Venice (June 10, 2002) with Pope John Paul II (1978–2005), the late Pontiff of the Roman Catholic Church:

It is not too late. God's world has incredible healing powers. Within a single generation, we could steer the earth toward our children's future. Let that generation start now, with God's help and blessing.

The same sentiments were jointly communicated with the current Pope, Benedict XVI, during his official visit to the Ecumenical Patriarchate on November 30, 2006:

In the face of the great threats to the natural environment, we wish to express our concern at the negative consequences for humanity and for the whole of creation which can result from economic and technological progress that does not know its limits. As religious leaders, we consider it one of our duties to encourage and to support all efforts made to protect God's creation, and to bequeath to future generations a world in which they will be able to live.

The natural environment—the forest, the water, the land—belongs not only to the present generation but also to future generations. We must frankly admit that humankind is entitled to something better than what we see around us. We and, much more, our children and future generations are entitled to a better and brighter world, a world free from degradation, violence, and bloodshed, a world of generosity and love. It is selfless and sacrificial love for our children that will show us the path that we must follow into the future.

VII.
FAITH AND FREEDOM

CONSCIENCE AND HUMAN RIGHTS

Created in the image of God, human beings are free by nature.
—SAINT MAXIMUS THE CONFESSOR (SEVENTH CENTURY)

INTRODUCTION: THEOLOGICAL PERSPECTIVES

In theological terms, we live in a world that is "fallen," that is to say, conditioned by sin and mortality. It is a world where every image of life is, to a greater or lesser degree, distorted and deformed by the reality of sin and mortality. Everything around us is somehow informed and shaped by the prevailing presence and powerful influence of what the Gospel of Love is not afraid of naming "the prince of this world" (John 14:30). If we move even a little outside our cocoon of complacency, it is not difficult to discern this truth in the world around us.

This by no means implies the lack of goodness in our world, where so much good is being accomplished on an individual as well as on an institutional level to resolve issues such as poverty, intolerance, and war. Yet the reality is that these noble expressions of charity and philanthropy face a constant struggle to resist evil; good is in combat with evil. A mere glance around us—in our neighborhood, in our nation, and on our planet—is sufficient to recognize that this world does not immediately reflect the sacred presence of the "Sun of Righteousness" (Mal. 4:2). In an open challenge to the divine plan and intent for creation, humanity has perverted the natural order of things and has consequently become alienated from any sense of true freedom.

As a result of this fundamental or "original" estrangement, Orthodox theology claims that humanity has become deprived of freedom, devoid of sanctity, and dependent on sinfulness. This is not a negative or pessimistic view of the world; it is a profound theological reflection on the world as we know it. Moreover, the body, too, which was once created "beautiful" (Gen. 1) by a loving God, blessed with potential for sanctification and destined to share in divine glory, has as a result of the same reality of sinfulness and alienation from God been "weakened" and "oriented toward death" (Rom. 8:3, 6).

The entire world has become wrapped—or perhaps we should say trapped—in the reality of the fall. And it is not merely certain people and places or certain professions and practices, that are affected. Even real knowledge—defined as the possibility of discerning and comprehending the reality of sin and estrangement—is sometimes tainted by sin and mortality. Recognizing that we are not ultimately free in this world is not something that comes naturally, especially in an age that claims to know so much about human freedom and human rights. In reality, freedom is a gift that is acquired through much spiritual effort and struggle. This is why Saint Paul speaks of enrichment "through all knowledge" (1 Cor. 1:5) while also warning that the wrong kind of "knowledge makes one arrogant" (1 Cor. 8:1).

An important distinction, from an Orthodox theological perspective, can be made between knowledge as *gnosis* and awareness as *epignosis*. A minimal capacity, at least, to recognize that there is a difference between good and evil is in fact natural, a part of human reasoning, an endowment granted by God at creation. It is the voice of conscience, which literally signifies the coming together of all possible human knowing (con-science). However, for the Church Fathers, true knowledge is only achieved through the personal experience of divine grace. As Saint Isaac of Nineveh remarked in the seventh-century desert of Syria:

> Knowledge that precedes faith is natural knowledge; knowledge that is born of faith is spiritual knowledge . . . Natural knowledge leads to God, as we learn to distinguish good from evil and to receive faith. The power of such knowledge is that we believe in the One, who has created all things. From this faith is born a sense of awe toward God. Thus, gradually, one comes to a spiritual knowledge, which is the sense of things hidden and transcendent. It does not contradict faith, but rather it confirms it. It is called faith through contemplation.[1]

So all of us—saints and sinners alike—dwell in a world that is deeply marked by the reality of evil, which in traditional theology is known as "the fall of Adam." In Western theological terms, this is called "original sin"; but in Orthodox theological language, we prefer simply to speak of "the reality of our mortality." This reality imposes no sense of guilt; it simply describes the situation that we human beings experience. Given that such a fundamental difference of understanding exists, it is not surprising that several other concepts, such as (individual or national) freedom and (personal or social) justice, vary in meaning according to the way we perceive sin and mortality. The distinctive Orthodox understanding of freedom is closely connected with faith. I often like to cite the profound comment of a prisoner in a concentration camp:

> [No knowledge of law can ever offer power to an individual.] What is needed is not power, but freedom. Yet, what enables one

to acquire such freedom is not knowledge, but faith. It is faith alone that empowers a person to submit to the inner voice, which no objective facts can verify.[2]

"Freedom" and "rights," then, are difficult and complicated terms, not only because they are variously understood by people in different periods or in diverse cultures, but also because the way we use these words depends on many particular circumstances. Nevertheless, one thing I feel able to say with confidence is that freedom presupposes respect in equal measure for all people and segments of society. Freedom cannot ultimately either exclude or discriminate.

FREEDOM ABSOLUTE AND RELATIVE

Whenever we discuss freedom in this day and age, we usually imagine the unimpeded possibility of choosing between certain things. Simply put, in our modern minds, freedom means choice. But for the Orthodox Christian, this definition is inadequate. However wide the range of earthly things or earthly activities that we are able to select, all of the available choices remain, from a spiritual point of view, tainted with the reality of the fall, of sinfulness or mortality. Freedom, then, is more than merely the difference between certainty and indecisiveness in confronting a finite range of options. This may perhaps be the focus of psychological freedom in the modern sense, which seeks to empower human frailty and bolster the human heart. Our spiritual attention should be directed at something much more profound, which is the struggle to overcome the consequences of human fallen-ness or the fragility of human existence. Moreover, in the contemporary mind, freedom may simply imply the possibility of doing whatever one pleases or desires. Yet this understanding is also flawed. Once we are blessed with proper understanding, could we truly ever hesitate between life and death, or between good and evil? Surely these would be false choices. It is important to recall that God alone grants the ultimate possibility of discerning evil and choosing good.

So we tend today to speak of human freedom and human rights as if they were unconditional realities and absolute concepts. Nevertheless, from a spiritual point of view, humanly defined freedom is always relative. The condition of true freedom, from a theological viewpoint, is divine grace; and human freedom is always related to and dependent upon the unconditional and absolute freedom of God, who is beyond all human categories, including our perception of freedom and justice. In fact, we believe that God is the one who grants freedom and justice, while at the same time transcending them. God is never defined; God simply is. Such, at least, was the revelation of God to Moses at the altar of the burning bush: "I am who I am." And such is the depth of apophatic theology, which we considered in Chapter 3.

It is my conviction that humanity derives its source and existence from God, whose image within human beings constitutes the essence and depth of freedom while at the same time planting the seeds for social justice within the world. This conviction underlies the theological origin and principle of human freedom as Orthodox Christians perceive it. At the same time, we believe that the end and purpose of human freedom will be revealed in the age to come, when humanity and all of creation will encounter the living Creator. Human beings will find themselves face-to-face with God together with the rest of the created world. At that time, we believe, human freedom will be reconciled and will reunite, once and for all, with divine will. This is what we call the eschatological dimension of freedom.

Until that time, however, we live in a world of spiritual tension and irreconcilable choices. The profound mystery of freedom is that it is both the source of utmost dignity and the cause of extreme suffering. In the Orthodox understanding, it is the ultimate mystery, with which even God does not interfere and which even God does not contradict. In the seventh century, Saint Maximus the Confessor (580–662) observed that God can do everything except one thing: God can never force or oblige any part of creation—human or other—to love Him. Faith, then, can only exist when there is an element of faithfulness to maintain. This is because the ultimate expression of freedom is love. Love is the ultimate content of freedom and of eternity. To say to someone "I love you" or "You are loved" is to assure that person that he or she will never die; it is to affirm that he or she is utterly free.

THE FREEDOM OF GOD

One of the fundamental dimensions of Orthodox theology is, as we have already noted, its emphasis on the apophatic way. *Apophasis* signifies negation; it is the denial of wrong or unhelpful ways of understanding reality. This in turn implies a dynamic understanding of God and the world. God—and for that matter humanity, or the world—can never be seen as a static reality. Herein perhaps lies a unique dimension and major contribution of Eastern thought and spirituality. For the central intuition of Orthodox theology is that one can never fully know God in the intellectual sense, even though one can everywhere encounter and know God through an ever deepening personal relationship.

The Church Fathers always underline the personal accessibility of God while never undermining the absolute elusiveness of God. This is why the Eastern Church Fathers distinguish between the essence of God and the energies of God. The divine essence is radically unknowable, inaccessible, invisible, and inexpressible by the human mind. The divine energies are able to be known, experienced, seen, and described, by the grace of God.

The apophatic way excludes the possibility of understanding God intellectually. God always transcends human knowledge and doctrinal formulation. Rather, it is a way of surrendering to God lovingly and of worshipping God liturgically. In this respect, it is the way of silence, a way of communion at its deepest and most intense. It is here that worship and silence coincide. All this means that God can never be exclusively comprehended or exhaustively known. No one person, no single belief, no institution or even religion can claim to contain the fullness of God. Certainly, no person, belief, institution, or religion can ever claim the right to judge or hurt others on the basis of its understanding of God.

This means that the apophatic way is the beginning and precondition of human freedom. It also implies that freedom in the true, spiritual sense ultimately leads to an acknowledgment of God and a sense of worship, since "the more authentically free a man is, the greater his certainty of God. When I am authentically free, I am also certain that I am not free through myself."[3] This means that the freedom of God determines and defines the freedom of humanity. Human rights, then, must be understood in a way that conforms to the right-eousness of God; in Greek, both "human rights" and "divine commandments" are implied in the same word, namely *dikaiomata.*[4] Human freedom and rights are ultimately informed by divine justice, truth, and love. Indeed, the person who realizes this truth also recognizes the mystery of God in all people:

> The divine Word is mystically present in each of the commandments . . . Thus, whoever carries it out also receives the Word that it contains.[5]

THE FREEDOM OF THE HUMAN PERSON

Although the human person can never be defined—it can never be exhaustively or exclusively contained in any single aspect or description—we are able to gain certain insights into the complexity and diversity of human nature. Thus, we are able to provide an ostensive perception into what it means to be human. Within humanity, there are unfathomable depths that contain a wealth of potential and beauty, as the author of the *Macarian Homilies* described the human heart in the late fourth century.[6] This is why the tradition of the Orthodox Church, in the writings of the Church Fathers, is anxious to preserve the *mystery* of the human person in the same way as it speaks of the unfathomable nature of God. Humanity contains the image and likeness of God (Gen. 1:26), the very breath of God (Gen. 2:7). We have God at the innermost part of our being.

Therefore, Orthodox theology never gives final or conclusive answers to the questions about human life and human nature. There are depths and dimensions within the heart that far surpass any conception or comprehension. The logical—or rather, the theological—basis is quite simple. If God can never be fully grasped, and humanity is created in the image of God, then humanity, too, can never be fully grasped. We speak, therefore, apophatically of the human person, in much the same way we speak apophatically about God.

The human person is a *microtheos*, an icon of God, according to Saint Maximus the Confessor in the seventh century. However, the human person is also a *microcosmos*, "a world within a world," as Saint Nilus of Ancyra (d. ca. 430) claimed in the fifth century, an icon of the world. Indeed, the role and vocation of the human person is precisely to reconcile these two icons: God and the world. The final destiny of humanity is to render God present in the soul, in society, and in the soul of the world.

Humanity stands at the center of creation, serving as a bridge and a bond between greatness and lowliness, between sacredness and frailty, between heaven and earth. As such, the human person acts as a mediator. Yet the way of mediation, otherwise known as the process of deification (divinization, or *theosis* in Greek), is long and arduous. It is what the Church Fathers call the journey from the divine image, as a gift from above, to the divine likeness as the realization and fulfillment of this initial endowment.

This implies a dynamic view of human nature, of human life, and of the human person. We are, as Irenaeus of Lyons (130–200) puts it, always on the way to becoming human beings. Beyond the fall, there is the full glory of God's image and likeness, which have yet to be revealed to us. In this life, the glory of God is only known "as in a mirror, dimly. But then, we shall see face to face. Now we know in part; then we shall know fully" (1 Cor. 13:12).

However elusive the nature of humanity may be, it should still be affirmed with certainty that all human beings are equal in value and share equal privileges.[7] This conviction was precisely what inspired the declaration on justice and human rights of the Third Pre-Conciliar Pan-Orthodox Conference organized by the Ecumenical Patriarchate in 1986:

Orthodox Christians should fight against every form of fanaticism and bigotry that divides human beings and peoples. Since we continuously declare the incarnation of God and the deification of humanity, we also defend human rights for every human being and every people. Since we live with the divine gift of freedom through Christ's work of redemption, we are able to reveal to the fullest the universal value that freedom has for every human being and every nation.[8]

Therefore, no single person can ever presume to cast a definitive moral judgment on any other person or action. Given our human limitations, we can only see one aspect or at most a few aspects of the people around us. We can never view those people or their actions in their entirety. We are never able to exhaust our knowledge of another person, whose heart will always elude us as a mystery. There is always more to know in another human being, whose life moves freely in God.

FREEDOM TO LIVE

In his Letter to the Romans, Saint Paul describes freedom as the power over death and as the triumph over mortality (see Rom. 8:10–11). This relates freedom to the grace of the Spirit, who is the "treasury of all good things and giver of life," to quote a favorite prayer of the Orthodox Church to the Holy Spirit, recited at the commencement of almost every service. Satisfying one's needs or desires is identified not with freedom but with captivity. In Orthodox ascetic terminology, it is in fact identified with submission to the passions.

Sin is not merely making evil choices, but in fact the result of an inability to make rightful—or righteous—choices. It is the state of captivity to compulsions or passions, where one is quite literally passive and not subjective, controlled and not creative, fallen and not free. It is subservience to the force of hardened habit. In contemporary language, it is called addiction. If I drink or eat whenever I like or whatever I want, I do not gain my freedom but in fact forfeit my freedom. For, in that case, I am constrained by the tyranny of passion, identified with the instinct of my nature. My "life is held captive; it is enslaved by the fear of death" (Heb. 2:15).

If the Holy Spirit is the defining dimension of human freedom, then the source of this freedom is to be sought in the opening chapters of the Book of Genesis, which describe the creation of humanity "according to the image and likeness of God" (Gen. 1:26). After God is said to have formed Adam from the dust of the earth, God then breathes life into him. This divine breath identifies Adam as an icon of the Creator while at the same time distinguishing him from the rest of creation. Adam's unique characteristic is freedom, the freedom to live in the fullest sense.

For the Church Fathers, the divine breath is the Holy Spirit, which Jesus Christ is said to have committed to the Father as he breathed his last on the Cross. Furthermore, the freedom of Adam is recognized by the same Church Fathers as precisely the content and essence of the divine image and likeness. For "where the Spirit of the Lord is, there is freedom" (2 Cor. 3:17).

Vladimir Lossky (1903–58), a renowned Orthodox theologian, once wrote that the same "self-emptying" (or *kenosis*) of God that occurred at the divine Incarnation (cf. Phil. 2:7), when the Word of God assumed human flesh in Jesus Christ of Nazareth (cf. John 1:14), is also reflected in the human heart, where the Holy Spirit empties itself in order to assume a dwelling place within the human race (cf. 1 Cor. 3:16–17). Therefore, whenever there is a spontaneous act of love and openness on our part, we can be sure that this is the motivation and inspiration of the grace of God. It is a genuine act of freedom.

This means, however, that we are never so free as when we are filled with the Holy Spirit. We are never more liberated than when our will is directed by the grace of God. Freedom is the action and activity of the Holy Spirit that is within us and around us. For as the same prayer of the Orthodox Church to the Holy Spirit also states: "The Comforter, the Spirit of truth, is everywhere present and fills all things."

It is the Spirit of God that empowers us to proclaim and promote freedom and justice in the world. This Spirit entitles us to reflect and respond in life-creating ways wherever we witness darkness, suffering, injustice, and evil. For we "are coworkers of God" (1 Cor. 3:9), and we are called to realize the divine plan of healing and reconciliation throughout the world "until all of us come to the measure of unity and maturity" (cf. Eph. 4:13). Then the Spirit of God will transform this world into the kingdom of heaven, the fallen world into the new creation, and every activity into true life.

FREEDOM FROM THE FALL

Spiritual captivity or enslavement inevitably leads also to social and political subservience and slavery. By the same token, liberation from the fall delivers us from any form of constraint, leading to social and political liberation and freedom. However, for the person guided by the Spirit, this in no way implies complacency or comfort. Indeed it primarily indicates and perhaps dictates a sense of identification and solidarity with the weak and vulnerable, "choosing rather to share ill-treatment with the people of God than to enjoy the fleeting pleasures of sin" (Heb. 11:25).

Just as any form of oppression and enslavement is the political and social expression of fallen-ness and sinfulness, so also the struggle for liberation and justice reveals the most profound spiritual symbol of freedom from the fall. This of course also implies that such struggle ought to transcend all racial competition and national rivalry, which only lead from one form of slavery to another. The sincerity and authenticity of the struggle for freedom are always measured by the degree of their spiritual depth as well as by the perennial value of their ultimate purpose.

ORTHODOX THEOLOGY AND RELIGIOUS FREEDOM

Christianity challenges the concept of the human person as merely an economic entity or consumer. The Christian tradition insists that, on the contrary, every human person is *zōon theoumenon*, to use the words of Saint Gregory of Nazianzus (329–89)—in other words, "an animal that is being deified."9 That means a creature called to share in God's glory and to become a "partaker of the divine nature" (2 Pet. 1:4). The most important fact about our humanness is our transcendent dimension: we are formed in the image of God (Gen. 1:26). We are endowed with God-consciousness, and so we are capable of prayer. We have the capacity to offer the world back to God in thanksgiving, and it is only in this act of offering that we become genuinely human and truly free.

We have spoken of personal freedom, but it needs also to be said that our freedom is not only personal but interpersonal. As human beings, we cannot be genuinely free in isolation, repudiating our relationship with our fellow humans. We can only be genuinely free if we form part of a community of other free persons. Freedom is never solitary but always social. We are only free if we become a *prosopon*—to use the Greek word for "person," which means literally "face" or "countenance"—only if we turn toward others, looking into their eyes and allowing them to look into ours. To turn away, to refuse to share, is to forfeit liberty. Freedom is expressed as encounter.

This indeed is specifically what is implied by the Christian doctrine of God. According to the teaching of the Greek Fathers, "in the image of God" means primarily "in the image of Christ"; to be human is to be Christlike, for Christ is the supreme model of what it is to be a person. But the phrase "in the image of God" also means "in the image of God the Trinity." As Christians, Orthodox believe in a God who is not only one but one-in-three. The Christian God is not merely personal but also interpersonal; God is not just a unit but a union. As Trinity, God is not simply the Monad, unique and self-sufficient. God is the Triad: Father, Son, and Holy Spirit, three divine persons united with one another in the unceasing movement of mutual love that the Greek Patristic tradition calls *perichoresis*. For Saint Basil of Caesarea (330–79), God is the mystery of communion: "The unity of God lies in the communion [*koinonia*] of the God,"[10] truly united in the interrelationship of the three persons. As a contemporary Orthodox theologian expresses it: "The being of God is a relational being: without the concept of communion it would not be possible to speak of the being of God."[11]

Now, if as humans we are formed in the image of the Trinity, then it follows that everything which has just been said about God should be applied also to humankind. We are called to reproduce on earth, so far as this is possible for us, the same *perichoresis*, or reciprocal movement of mutual love, that in heaven unites the three persons of the Trinitarian God. This we seek to do not only on the level of our interior life of prayer, and within the immediate circle of our family and friends, but also more broadly on an economic and political level. Our social program is the doctrine of the Trinity, a God in communion, a social God. Every form of community—the workplace, the school, the city, even a nation—has as its vocation to become, each in its own way, a living icon of the Trinity. Nations are called to be transparent to one another, just as the three persons of the Trinity are transparent to one another. Such is surely part of the role of religion in a changing world—namely, to promote freedom among human beings as the basis of encounter and communion.

THE ECUMENICAL PATRIARCHATE AND
RELIGIOUS FREEDOM

Part of the problem with understanding the Orthodox attitude to religious freedom derives from the reality and recent history of the Orthodox churches. On the one hand, even as recently as the twentieth century, the greater majority of Orthodox Christians throughout the world lived behind what was then known as the Iron Curtain. Many millions of these, together with many thousands of others elsewhere, experienced several decades of either persecution verging on martyrdom or else precarious toleration. Several millions encountered—and some continue to encounter—a religious intolerance that limited and even isolated them as minorities through social and economic pressures.

On the other hand, to this day, in one European country (Greece), the Orthodox Church comprises the state religion, while in another predominantly Lutheran country (Finland), the small but dynamic Orthodox presence enjoys the status of a state church. In today's world, Orthodoxy has to discern its place within a huge variety of political cultures and regimes. In 1959, the fewer than one million citizens of Cyprus elected their Orthodox Archbishop, Makarios III (1913–1977), as the president of their democratic nation. In the United States, a country of secular governance but relatively strong religious affiliation, the Orthodox Christian presence predates the Constitution. Meanwhile, the Orthodox Ecumenical Patriarchate in Constantinople (present-day Istanbul, in modern-day Turkey) retains its status as the "first among equals" for Orthodox Christians throughout the world, but it is denied any legal recognition of its "ecumenical" status by the government of Turkey.

Despite the difficulties it faces, the Ecumenical Patriarchate enjoys the privilege and the responsibility of being situated at a critical crossroads. The Bosphorus marks the geographical border between two continents, Europe and Asia. Historically, the ancient city of Constantinople always served as a meeting point of diverse civilizations and of the three monotheistic religions: Judaism, Christianity, and Islam. This is why we have always regarded our role within contemporary interreligious dialogue as a pivotal one, serving as a bridge of goodwill and peaceful cooperation between vastly different worlds. In 1996, Professor Joël Delobel of the Catholic University of Leuven rightly described our hometown as "truly the city that builds bridges." Accordingly, the Ecumenical Patriarchate bears a unique role and responsibility within the broader relationship between East and West.

HUMAN RIGHTS AND RELIGIOUS TOLERANCE

By virtue of its history, as well as its location at one of the world's most sensitive meeting points between continents and civilizations, the Ecumenical Patriarchate feels strongly about the issue of religious tolerance. As Orthodox Christians, we are called to support and stand up for the innocent and defenseless victims of religious oppression, racism, and intolerance. Ultimately, we are called to work for peace in every part of our world. Prayer for peace is the opening petition of Orthodox liturgy, immediately followed by the petition "for the peace of the whole world." While we may not be immune to the forces of history, we are also not helpless before them. We are obliged to respond to the fratricide and fragmentation of nationalism with the love and integration of ecumenicity. We must remind people of the significance of tolerance, which is ultimately grounded in respect for the sanctity of freedom and the sacredness of human justice.

For those of us who place our faith and trust in spiritual commitment and religious community, the first principle must always be the fact that each person contains the divine spark of freedom and is "ordained" to be an authentic child of God. Every human being has been created in the image and likeness of God; every human being is a child of God, endowed with the freedom to live and preordained to live with freedom. This means that a different standard cannot be applied to people in Europe or the United States from those in Asia or Africa. Culture may be relative; humanity is not.

The Orthodox Church has long searched for a language with which to address nationalism, amid the strife that this new ideology created in countries of Eastern Europe for much of the nineteenth century. In 1872, a great synod held in the Patriarchal Cathedral of the Phanar in Constantinople issued an unqualified condemnation of the sin of racism. The council was attended by members of all of the ancient patriarchates and was, therefore, broadly representative in its intent and scope:

> We renounce, censure, and condemn racism, namely racial discrimination, ethnic feuds, hatred, and dissensions within the Church of Christ.

Unfortunately, however, the problem of racial discrimination continues to this day, even within—and sometimes especially within—religious and church circles. It is our hope that all religious leaders will exercise particular attention, pastoral responsibility, and sacred wisdom in order to avoid and dispel the exploitation of religious sentiment for political, fanatical, or nationalistic reasons. Any peace that comes at the tip of a sword is no longer acceptable. Any crime supposedly committed in the name of religion is a crime against religion itself and an offense to God. Appeals to and exploitations of religious symbols and precepts in order to further the cause of aggressive nationalism are a betrayal of the universality of religious faith.

Freedom of conscience and freedom of religion are imperative for every minority. We cannot accept those who violate the sanctity of human life and pursue policies in defiance of moral values. We cannot tolerate and can in no circumstances justify ethnic cleansing. We must become alert and respond promptly when we learn of the forced migration of refugees and the displacement of populations. We must condemn those who tear apart families in the name of false nationalism or fanaticism.

Freedom of conscience is the greatest of divine gifts conferred upon humanity. It represents most clearly the reflection of God in the human person. In claiming and proclaiming that God created humanity in the divine image and likeness (Gen. 1:26), we imply that human beings are endowed with spiritual qualities that correspond to God, including and especially free will and freedom of conscience. Whenever the freedom of conscience is subjected to any kind of external or internal necessity, particularly in the form of the restriction of divine worship, this does not reflect the original blessing bestowed indiscriminately by God on all human beings.

Freedom of conscience and the free practice of religious conviction are fundamental principles, which from an Orthodox perspective derive from the words of Jesus Christ: "Whosoever wants to follow me . . ." (Matt. 16:24). The freedom conferred by God at the moment of creation, and the freedom confirmed by the Son of God at the moment of the Incarnation or re-creation, cannot be denied or withheld without at the same time denying and rejecting the very presence of God. Emphasizing the element of freedom in God's relationship with the world, the second-century *Epistle to Diognetus* affirms, "God persuades, He does not compel; for violence is foreign to Him."[12]

Consequently, the legal consolidation of freedom of conscience, and especially of religious freedom, is a critical benefit of the civilized world inasmuch as it hinders the oppression of one person by another on the grounds of religion. Some people may express the fear that this may in turn lead to a supposed fragmentation of society, which until recently glorified homogeneity and uniformity. Yet the very fact that such fear exists is proof that the sort of homogeneity and uniformity which is imposed by external forces does not reflect the will of God.

Of course, politicians alone cannot heal the rifts brought about by extreme nationalism. Religious leaders have a central and critical, indeed an inspirational, role to play in this regard. We must help bring the spiritual principles of genuine ecumenicity and tolerance to the fore. Our deep and abiding spiritual message stands as a complement, even if sometimes in stark contrast, to the secularism of modern politics. There will always be a limit to what purely secular approaches to healing the wounds of human society can achieve. The famous psychologist Carl Jung (1875–1961) once noted: "Among all my patients in the second half of life, every one of them fell ill because they had lost what the living religions of every age have given their followers; and none of them has been really healed who did not regain this religious outlook."

Communities of faith are able to provide a counterbalance to secular humanism and exclusive nationalism by proposing a more spiritual form of humanism. That applies to Christians, Jews, and Muslims alike; while we cannot deny our differences, neither can we deny the need for solidarity and fellowship in order to deter and dispel the forces of intolerance and racism. If we believe in a "God who is love" (1 John 4:16), then we must proclaim that "perfect love casts out fear" (1 John 4:18) and "pursue what makes for peace" (Rom. 14:19). And peace is more than the mere absence of war. Peace is the invocation of a divine name; it is the very presence of God (cf. John 14:27).

Nonetheless, in order to recognize and understand this kind of peace, we require a complete change in our worldview, a Copernican revolution of the divine Spirit so that the human heart will center no longer on the ego, be it individual or collective, but rather on the divine light of Christ, the Sun of Righteousness. Yet religious people are not normally supposed to act as statesmen or military generals. We can only act when we allow God to act through us. And God is never the source of vengeance and tyranny, but only the source of love and peace. We are called, then, to become prophets of this loving and peaceful God, "walking humbly with our God" (Mic. 6:8).

REMEMBERING THE HOLOCAUST

I still vividly recall the horrific consequences of religious intolerance and shameful racism that I witnessed when I visited the Yad Vashem in Israel in 1999 and, two years earlier, the Holocaust Memorial Museum in Washington, D.C. Both these sacred monuments of remembrance are striking icons, articulating the unspeakable depth of suffering that was endured by people who were living images of God. Even to contemplate the terror seems impossible—the pure depravity of human nature at its lowest. It is our responsibility to remember in order never to repeat; it is our obligation to acknowledge in order forevermore to avoid. How could I ever forget the memorial tribute to the children of the Holocaust in Israel—a single flame reflected in a million mirrors? How could I not, as an Orthodox Christian, identify these children with the infants massacred by Herod (Matt. 2:16–18)? Or how could I not relate them to the infant Jesus, whose name Yeshua in Hebrew means "the Lord saves" and who chose to be born in the land of Palestine, with the legacy of the Patriarchs and the Prophets of Israel?

In the Orthodox Church, we recall the story of Chrysostomos, Metropolitan of Zákynthos (1890–1958), of whom the Nazi authorities demanded a list of all Jews living on his island. In response, he returned the letter with a single name, his own. He, like so many others in Greece, is an authentic lesson of love, which speaks with courage before the dark principalities and powers of the world (Eph. 6:12). These people overcame evil with good (Rom. 12:21) and fear with faith. In their lives, freedom reigned.

The truth is that, in preserving such moments of evil and terror, these museums simultaneously create an icon of hope and renewal. Similarly, in facing one another as human beings, we can discover the way of tolerance and love. I sometimes wonder how it can be humanly possible to remain indifferent to the slaughter of human beings in the name of prejudice and hatred. Yet I always especially recall in my prayers the innocent suffering and unjustifiable death of children in recent wars, such as in the Balkans and Iraq, and in genocides, such as Rwanda and Darfur. These atrocities continue to take place before our very eyes. And we have the audacity to claim that we are free?

Still, I am convinced that the faith communities are able—indeed are obliged—to awaken people from such indifference. For "human rights" are not the invention of the Enlightenment; they belong rather to the essence of religion itself, which inherently espouses and promotes religious freedom and tolerance. When, as believing persons, we fail to speak up in the face of intolerance and torture, we are neither religious nor human. Certainly, we are not free. When, as religious believers, we silently endure prejudice and discrimination against others, we fail to recognize the image of God in others. At that moment, we deny ourselves the privilege of freedom. And when, as religious people, we ignore the suffering and torture of other people, we ultimately refuse to recognize ourselves in others. Faith and tolerance share the same language. Its alphabet is freedom.

FAITH AND TOLERANCE

Religious faith is not an inactive force. Even among agnostics and declared atheists, it is considered an active cause with numerous implications and consequences. There are those who attribute to faith the responsibility for historical progress. Others profess a divinely supreme Being, who intervenes and defines the flow of historical currents. Sometimes, faith precedes and informs life. At other times, life is predetermined and faith merely validates. One way or another, however, faith can transform the life of an individual as well as the direction of an entire society.

Moreover, certain religious faiths acknowledge and accept their relativism before other religious convictions, whether in the form of many roads that lead toward perfection or as many spiritual deities that are manifested in all people. The first implies tolerance as a social reality; the latter leads to a form of religious syncretism. However, these are not the only ways of emphasizing religious tolerance and religious freedom.

Against these relativistic faiths are the absolutized ones, some of which believe that they are bearers of the whole truth and merely tolerate others, including some who may hold the same claims of absolutism. Others exclude the possibility of truth outside of their own religion, in which case they can pose a social danger. Finally, religious faith may even be used to mislead believers into bad actions for reasons of personal or collective expediency.

In the chapters that follow, I shall endeavor to develop an argument of mutual respect in religious tolerance. In the course of such an argument, however, it is worth remembering some basic principles. For even if there are numerous ways of asserting truth—some of which may be diametrically opposed and sometimes even mutually exclusive—God cannot possibly be self-contradictory. God cannot, for instance, at the same time proclaim love and hatred, peace and war, humility and arrogance, tolerance and prejudice. Surely, then, it is not God but humanity that expresses these contradictory teachings. Therefore, it is humanity that must also discern and differentiate between the same contradictory teachings. It is up to humanity to agree to the mutual respect of diverse religious convictions.

As a corollary to the belief that the fullness of truth lies in belief in one God, the Orthodox Church also acknowledges that the God whom we worship can never be imposed on anyone. The God of Revelation says:

> Behold, I stand at the door and knock. If you hear my voice and open the door, I will enter and eat with you, and you with me. (Rev. 3:20)

The principle of revelation permits no room for misinterpretation or justification of any forceful imposition of the Orthodox Christian way of faith and worship. Such faith can never be propagated or proselytized. Otherwise, both the door of the human heart and the sanctuary of God are violated. The spreading of the Gospel can never assume the form of (economic) compensation or (military) retribution. The only viable means of spreading the Gospel, at least in the Orthodox Christian view, is the cultivation of one's own soul in order to become sufficiently spacious to embrace all people. In this way, social peace is maintained and religious tolerance is preserved.

Although I do not aspire to religious pluralism as a value in itself or as a religious principle in itself, I do recognize that religious freedom and pluralism have an immense moral and social value as confirming the incomprehensible breadth, grandeur, and mystery of God's freedom as well as of God's respect for human freedom. Such respect is the supreme expression and confirmation of the same value within human beings in their relationship with other human beings. We cannot impose upon the religious freedom of human beings without impinging upon the freedom of God.

CONCLUSION: HUMAN RIGHTS AND
MATERIAL CREATION

Secular culture sometimes accepts the principle that human rights are God-given. Yet at the same time, it maintains that the relationship between God and humanity remains individual and private. The Orthodox faith offers a different perspective, seeking to understand the entire cosmos—as well as everyone and everything within this cosmos—as a seamless garment of God's vast creation. The individual exists not separated or isolated from the rest of creation and fellow human beings but in constant relationship, which informs our understanding of human existence as being derived from a divine Creator and as being rooted in the created order.

Within this context, we are valued as part of the cosmos. It is within such a context that a just society is also founded and sustained. For the Orthodox concept of *theosis* (or deification) is more than merely individual or personal; it is also deeply communal and social. Society, too, is transformed as we strive to respect the image of God—the very source of freedom and the inalienable right to justice—in every human being. Freedom, moreover, is the key to the transformation of the natural environment, whose silent voice must be articulated by the children of freedom:

The entire creation waits with eager longing for the revealing of the children of God. For the creation was subjected to futility, not of its own will but by the will of the one who subjected it, in hope that the creation itself will be set free from its bondage to decay and will obtain the freedom of the glory of the children of God. We know that the whole creation has been groaning in labor pains until now; and not only creation, but we ourselves, who have the first fruits of the Spirit, groan inwardly while we wait for adoption, the redemption of our bodies. (Rom. 8:19–23)

VIII.
TRANSFORMING THE WORLD

I. SOCIAL JUSTICE:
POVERTY AND GLOBALIZATION

Your goods belong to God; and they must
be shared with your neighbor.

—SAINT JOHN CHRYSOSTOM (FOURTH THROUGH FIFTH CENTURIES)

The world of faith can prove a powerful ally in efforts to address issues of social justice. It provides a unique perspective—beyond the merely social, political, or economic—on the need to eradicate poverty, to provide a balance in a world of globalization, to combat fundamentalism and racism, and to develop religious tolerance in a world of conflict. It is precisely the role of religion to respond to the needs of the world's poor as well as to vulnerable and marginalized people. In fact, it has been rightly observed that "it is a rare instance where a faith institution is not a defining marker of the space and character of a community . . . Religion is arguably the most pervasive and powerful force on earth."[1] This is why it comes as no surprise to me that religion and the faith communities are proving to be the subjects of renewed interest and attention in international relations and global politics, directly affecting social values and indirectly impacting state policies.

Not only does religion play a pivotal role in people's personal lives throughout the world, but religions play a critical role as forces of social and institutional mobilization on a variety of levels. Although the theological language of religion and spirituality may differ from the technical vocabulary of economics and politics, the barriers that at first glance appear to separate religious concerns (such as salvation and spirituality) from pragmatic interests (such as commerce and trade) are not impenetrable. Indeed, such barriers crumble before the manifold challenges of social justice and globalization. Whether we are dealing with the environment or peace, poverty or hunger, education or health care, there is today a heightened sense of common concern and common responsibility, which is felt with particular acuteness by people of faith as well as by those whose outlook is expressly secular.

Our engagement with such issues does not of course in any way undermine or abolish the difference between the various disciplines as well as the disagreements that arise between those who look at the world in different ways. Yet the growing signs of a common commitment to work together for the well-being of humanity and the life of the world are encouraging. It is an encounter of individuals and institutions that bodes well for our world. And it is an involvement that highlights the supreme purpose and calling of humanity to transcend political or religious differences in order to transform the entire world for the glory of God.

THE EARTH AND ALL WITHIN

In recent years, we have learned some important lessons about caring for the natural environment. However, we have also learned that environmental action cannot be separated from human relations. What we do for the earth is intimately related to what we do for people—whether in the context of human rights, international politics, poverty, social justice, or world peace. It has become clearer to us that the way we respond to the natural environment is directly related to and reflected in the way we treat human beings. The willingness of some people to exploit the environment as the "flesh of the world" goes hand in hand with their willingness to ignore human suffering in the flesh of our neighbor. By analogy, willingness to respond to the needs of creation and our neighbor reflects our willingness to respect the commandments of God. This is precisely why, in the fourth century, Saint John Chrysostom underlined the universal application of the Lord's Prayer. Indeed, by praying to "our Father in heaven," we also embrace a universal—even global—vision of the world. For Christ asked us to implore: "Thy kingdom come; Thy will be done, on earth as it is in heaven" (Matt. 6:10). Chrysostom points out that Christ does not say, "Thy will be done in me or even in us," but "everywhere on earth."[2]

Nevertheless, at the same time, we have to admit that while we have become more sensitive to environmental issues, we continue to ignore some fundamental issues of human welfare. This, however, amounts to an unbearable contradiction. In reality, extending our concern toward created nature implies and necessitates a change also in our attitudes and practices toward our fellow human beings. The world is a gift from God, and it is offered to us for the purpose of sharing. It does not exist for us to appropriate selfishly, but rather to preserve humbly. The way that we relate to God (in heaven) cannot be separated either from the way we treat other human beings or from our treatment of the natural environment (on earth). To disconnect the two would amount to nothing less than hypocrisy. Whoever can discern this simple truth will no longer be surprised that the Christian God chose to be born in a manger.

In our efforts, then, for the preservation of the natural environment, we must ask ourselves some difficult questions about our concern for other human beings and about our way of life and daily habits. Just how prepared are we to sacrifice our excessive lifestyles in order for others to enjoy the basic right to survive? What are we prepared to surrender in order to learn to share? When will we learn to say: "Enough!"? How can we direct our focus away from what we want to what the world and our neighbor need? If we are not allaying the pain of others, and only see or care about our own interests, then we are directly contributing to the suffering and poverty of our world.

THE WAY OF THE GOSPEL

In the New Testament parable of the sheep and the goats (Matt. 25:31–46), we are told that we shall not be judged on how many prayers we made, or how strictly we fasted, or how many converts we persuaded, or how many formal good deeds we performed. We shall certainly not be asked how much we achieved in worldly terms, what reputation we gained, what level on the corporate ladder we reached, or how we measured our success. We shall be asked only one question: Did we share? Did we feed the hungry and clothe the poor? Love for God can only be demonstrated through love for other people. There is simply no other way; any other way is deceit (cf. 1 John 4:20).

It is curious how in the same Gospel parable, Christ says "I" about every person that is in need or distress: "I was hungry," "I was thirsty," "I was a stranger, sick, naked, and a prisoner." In effect, God is looking at us through the eyes of all those who suffer. How can we turn away? How frightening a reminder, especially at a time when almost everywhere in wealthier cities our streets are filled with the hungry and the homeless, with young women and even children trapped in the ways of prostitution and poverty, and with those who have been irreparably wounded by the greedy ways of our society. These men and women are God in our midst; they reveal the suffering of a wounded God in the crucified Christ, even as He walks through our cities. These wounds become our judgment; yet they also hold our healing and hope. Will we ever respond to them? More important, can we even notice them?

In another parable from the New Testament, Jesus tells of a poor man, Lazarus, who lay at the gate of a rich man, "longing to satisfy his hunger with what fell from the rich man's table" (Luke 16:21). The rich man never once invited Lazarus to eat with him. What is worse, the rich man probably did not notice Lazarus, who was so close to his table. I wonder sometimes whether we even notice what goes on around us. And yet how can we respond if we do not notice, if we are unaware or uninformed? Moreover, how many people do we invite to sit at our table? How many are we willing to embrace? What sorts of issues—whether poverty, or peace, or the environment, or health care, or education, or social justice, or human rights—are we willing to place on our table of life? How open and inclusive—or just how closed and exclusive—is the table at which we have chosen to sit?

In my ministry as Patriarch of an ancient and historic Church, I have set out to address some of the more radical challenges of our time, including poverty, racism, fundamentalism, and conflict. They are the ones I come across daily in my encounter with individuals, as well as with religious and national leaders. Yet there are many other problems, so very close to each of us and to our ordinary lives, that need to be addressed and resolved; and in many cases, they affect us even more directly. These include the challenges of ensuring basic education and adequate wages and of providing decent, affordable health care. Then there is also the growing problem of proper care for the elderly. Indeed, no less pressing are the questions of inclusiveness for those with disabilities, the status of refugees and minority groups, the systematic abuse of women or children throughout the world to exploit their bodies or their labor. I also encounter many and diverse issues related to the sanctity of life from birth through death. Those issues range from sensitive matters of sexuality to highly controversial questions like the death penalty. In all such social and moral issues, it is not one or another position that the Orthodox Church seeks to promote in a defensive spirit. Indeed, we would normally refrain from expounding a single rigidly defined dogma on social and moral challenges. Rather, it is the sacredness of the human person, created in the image and likeness of God, that the Church at all times seeks to underline.

Recent years have undoubtedly been a critical time in the gradual awakening of people's environmental consciousness and the transformation of their attitude toward the future of our vulnerable planet. Yet even as my Church has been honored through my ministry with numerous awards and been heralded as "champion of the earth" by the United Nations Environment Programme in 2005, I humbly recognize that our work is far from concluded. This is by no means a false sense of humility; it is a genuine sense of reality. For if I have struggled—and continue to struggle—in order to alert and educate the citizens of the world about the imminent threat facing the water that we drink, the air that we breathe, and the earth that we tread, I know very well that we are only in the early stages of bringing about the truly radical change that is needed in people's behavior and lifestyle. All over the world, people are becoming increasingly aware of the global problems of water pollution. Yet we still stubbornly persist in our selfish patterns of consumption and waste, which have set our world on a dangerous road toward self-destruction. We require nothing less than a radical vision of transformation for ourselves and our world.

THE WAY OF THE SPIRIT

The transformation of the heart can and must lead to the transformation of society. This, after all, is ultimately the way of encounter. Transformation in this sense is essentially a vision of connection and compassion. It is the way of acting in community. We Christians have disassociated our spirituality from responsibility for the community. Looking inward should not be contrasted sharply with looking outward; what we aspire to achieve is a way of seeing more clearly what lies inside us and also around us. When as Orthodox Christians we leave the transforming event of the Divine Liturgy, we move out into the same world, continue the same routine, and face the same problems. Yet in the light of the liturgy, we should be able to see things in a new way, for we know the world differently. And we should feel impelled—indeed inspired—to act in a new way, in a spirit of grace. When we are transformed by divine grace, we shall be able to seek solutions to conflict through open exchange without resorting to oppression or domination.

We have it in our power either to increase the hurt inflicted on our world or to contribute toward its healing transformation. So when will we realize the detrimental effects of wasteful consumerism on our spiritual, social, cultural, and physical environment? When will we understand how religious and racial intolerance simply cannot lead us out of our impasse, and the way they lock us instead in a vicious cycle of hatred and violence? When will we recognize the obvious irrationality of military violence and national conflict, both of which betray a lack of imagination and willpower? Transformation involves an awakening from indifference. It extends our compassion to victims of poverty, discrimination, and all forms of social injustice.

The above-mentioned parable of the sheep and the goats is so telling in this regard. It is a story about transforming the world. I recall on the day of my ordination to the order of deacon how my ordaining bishop, the late Metropolitan Meliton of Chalcedon (at the time, Metropolitan of Imvros), preached on the New Testament reading about the Transfiguration of Christ, from the Gospel according to Saint Matthew (17:1–8).[3] At that precious moment of glorious transformation, when the disciples "looked up," we are told that "they saw no one except Jesus himself" (17:8). When we look around us at people in distress, what or whom do we see? Do we see strangers or do we recognize Jesus? On the day of my ordination, it was deeply seeded in my heart that I should look around and everywhere see Jesus, "no one except Jesus himself." That should be the focus of our vision and worldview; that is the firstfruit of transformation: the possibility of seeing God—and no one less or other than God—in our brother and sister, irrespective of social status, religious persuasion, or racial origin.

Transformation is our only hope of breaking the vicious cycle of poverty and injustice. It is vicious precisely because it is the fruit of vice and selfishness. Yet this vice is not incorrigible; it is again a matter of choice for us—as individuals and as institutions. Furthermore, it is a matter of choice that calls for change in us—both in personal practices and in collective policies. For this to happen, however, as the precondition of such change, transformation requires conversion or *metanoia*, the Greek word for "repentance." Transforming our world requires commitment, courage, and conversion. It demands of us a willingness to become communities of transformation and to pursue justice as the prerequisite for global transformation. It is the way of sacrifice; but it is especially the way of generosity. Where do we stand along this way?

As defined in the Orthodox spiritual classics, the transformation of the human person is not some unique occurrence. Rather, it is perceived as an ongoing process; it is a never-ending development. In a quite different sense, the globalization of the world's economy is also a continuous process, which cannot be understood even minimally without patient, careful analysis. Indeed, since its consequences are both positive and negative, it would not be correct simply to say that globalization is detrimental in all circumstances, simply because it has not resolved the global issues of poverty and environment. On the contrary, it is worth reflecting on how much has been achieved in recent years, in particular for the 800 million people in Asia—especially in India and China—whose poverty has been alleviated and whose quality of life has improved through education, health, and technology. To say this does not imply a naive sense of optimism—the persistent poverty and rampant diseases in Africa prove humbling reminders in this respect. Yet individuals and institutions may be more positively inspired and encouraged if they are also reminded of the progress that has been accomplished through the good grace of God and the goodwill of many. That is one aspect of the paradox of globalization.

GLOBAL ECONOMY AND GLOBAL ETHOS

The relatively recent and rapid growth of the global economy presents numerous critical challenges to religions throughout the world. While this phenomenon promises so much to so many, it also threatens to marginalize millions more. It is crucial for us to be informed about its complex dimensions; it is also critical for us to recognize our responsibility and role within the global network. We must be able to recognize the complex ways in which economic decisions and actions undertaken in one part of the world have direct consequences for people many thousands of miles away. Unless we understand those connections, we will surely fail to grasp the serious consequences of globalization; indeed, we will also have little hope of channeling its consequences in a positive manner and direction.

The truth is that globalization is often not as global as we might imagine. It is sometimes more exclusive and more parochial than its name conveys. There are so many areas where our global society is merely transnational and insufficiently global, that is to say not truly global by representation. Entire nations and regions are omitted from critical discussions and important organizations. Major policy makers, such as the United Nations, the World Economic Forum, and the World Bank, are not as global or open as one might at first suppose or expect. Such bodies are founded on the political realities that emerged in the mid-twentieth century, resulting from the conclusion to World War II. This means that certain regions are inevitably less than fairly represented. In any case, we cannot rely on institutions alone to guide our behavior as inhabitants of a planet that serves as home—or *oikos*—to human beings and all ethnic cultures. We must learn, therefore, both to think and to act in a global manner.

Whether one speaks about economy or ecology, from the perspective of the Ecumenical Patriarchate, it is important to recognize that this world is our home—which, as we have already seen, is precisely what the Greek root (*oikos*) or the prefix "eco-" implies. Indeed, this world is the home of everyone and of all creation. *Oiko-nomia* (or the care and "management of our household"), *oiko-logia* (or the appreciation or "study of our household"), and *oikou-mene* (or the way of "inhabiting the world" as our home) are all derived from the root word *oikos*.

Therefore, when Orthodox theology considers the word "economy," it immediately reflects on God's compassionate and merciful

concern "for the life of the world" (John 6:51). In theological terminology, this is called the "divine economy." According to the literary
classics of Christian spirituality—the writings of the great Fathers
of the Church—it is the mystery of divine economy that led God in
the first place to create and to provide for the world. This mystery is
at the very heart of the Orthodox spiritual worldview.

Moreover, in Christian theology, the supreme example of this
divine economy was revealed in the Incarnation of God's unique
Word, who "assumed flesh and lived among us, and we have seen
His glory" (John 1:14). For "God so loved the world, that He gave
His only Son" (John 3:16). Indeed, Orthodox theology is so convinced that divine economy is the source of all life that it would cut
short this definitive phrase of Saint John the Divine: "God so loved
the world that He—quite simply—GAVE!" We are, therefore, called
to give in generosity. We are called to give selflessly and unconditionally. We are called to exercise this love globally and indiscriminately, despite any opposition, violence, or terror that may stand in
our way.

This recognition is surely one of the simplest yet greatest lessons
we have all learned about globalization. None of us can any longer
pretend to live as if the rest of the world does not exist. We engage
with the rest of the world in our many travels, in our everyday conversations, in our newspapers every morning, and on our television
sets every evening. We have an ethical responsibility to consider
carefully the way that we inhabit the world and the lifestyles that we
choose to adopt. We can no longer live as isolated individuals, disengaged from events in our world. We are created for encounter,
and we are judged based on our response to each encounter. We are
social beings; we share the world; we live in community.

Moreover, the borders of this community have today been
broadened to encompass our entire planet, and beyond. Today, we

know all too well the sins associated with cheap labor and economic inequality. We are all able to perceive how assets or investments are transferred from one country to another in a way that leaves ordinary people feeling bewildered and disenfranchised while at the same time making it impossible for anyone to hold investors accountable for their social and environmental behavior. We can see clearly that in global competition for economic gain there are losers as well as winners, victors as well as victims. We often feel that we lack the knowledge or the instruments that would be needed to exercise some control or restraint on this global market. And, through our own behavior or consumer choices, as well as our generally unquestioning acquisitiveness, we may also be encouraging bad behavior by the companies that dominate the global economy, instead of using whatever influence we may have in a positive way.

ASSUMING RESPONSIBILITY

We could put the matter still more simply. The way we work, the salaries we earn, the houses we construct, the cars we drive, the money we spend, the luxuries we enjoy, the goods we consume, the resources we waste, even the channels we decide to watch or ignore on television—all of these, we now know, impact directly on our neighbors within our own society, in our neighborhood, and more broadly in our world. Our way of living, we now know, either enhances or endangers the rest of the earth's inhabitants as well as all future generations. Perhaps this is the unique responsibility and historical privilege that we share as human beings in the twenty-first century. Are we prepared to assume this responsibility and accept this challenge?

It is true, of course, that many people are uncomfortable speaking about money and wealth; this is perhaps more true of religious people, who will either denounce money as demonic (see Matt. 6:24) or silently idolize wealth as a blessing. Theologically and spiritually, however, the significance of money depends very much on what we do with it. The Greek word for "money" (*chrema*) literally implies something that has the potential of being "used." All of us are called to remember that people should matter and that money should be used for constructive purposes. How tragic it is that we have reversed this principle and have come to believe that money matters while people are there to be used in our effort to acquire wealth. When people matter and the welfare of human beings as well as the sacredness of human life is our priority, we will try to learn just how we can make a difference in our world. What is more, we will act accordingly.

The issues of free trade, global commerce, and market growth should be of concern to everybody, not just a few people. Unless that is clearly recognized, there will be a deeper and deepening chasm between the individual and the community, as well as between the rich and the poor. The notion of community involves values that are shared; these values transcend national, political, religious, racial, or cultural boundaries. Those who live in Western countries must stand back and appreciate how competing in markets and investments does not merely serve to improve the benefits that they enjoy or affect the lifestyles that they are privileged to lead. This privilege comes with a cost, leading to the impoverishment of the rest of the world's population. For it becomes a harsh awakening when we realize that the amount of things we "possess" has implications for those on the other side of the mirror, namely for those who do not possess these same things. Yet this harsh realization is precisely the meaning and mystery of encounter. When we ignore this truth, we are no longer what we are created and intended to be.

Furthermore, the test of our ethical awareness lies not in whether, as adherents of whatever religion, we remember the poor in our prayers but in whether we recognize and act upon our responsibility for the poverty of others. We must all ask ourselves whether we are part of a system that thrives on the exploitation of other nations—and so many of us are. We must consider whether we are in some way complicit with banking or investment practices that manipulate profits and resources in unfair or immoral ways— and so many of us are. We must genuinely examine whether we are part of a system in which unconstrained or poorly regulated development is promoted by national leaders or greedy creditors—and so many of us are. Finally, in light of all these issues, we must begin to address serious questions about personal responsibility and - accept some blame or ethical liability for the choices we make. Addressing these issues means redressing the balance of our involvement in the world; it means learning to be generous where we have previously been greedy. This is not an easy lesson to learn; but it is one that religions must teach: namely, that what happens in the world depends directly on decisions we make as individuals in our lives, in our homes, in our professions, in our churches and temples, in our society, in our politics, and in our nation.

GLOBALIZATION AND ECUMENICITY

Across the world, the power of sovereign governments to act for good or ill is being eroded as private companies extend their business to every corner of the earth. Globalization has been driven forward, to a large extent, by private companies whose almost exclusive purpose is to trade and invest profitably wherever that is possible. These companies have benefited from, and in turn stimulated, the incredible development of technology and communications, which have facilitated immense economic growth and international economic activity of all kinds. For better or worse, the influence of individual states has been downgraded, while the power of a few economically prominent corporations has grown to new heights. Nevertheless, this is not the only kind of global development that is known in the world.

In the Orthodox Church, we have experienced and cultivated a different form of globalization, a notion that we call ecumenicity. We adopt that word to refer to a global outreach that proclaims the unity of all human beings through a bond of love and cooperation, irrespective of racial or ethnic background. While it is true that the Orthodox Church invites all people to one faith, its love for all people is never contingent upon adherence to this faith. Moreover, the ecumenicity of our faith is not related to worldly structures of power and authority. From this point of view, then, the ecumenicity of the Orthodox Church, and in particular of the Ecumenical Patriarchate within the worldwide Orthodox Church, differs substantially from the recent phenomenon of economic globalization. The former is based on love for all people and respects the human person, whom it serves in its totality. The latter is primarily motivated by the desire to enlarge the economy. It can also have the effect of merging different cultures into something new and relatively uniform, in which the common denominators are mass entertainment and the consumption of globally successful products or brands.

GLOBALIZATION AS AN OLD PHENOMENON

People today generally understand globalization as an economic phenomenon. However, the Gospel saying that "man shall not live by bread alone" (Matt. 4:4) should be interpreted and understood more broadly. The truth is, as the saying goes, that bread for myself is a material value; bread for my neighbor is a spiritual value and a moral obligation. We cannot live by economic development alone, but we must seek "every word that proceeds from the mouth of God" (Matt. 4:4). This means that we must pursue values and principles that transcend economic concerns. Once we accept these, the economy becomes a servant of humanity, not its master.

It is my firm conviction—and I believe it can easily be understood by all, independently of religious or political persuasion— that economic development in itself and the globalization that serves it lose their value when they cause deprivation among the many and excessive concentration of wealth among the few. Moreover, the evolution of globalization in this direction cannot be limitless; at some point, we shall face a dead end in the world's economy. Beyond a certain limit, an individual or small group obsessed with financial gain receives a response that has been well-known since ancient times: "You cannot take from someone who does not have." Solon (638–558 B.C.E.), the legislator and one of the seven ancient wise men, once declared that Athenian society was not functioning properly because of the excessive indebtedness of the majority of its citizens to the few. He therefore instituted what was called *seisachtheia*, namely the writing off of all debts. The debate, then, about world debt is not new. Although Solon's initiative seemed at first to be to the disadvantage of the rich, in the end it benefited the entire Athenian community because it allowed all of its members to act as free, creative, and self-motivated citizens rather than as each other's slaves.

The example of Solon, and many others like this through the centuries, reveals—at least in a general manner, since economy is a very complex phenomenon—how economic progress is morally justifiable and successful only when all the members of the global community are able to participate. The current situation in our un-

able bedrock of all existence and coexistence? "For what will it profit [us] to gain the whole world and forfeit [our] life?" (Mark 8:36)

The Orthodox Church is not opposed to an economic progress that serves humanity as a whole. Rather, our desire is always to safeguard the possibility for people throughout the world, for members of every religious or cultural minority, to maintain their distinctiveness and to preserve the particularity of their culture. We are in absolute agreement with advancement and progress when globalization opens doors for the closer cooperation and greater welfare of peoples, when globalization becomes a powerful means of encounter and openness. In the past, I have frequently invited adherents of divided ideologies and diverse interests—both religious and political—to lay aside their differences in order to be reconciled and work together on a practical level. The truth is that our destiny on this planet is closely intertwined. In the past, civilizations proceeded to act upon their natural environments largely in isolation. However, in today's increasingly globalized world and interdependent economy, the behavior of every nation or group of nations affects the whole of humanity.

Such is the positive dimension of globalization, whereby people all over the planet recognize their common purpose, if only by realizing their common fate. However, globalization as a mechanism for controlling patterns of consumption or the opportunity to influence people's consciousness, thereby creating more homogeneous or uniform modes of thought, will always find me firmly opposed. This form of globalization shuts doors and precludes encounter. For the same reason, I would also regard the use of globalization for the exclusive enrichment of the few to the detriment of the many as something unacceptable and unjust, as something to be avoided and condemned.

POVERTY AND WEALTH

In this respect, I would invite everyone, both rich and poor, to cooperate for the improvement of the standard of living of all people. After all, this, too, is ultimately in the best interest of the "haves," perhaps more so than any one-sided increase of their economic worth. Human welfare is affected not simply by the amount of wealth created in the world but by how it is distributed. Yet never before in human history has the inequality between rich and poor on a global scale been so acutely felt. The global economy has allowed the international elite to enjoy new heights of wealth, while the fate of the poorest has visibly worsened. Thus, technology and global communications have enabled the richest and most successful members of the human race to accumulate new privileges, while large segments of society and areas of the earth—especially in Africa and Asia—have been ravaged by disease, anarchic violence, and environmental destruction. The effects of inequality—in the areas of basic health care and education—impact upon the world as a whole, whether or not we recognize it, or indeed whether we like it or not. Eradicating poverty—by improving health care and providing appropriate education—would ultimately stabilize the entire planet's population and environment. Therefore, even from a "selfish" perspective, all of us should become involved in and support the reduction of world debt—for instance, by cutting consumption patterns and reducing energy waste, by developing sustainable patterns of life in cities, and by addressing social injustice within our communities.

While the picture appears gloomy, the reality should not be presented as pessimistic. In reality, never before in history has there also been such a widespread interest in and concern for the eradication of poverty and the future of our planet. This is precisely where globalization carries the potential for a positive impact and change within society and our world. For while it may be true that the gap between rich and poor has never seemed greater, the very fact that such inequality is now palpably obvious, thanks to the images and information that flow so freely around the world, gives humankind a new priority and renewed responsibility. Above all, our attention should instead be directed toward improving the situation of the poor in our world and the poorer nations of our planet. Of course, there is still much to be desired, but in truth there is also much that can realistically be done. No longer is poverty a matter of fate or inevitability. In our age, poverty does not have to be the "lot" of the poor; it is being positively addressed, and it can indeed be resolved through purposeful and compassionate action.

The logic is simple, though not simplistic. Much wealth in the hands of the few in the short term deepens the relative poverty of the many. Yet poverty for the many is ultimately far worse in the long term for the rich than it is for the poor, both from a spiritual perspective and from a secular perspective. The stress that arises from sustaining and developing one's excessive belongings as well as from the consequent imbalance wrought upon the poor reminds me of another ancient Greek proverb: "The protection of goods is much harder than their acquisition." How, then, do we break the vicious cycle?

POVERTY AND RELIGION

Practically speaking, when we fall into the trap of accepting a worldview based exclusively on *homo oeconomicus*—in other words, when human nature is understood in purely materialistic terms—it can prove extremely difficult to resist the uncontrollable impulse of unrestrained acquisitiveness, which is one of the most pervasive and powerful phenomena in our secular age. Religious leaders and believers may not be able to take drastic steps to correct this trend. Nevertheless, we are able to sensitize and move consciences as well as to take measured practical steps with potentially unlimited consequences. The most politically significant step is sometimes the most personal and the most practical of all steps: a change in our way of perceiving the world. The point is that we can no longer remain mere spectators. Each of us is involved; each of us must take appropriate steps.

And the blessed reality is that, increasingly, more individuals and companies are assuming social and moral responsibility. Institutions and corporations are beginning to pledge and show some commitment to respect those in society and our world that are in need; but they are also beginning to appreciate the importance of involving and including their stakeholders—shareholders and markets, as well as employees and consumers alike—in the business of responsibility and philanthropy. While these steps may constitute mere drops in an ocean of needs, they are critical for the development of a moral sense and social conscience.

I am also not naively ignorant of the limited influence of religious leaders. The great majority of people in our affluent societies appear to be caught up, tempted by the illusion that maximal gain and material profit can be pursued without limit. I say "appear" only because it is abundantly clear that the majority of people in our world are in fact victims of this mentality. At the same time, most people can see that poverty is not an illusion; it is a painful reality. Religious leaders must remind their faithful that the economy is not an altar on which human welfare is to be sacrificed. Rather, as I emphasized to participants of the World Economic Forum in Davos, in February 1999, it is the economy itself that should always be at the service of the human person.

How, then, can the many in Western societies—who are the few by comparison with the rest of the world—be convinced to lessen their demands? How can they be inspired to share, to spread their privilege, to open up the scope of their vision? It is my firm belief that religious leaders must seek ways of convincing the affluent that the ultimate gain, the utmost profit, is achieved through the dignity of compassion and philanthropy. What at first appears to be sacrifice is in the final analysis the seed of transformation for one's immediate environment, for the broader interests of society, and for the world in general. Philanthropy is demeaning neither for the giver nor for the recipient, so long as it is practiced as a way of sharing resources for the sake of all people and future generations. The benefits reach out in every direction, returning as ultimate blessing to the giver. This means that the final result benefits both the benefactor and the receiver. The mandate of giving is not simply a metaphysical principle; it is dangerous to distribute wealth for the sake of spiritual reward alone. It is the foundation on which the world rests and grows as community. It is the only way in which the world is nourished and thrives. This is precisely why God becomes involved, extending blessing and offering grace. God is a God of communion, of community, and of love, a God of encounter: "God is love . . . and we love because God first loved us" (1 John 4:8, 19). We can understand generosity and charity to the degree that we have experienced and received these from God through our life.

Moreover, the fundamental religious response to poverty is embracing others as part of our own community and even our own body. The Judeo-Christian Scriptures would say: "Love your neighbor as yourself" (see Lev. 19:18 and Matt. 5:43). This ultimately means recognizing in our neighbor the very face of God and, indeed, the face of our own selves. If only we are able to discern in others (no matter how distant they are from us geographically or culturally) our very own flesh and destiny, then we would respond to their needs in the same manner in which we would respond to members of our own family.

This "re-membering" of our relationship with the rest of the world—namely, the recollection that "we are all members one of another" (Eph. 4:25)—is the most dignified way of resolving poverty. If we consider our neighbor as our own selves, if we look upon those in need as members of our own family, then we care deeply for them, share our resources generously with them, and are sufficiently concerned about their welfare and progress so as to enable them to stand on their own feet in order to support themselves. The truth is that the world as a whole contributes in essential ways to the life of each one of us; we can never isolate ourselves from the fate of the rest of the world.

This is the concept on which all successful programs of developmental aid through financial grants and technical assistance are based. And the final result, as specialists confirm, is that (perhaps rare) instances of well-administered aid bring manifold returns to the ones who offered it at the outset, not as material gain for a few markets or a few nations, but as growth for all of humanity and as sustenance for the entire planet. Aid offered for immediate consumption is never productive or very profitable—either for the one who receives it or for the one who offers it. The kind of aid that is required is such that the recipient will be enabled to produce and be empowered to thrive as a particular and unique nation in a global market. Then the act of giving—which is transformed into the art of communion and encounter—becomes an enrichment and blessing for all.

Such aid may be developmental and financial; but it is not restricted to the economic level. It may also be social and moral aid. The usefulness of the first type of aid is generally accepted. However, as far as the second type of aid goes, there needs to be an important clarification. For the truth is that we all too hastily and habitually determine morality from productivity. Nonetheless, social injustice and moral corruption may well become obstacles to material prosperity and financial productivity. They invariably raise the cost of security and repel the interest of foreign markets. And they threaten the welfare of all citizens by damaging the wider reputation of a nation. Social injustice and moral corruption impair the functioning even of basic economic processes, thereby deterring or delaying overall development. In this respect, for instance, education is yet another area that should attract our attention and assistance. Globalization often tends to benefit the better educated and to neglect the less skilled. Entire communities and nations are being marginalized by the forces of integration within the global economy because people are not benefiting from the basic right of education.

This certainly does not mean that Western nations should in any way impose on or interfere with the ethnic, religious, and cultural sensitivities of a particular nation. So often Western nations and religions have created havoc in poorer nations, where they suppose it to be in *the recipients'* best interests—when almost always it has been in *our own* best interests—to offer the enlightenment of the Western world. Of course, one cannot overlook the critical emergency relief aid, where citizens of the West generously respond by feeding the hungry or providing for refugees after natural disasters. Unfortunately, however, the allocation of sufficient and appropriate aid in order to address issues related to social injustice and moral corruption does not receive necessary and deserved attention. We prefer to compartmentalize our efforts and our interests, concentrating on economic and environmental dimensions while continuing to ignore social and moral issues. But surely the social and moral development of a nation determines also its economic or other progress. The social and moral values of a nation are defined by the way it responds to those who have no power and those who have no wealth.

POVERTY AND POWER

Western societies have not really found any more beneficial economic mechanism than the markets to regulate the activities of labor and capital. The Western system of capitalism forever seeks new ways of reducing costs and increasing gains. Nevertheless, not even the strongest advocates of capitalism would claim that it can serve as a basis for human society unless its activity is underpinned and regulated in the light of moral and spiritual values, which recognize the ultimate value of human beings. Far too often, unrestrained and unregulated markets have led to poverty and pollution. They have failed to curb unemployment and inequality or to protect noneconomic goods, such as culture and ethnic particularity.

There is no specific political agenda behind my words. I am by no means advocating sharing of wealth or eradication of poverty through some abstract dogma or Marxist formula for the redistribution of wealth. The reader should remember that the Ecumenical Patriarchate is nonpolitical in its role and responsibility; it seeks to underline the spiritual value of social justice and to challenge the spiritual dangers implicit in the vice of greed. Yet the fact is that governments often fail to fulfill their responsibility as guardians of the public interest. And the "prophetic" role that religious institutions can play is crucial for a more balanced and fair society.

In response to the power of markets, governments have a duty to exercise greater responsibility and vigilance. However, for better or worse, many governments fail to exercise this responsibility to monitor the activities of international companies and ensure that their productive power is not abused. Companies are better at making cross-border connections than regulators or nongovernmental organizations. Therefore, religious institutions and other independent agencies have a particular obligation to speak out wherever they see that unrestrained globalization is having negative consequences. Nevertheless, irrespective of our efforts, a global economy will inevitably have its victims as well as hundreds of millions of beneficiaries; it will invariably further sharpen the sense of inequality between the rich and the poor. While, then, there are many advantages to the phenomenon of globalization, there are also serious negative consequences, such as heightened inequality and increased conflict over social, economic, and political priorities. Thus, religious institutions must insist on the priority of human rights and of social justice, both of which are deeply rooted in civil society and inspired by the faith communities. Together with nongovernmental organizations, religious institutions should stand in opposition to trends that favor the concentration of global economic power in the hands of a small number of economically powerful institutions or politically powerful dictators.

CONCLUSION: THE RETURN OF THE KING

Christians read the parable of the sheep and the goats as a narrative symbolic of the criterion according to which they will be judged on the day of reckoning, when the Lord of life and death will return. Nevertheless, how striking it is that the measure of judgment adopted in the Gospel story is neither abstract nor arbitrary. Our responsibility, indeed our vocation, is not to transform the entire world but to effect a healing and transforming change in the small area where we have lived, in the few encounters we have had, and in the limited scope where we have acted. In the words of a twentieth-century writer with renewed popular interest:

> It is not our part to master all the tides of the world, but to do what is in us for the succor of those years wherein we are set, uprooting the evil in the fields that we know, so that those who live after may have clean earth to till. What weather they shall have is not ours to rule. (Book 5, IX)[6]

II. RELIGION AND SOCIETY:
FUNDAMENTALISM AND RACISM

Despise no one; condemn no one;
and God will grant you peace.
—ABBA POEMEN (FIFTH CENTURY)

THE ECUMENICAL PATRIARCHATE AND
INTERFAITH DIALOGUE

Two symbolic images adorn the foyer at the entrance to the central offices of the Ecumenical Patriarchate in Istanbul. They silently represent decisive moments in the rich and complex story of a city where Orthodox Christians, Muslims, and those of many other faiths have coexisted over the centuries. One of these images portrays Saint Andrew, the "first-called" of the Apostles and patron saint of the Ecumenical Patriarchate, whose feast day is celebrated on November 30. Beside Andrew stands Stachys, the first priest and successor to Andrew as bishop from 38 to 54 C.E. in a long line of bishops in the city, variously known through history as Byzantium, Constantinople, and Istanbul. Facing this icon of the beginnings of our Church is another image, a magnificent mosaic depicting Gennadios Scholarios (1405–72), first Ecumenical Patriarch of the period under Ottoman occupation. The Patriarch stands with hand outstretched, receiving from the sultan Mehmet II (1432–81) the firman, or legal document, guaranteeing the continuation and protection of the Orthodox Church and the protection of its traditions throughout the period of Ottoman rule. It is an icon of the beginnings of a long coexistence and interfaith commitment whose legacy is still felt and lived by Greeks, Turks, and others in the region.

The Ecumenical Patriarchate has always been convinced of its wider role in the world and of its ecumenical responsibility in several senses of that term. This keen sense of obligation and leadership before other people and before God has inspired manifold initiatives, such as the Patriarchate's tireless efforts to consolidate the unity of the Orthodox Church worldwide, an effort that has often been fraught with national tensions and political divisions. The Patriarchate's involvement in ecumenical dialogue dates back at least to the sixteenth century with the "Augsburg-Constantinople" encounter, which consisted of a series of exchanges between Lutheran theologians from Tübingen and Ecumenical Patriarch Jeremias II (at various times from 1572 to 1595). Although not dialogues in the formal sense, these exchanges were indicative of the general philosophy of the Ecumenical Patriarchate with regard to other churches and other faiths.

The same philosophy has also inspired our encouragement in principle of ecumenical discussions from the early twentieth century onward as well as our involvement in ecumenical organizations, such as the World Council of Churches, of which the Ecumenical Patriarchate has been a founding and active member since its inception in 1948.[7] Moreover, it has provided the impetus and foundation for several bilateral discussions with other Christian churches. Beyond the agreed statements between the Orthodox and the Oriental Orthodox churches,[8] the most effective and to date fruitful of these theological dialogues has been engaged with the Roman Catholic Church. Some of the highlights of this dialogue include the historic meeting between Ecumenical Patriarch Athenagoras (1886–1972) and Pope Paul VI (1897–1978) in 1964, which led to the mutual lifting of the anathemas from 1054, and the equally historic visit between the late Pope John Paul II (1920–2005) and my predecessor, Ecumenical Patriarch Demetrios (1914–91), in 1979, which led to the announcement of the official bilateral dialogue between our two churches, which officially commenced in 1980. The visit of the present Pope Benedict XVI to Turkey, in response to my invitation to attend the Thronal Feast of the Ecumenical Patriarchate on November 30, 2006, led to a renewal of the commitment to dialogue.[9] Another important result of such initiatives has been a conversation with the Anglican communion, under way since the Lambeth Conference of 1930, and an ongoing dialogue with the Anglican communion about specifically theological matters that has been in progress since 1973.[10]

However, even at the cost of much defamation for "betraying" the Gospel truth, we have never restricted these engagements merely to the various Christian confessions. Standing as it does at the crossroads of continents, civilizations, and faith communities, the Ecumenical Patriarchate has always embraced the idea and responsibility of serving as a bridge between Christians, Muslims, and Jews. Since 1977, the Ecumenical Patriarchate has pioneered and been directly involved in a bilateral interreligious dialogue with the Jewish community (on such topics as law, tradition, renewal in a modern world, and social justice); in 1986, we initiated a bilateral interfaith dialogue with the Islamic community (on such matters as authority, coexistence, peace, justice, pluralism, and the modern world); and since 1994, we have organized a number of diverse multi-faith dialogues, in particular hosting several international gatherings, which have made possible deep, multilateral conversations between the Christian, Jewish, and Muslim communities (on such issues as religious freedom, tolerance, and peace).

At various points in my tenure as Ecumenical Patriarch, I have had the opportunity to address the issues of peace, racial discrimination, religious tolerance, globalization, and secularism before diverse audiences in Western as well as Eastern Europe, the Middle East, Africa, Australasia, and the Americas. Their questions have ranged in character from political to religious and interreligious concerns, as well as from economic to scientific and academic interests. Undoubtedly, however, one of the most rewarding aspects of my humble ministry has been the blessing of either hosting or sponsoring international initiatives,[11] such as:

- the Peace and Tolerance Conference, which met for the first time in Istanbul in 1994 and published the Bosphorus Declaration, affirming (based on the Berne conference on peace in 1992) that "a crime committed in the name of religion is a crime against religion";

- the Conference on Peaceful Coexistence between Judaism, Christianity, and Islam held in Brussels in 2001, in the aftermath of September 11, which published the Brussels Declaration, "rejecting the assumption that religion contributes to the clash of civilizations," and pointing out the role of faith in "providing a constructive and instructive platform for dialogue among civilizations";

- a special session held in Bahrain in 2002 on the occasion of the tenth anniversary of the commencement of our Christian-Muslim dialogue; this led to the Bahrain Declaration, which asserted the need to cooperate "in healing the traumatic experiences of the historic past, by taking concrete initiatives addressed to the local society, so as to remove negative prejudices and to foster respect among their faithful for the particularity of other religious traditions";

- the Conference on Religion, Peace, and the Olympic Ideal held in Athens in 2004, on the occasion of the imminent Olympic Games, which "repudiated all forms of nationalist, racist, religious, social, and other discrimination, by means of which morbid religious intolerance and fanaticism is harbored";

- the Peace and Tolerance Conference, held again in Istanbul in 2005, stating: "As spiritual leaders of the children of Abraham, it is incumbent upon us to diminish ethnic and religious tensions" while "deploring those who preach violence toward other faiths and ethnic communities" and "rejecting violence and totally and unconditionally condemning the use of force, ethnic cleansing and brutalities."

These gatherings, and others like them, have proved both pioneering in purpose and historic in substance. Yet, above all, they have opened our eyes to the diversity of cultures and religions in our fragmented world, as well as to the manifold complexity of the global reality. They have also widened our perspective and appreciation of pluralism and secularism, as well as of racism and fundamentalism.

THE RISE OF PLURALISM

As I consider our changing world, two significant and defining features immediately come to mind: pluralism and secularization. First, the national boundaries separating one country from another are becoming increasingly less clearly marked. This is more evident in Europe than in other parts of the world; and it is happening on many different levels, political, economic, and social. None of us any longer lives in a monolithic, mono-ethnic, or monocultural milieu;

all of us either belong to or find ourselves cast into broader and multiple cultural currents. One aspect of this multicultural trend is the ever-increasing scale of immigration throughout the world. This is again especially but not only true of Western Europe. In Europe today, for example, there are between fifteen and twenty million Muslims. In Britain, Muslims constitute 2.7 percent of the population, but in most other countries the proportion is higher: in Germany, 4.9 percent; and in France as much as 8.3 percent (no fewer than five million).

This is a social and political reality to be welcomed as an opportunity and a challenge, rather than perceived as a problem or a threat. Nations in the contemporary world are beginning to recognize how we all belong to and look to one another; they are learning that, as states, they are not self-sufficient but interdependent. To Cain's question in the Old Testament story of Cain and Abel—"Am I my brother's keeper?" (Gen. 4:9)—there is only one answer on the personal, the institutional, and the international levels.

This does not mean that national loyalty, patriotism, and love for one's native homeland have ceased to have any meaning. On the contrary, what Alexander Solzhenitsyn (b. 1918) said in his Nobel Prize speech some thirty-five years ago still remains fully valid today: "The disappearance of nations would impoverish us no less than if all humans were to become alike, with one personality and one face. Nations are the wealth of humankind, its collective personalities; the very least of them wears its own special colours and bears within itself a special facet of divine intention."[12] Naturally, then, the experience of our own national identity has today to be lived out within this pluralist and multicultural context. This implies, at the same time, that we must learn to be more tolerant and understanding of one another.

THE EUROPEAN UNION

The most striking expression and contemporary embodiment of this multiculturalism is of course the emergence of the European Union. From its early beginnings in 1950, when Robert Schuman (1886–1963), as French minister of foreign affairs, proposed the establishment of the European Coal and Steel Community, the European Union has now come to embrace no fewer than twenty-five member states, and continues to expand. As a Turkish citizen, I hope that in due course Turkey will acquire full membership in the European Union, especially when the necessary preconditions of membership have been met, including in particular the recognition of the religious and other rights of minority communities in that country. The admission of Turkey to the European Union will, I believe, significantly contribute to the rapprochement and reconciliation between the Muslim world and the West.

It is true that the European Union has gone through periods of crisis. The idealistic vision of its founders has sometimes been blurred or even somewhat faded. Yet this should not blind us to its remarkable achievements. For more than sixty years there has not been a major war in Europe; probably, since the fall of the Roman Empire, there has never been in Europe such a prolonged period of peace. With a minimum of violence and bloodshed, the Iron Curtain was torn down before the eyes of the world. To a degree that would have been unthinkable in the 1930s, the peoples of Europe are today committed to embracing the principles of freedom, justice, and democracy. Therefore, when we Orthodox pray, as we do at every celebration of the Divine Liturgy, "for the peace of the whole world," we have good reason to reflect with gratitude on these historic developments. At the same time, we know that there is no room for complacency. Peace and freedom are not only gifts from God; they are also unceasing tasks.

The problem is not that Islam is undoubtedly growing as a presence in the West, or that it is increasingly visible and vocal as a presence in the world. The problem lies in the unprepared nature of the West to understand and embrace this presence. Indeed, the reality is that, in contrast with the self-confidence of militant Islam, the West finds itself in an era of postmodern moral indifference. The greatest vulnerability of the West is not so much the rise of Islam as the rampant growth of secularism. Christianity seems to have abdicated its responsibility to inspire and guide Western civilization. It has retreated from the public square, where it naturally belongs and thrives. It has conceded to an agnosticism, even atheism, that appears to be riding the crest of an intellectual wave throughout the Western world.

THE GROWTH OF SECULARISM

Along with multiculturalism, then, a second major feature in today's changing world is the growth of secularism. In earlier centuries, religion played a definitive and formative role in all facets of life, profoundly influencing philosophy, medicine, law, art, and politics. This was most certainly the world of the Byzantine era, as well as of the Middle Ages. However, this reality is no longer characteristic of our world and time, where each of these areas of life has acquired a distinct existence. Religion, therefore, must first of all discern and affirm its proper place and unique role among the new forces that shape and unite global humanity. Above all, religion must maintain a prophetic and authentic role among these forces, addressing problems with clarity and criticism in order to focus— and sometimes even awaken—the spiritual vision of our world.

Thus, the role of religion is to remind the world of the divine mystery, sometimes overlooked in the diverse masks of secularism, which run the risk of concealing the divine beauty in all things.[13]

Today, at least in most countries throughout the world and especially the Western world, there has been a dramatic decline in attendance at religious places of worship. Almost everywhere, with certain notable exceptions, religious groups (and especially Christian denominations) are lamenting a lack of candidates for the priesthood and the religious life. Although this does not seem to be a problem for the Orthodox churches at present, they, too, have been deeply marked by secular trends. In education and in the total life of society, Christianity—including Orthodox Christianity in traditional lands—is becoming marginalized.

By secularization, I mean the marginalization of religion through a dangerous compartmentalization of the religious worldview. Ultimately, it is an abandonment of the sacramental view of life and the world, a loss of the sense of mystery. Secularism is the heresy that isolates humanity from God and the world; it ignores the original calling of the human person as a eucharistic and ascetic being.[14] For, as we have already seen in earlier chapters, the original and ultimate purpose of human life is to worship and glorify God while at the same time sharing the gift of the world with all of humanity. Secularization can mean the erosion and distortion of our proper understanding of the world as sacrament. A secular society may well nominally accept the idea of an existing God, even while emphatically rejecting the sacramental nature of the world and of the human person.

In this respect, secularization has infiltrated even traditionally Orthodox nations, although the process may have taken longer than for other Western societies. Already evident as early as the seventeenth century, the impact was certainly profound in the twentieth century. Today, secularization is as present and pervasive in Orthodox cultures as in Western societies. This means that, like other Western citizens, Orthodox Christians struggle to maintain the integrity of their faith in the face of national tensions and within a globalized world.

All of this leads us to ask: Does religion any longer have a role in the future of the world? Yet we must be careful not to exaggerate. Even if levels of religious attendance have dropped in many places, the greater majority of people still affirm that they believe in God. In some countries, the proportion of those who do so is surprisingly high, such as in European nations like Malta, Cyprus, and Romania but also in the United States. Nonetheless, while people are inclined in recent years to claim some form of faith, it is true that their confidence in institutional religion, and in a doctrinal expression of that faith, has certainly been shaken.

FUNDAMENTALISM AND FANATICISM

At the very time when Christian confessions appear to be experiencing a crisis from within, there seems unfortunately to be a rapid rise in popular interest worldwide—whether out of conviction or fear— in religious fundamentalism. However, I believe firmly that, as the Koran itself also explicitly states (2:257), "religion cannot be imposed." Instead, religion depends on the free will of the individual. The notion of the "free individual" is of course more germane to eighteenth-century Western thought. The notion of free will is perceived differently in the Orthodox Church, as in organic societies.[15] Nevertheless, the Orthodox Church would strongly emphasize the importance of personal respect and freedom of choice with regard to one's religious convictions. As Orthodox Christians, we would vehemently disapprove of any form of proselytism, in the sense of placing unbearable pressure on others to change their religious affiliation. We are as uncomfortable with those who seek to proselytize within traditionally Orthodox countries as we are with those within Orthodoxy who seek to impose our faith on others. We do not participate in dialogues with Muslims or Jews simply in order to convince them to accept our own faith; that in itself would imply a sense of arrogance and prejudice, defeating the very purpose of encounter and dialogue. Moreover, we have sensed no such intention directed toward us by our Muslim or Jewish colleagues at these bilateral discussions.

If there is one fundamental principle that draws Christians to the discussion table with Muslims and Jews alike in a world torn by division and turmoil, it is the passionate desire to recognize and declare more widely that it is not religious differences which create conflicts among human beings. After all, if indeed the cause of human conflict was the differences among religions, then surely there would be no tensions among the faithful of the same religion. Yet we know of plenty of tensions and conflicts, even wars, that have divided followers of one and the same religion, indeed even within one and the same region. In our times of tension and conflict, many Westerners and other secular-minded people often single out religion as the forum or as a scapegoat to blame for the various problems that plague our world. Indeed, as global conflicts intensify, they argue ever more passionately against religion and for a secular approach to international relations. And to some degree, these critics may be right. Nevertheless, religion is not the issue at stake here; religion is not the source of the problem at hand; and religion is certainly not the primary cause of the growing tensions throughout the world.

At times, misinterpretations of the sacred texts of one religion have unfortunately been deliberately promoted in order to justify human pursuits or selfish interests and also to attract religious believers to support a particular leader. Although it is true that there are many misconceptions about religious fundamentalism, religion has undoubtedly been used as a means toward political ends or personal interests.[16] Nonetheless, honest individuals of every religion must struggle to respect God and not be fooled by such self-serving interests while remaining steadfast in virtue, mercy, forgiveness, and compassion. Of course, I am also aware that among the followers of all religions, whether among Christians of all denominations, among Jews of all congregations, or among Muslims of all persuasions, there are always minorities that will espouse different views, some of them quite extreme. However, as a Christian leader, I cannot surrender my hope that the evangelical gospel of consent, reconciliation, and peaceful cooperation will in the end prevail. Surely this is what the Apostle Paul refers to when he writes: "If possible, so far as it depends on you, live peaceably with all people" (Rom. 12:18).

RELIGION AND ABSOLUTISM

The most delicate and at the same time awkward issue with which we must deal in relation to religious fundamentalism is absolutism. It is well-known that every religion asserts that it contains the absolute truth concerning God and the world. Furthermore, it is also well-known that God is the absolute being, the one to whom all pure attributes belong and from whom all evil attributes are entirely absent. This is fairly common ground among the three monotheistic religions of Christianity, Judaism, and Islam, and beyond.

Moreover, as all monotheistic religions confess, God is one—although Christians would prefer to recognize and refer to the One God in Trinity. This means that all believers of the monotheistic religions should have at least some perception of the one, immutable, and perfect God. The fact that the perception of adherents to one religion differs from the perception of adherents to another faith community means little other than the fact that as "creatures" of God and "observers" of the world, we naturally differ from one another. In other words, our perceptions as human beings and religious believers are essentially determined not by the object/Subject that is observed (if we can ever truly speak in this way about God) but by our condition as observers. The variation of opinions, then, derives not from the relativity of the One God or of God's creation but from the cultural and religious diversity as well as from the human and rational limitations of us as people.

The confession of this fundamental truth about God and ourselves incites within each of us the Socratic admission with regard to our ignorance: the one thing that *we do know* is that *we do not know* anything! In other words, we humbly accept the fact that when we speak of absolute values, we are dealing with truths beyond our intellectual capabilities and experience. We are dealing with truths beyond rational debate and logical discussion. As a direct consequence of this humble recognition—namely, as a direct consequence of our responsibility to the truth about the One God, whom alone we worship—we are at the very least obligated to be open to and tolerant of the views of others. For insofar as we stand in some relationship to one another before the truth about God, we can only be united in complete silence before God's transcendent being and inaccessible presence. Even the most complete and comprehensive sentence or definition of God can neither appropriate nor approach the fullness of divine nature, which always remains incomprehensible, indeterminable, and unqualified. As Saint Paul was raised to the third heaven, he wrote in his Letter to the Corinthians: "For now we see only dimly [that is to say, through puzzling riddles or reflections], as in a mirror. But then [one day], we shall see face to face" (1 Cor. 13:12).

APOPHATIC THEOLOGY IN POLITICAL PRACTICE

We do not know God's inner being or nature; we can never know God's essence; at all times, this eludes us. Any certainty with regard to God is dangerous; it tends to polarize cultural discourse and deepen cultural division. One cannot debate with fundamentalist Muslims, any more than one can debate with fundamentalist Jews or fundamentalist Christians. Their certainty about God renders global discourse or religious discussion almost impossible. The alternative is humble engagement and moderate conversation. It is an expression not only of a dignified respect toward other human beings but of a due response to God, who remains beyond all certainty and comprehension. Moreover, it is a reflection of a proper self-respect, inasmuch as one readily admits one's limitations and imperfections.

Some Christians will be quick to retort with doctrine, which expounds the fullness of truth; or with the sacramental life of the Church, which expresses God as fully present; or with the mystical witness of the saints, which experiences God as totally intimate. Although that is the tradition within which I have been formed and for which I am responsible as a leader, it is not the level on which I am called to communicate with my fellow human beings who are Muslims and Jews. The point is that God is by definition and by nature beyond all human understanding and perception; otherwise, God would not be God. This is the teaching of the great theologians and mystics, like Saint Gregory of Nyssa in the fourth century and Saint Gregory Palamas in the fourteenth century, both of whom underlined the radical transcendence as well as the relative immanence of God: God as unknowable and yet as profoundly known; God as invisible and yet as personally accessible; God as distant and yet as intensely present. The infinite God thus becomes truly intimate in relating to the world.

There is always something in God that we can never and will never grasp fully; God is beyond all human faculties and categories. By contrast, the definition of human nature will always include weakness and limitation, uncertainty and imperfection. This conviction allows us the freedom and the space to sit with our Muslim brothers and sisters, as well as with our Jewish colleagues, in order to determine how best to dwell with one another in peace and harmony. All of us recognize that love transcends law, that mystery transcends doctrine, and that practice transcends theory. A genuine and humble faith will, therefore, be tolerant of other faiths. It will not feel threatened by other faiths, but instead will freely and fearlessly embrace the adherents of other faiths.

After all, the Old Testament's Book of Exodus, revered by all three monotheistic religions, itself reveals the same apophatic truth, namely that "no one shall see the face [of God] and live" (Exod. 33:20). The language of Scripture here is metaphorical and symbolic. Its goal is to preserve—and not dispel—the mystery of God; the purpose is to pray to—and not dismiss—the transcendent God. God "is who God is" (Exod. 3:14); the face of God is veiled in mystery. Therefore, we can only confess *that* God is (cf. Judg. 13:15ff.); we can never define *who* God is. No one can imagine a God that resembles us; this would be an "anthropomorphic" God.[17] This is the God about whom we may genuinely be taught as young children, but whose understanding must be continually refined. For God can never be either fully contained or exhausted. "The face of the living God" signifies the true nature of God. This means that no living person can know God, although we can know something about God from the way God is manifested in the world, for instance, as love and justice and peace. Yet even in our understanding of these actions—which in Orthodox theological discourse are called "energies"—we still know God in a limited fashion, which inevitably results in differences. Indeed, if we are honest with ourselves and with God, then we shall admit that there are times when we confuse our imperfect and limited knowledge with our prejudices and passions, thereby conforming our understanding of God to our condition. The ancient Greeks long ago understood this notion of projection. The Greek Fathers of the early Church labeled it the creation and worship of idols!

Nonetheless, even this reality of projecting onto our understanding of God our limited conditions is understandable, given the inherent weaknesses of human beings. What, however, is entirely unacceptable is the desire to *impose* on others our image of God, which may be refracted—perhaps even deformed—through the prism of our personality and passions, presenting this as the only and absolute truth about God. This "God" could even be manipulated and invited to bless someone's fundamentalism and fanaticism, pitting the cross against the crescent.[18] The Koran itself recognizes this: "Some falsely refer to the Lord, knowingly" (3:78).

The many names of God in Islam surely offer another point of encounter with Muslim believers, who likewise submit before the living and loving God. Indeed, while the correspondence may not be precise, the diverse, wonderful names of God in Islam resemble the names attributed to God in Christianity and are eloquently preserved in the Eastern Orthodox theological and liturgical traditions.[19] Both religions describe God as merciful, compassionate, and holy. Both religions call God Creator, king, peacemaker, and repairer. Both religions pray to God as forgiver, provider, and judge. Both religions refer to God as first and last, but also as light and hidden. Nevertheless, above and beyond such similarities—some will be quick to add numerous contrasts and dissimilarities—the various names in both religions underline an important truth: that the names of God reflect the power both of encounter and of mystery. They reveal a personal relationship between God and the world, initiated and sustained by God through love and forgiveness. Moreover, they conceal the ultimate incomprehensibility of God, which is especially preserved by the people of the Old Testament. The names, then, are metaphors and symbols, albeit powerful and personal, of the nameless God. It is the same truth that mystics have known through the centuries.

Thus, the great monotheistic religions may be said to agree not only on the one name (or the many names) of God. More fundamentally, they agree on the ultimate namelessness of God. For while they may disagree on the precise content of the names themselves—that is to say, on the details of the faith that they confess—they agree on the mystery of God, who transcends all names and knowledge. Put more simply: while Jews, Christians, and Muslims may disagree on the partial truth that we know dimly about God, they in fact approach one another in their recognition that the absolute truth cannot be conceived, contained, or exhausted.

THE ROLE OF RELIGION

As religious leaders responsible before God to preserve the teachings and traditions of our faith, to whatever degree we are of course cognitive of this faith, we are obligated consciously to reject any projection of personal whim that seeks to replace the will of God. At the same time, however, we are obligated humbly to demonstrate a profound mutual respect, which allows our fellow human beings to journey on their own personal path to God, as they understand the will of God, without interfering with the journey of anyone else. This kind of profound mutual respect on the part of one person toward the religious journey and conviction of another is the foundational responsibility of each of us. It is also the fundamental presupposition for peaceful coexistence and goodwill among people.

Even in the sacred texts of the monotheistic religions, there is no evidence whatsoever that God is in any way pleased with conversion by means of force, obligation, or deceit. Indeed, there is no evidence that God forcefully draws people to the divine will or way. On the contrary, at least from the Judeo-Christian Scriptures, as we have already observed, the idea that emerges is of the human being created in the image and likeness of God, adorned with the divine characteristic of personal freedom. Surely it would be paradoxical, if not contradictory, for God to endow humanity with free will on the one hand while forcefully curtailing that freedom on the other hand. Therefore, what modern and even secular Western society promotes as cultural achievement, namely the expression and protection of free will in relation to the inviolability of religious conscience, is also essentially espoused by and directly derived from the teaching of the three monotheistic religions of Christianity, Judaism, and Islam. This is what forms the basis of interfaith encounter and dialogue.

The personal encounter among the adherents of these religions, and perhaps especially the conversation between those who—like Moses—seek to encounter the true face of God, is the only way that is worthy of the God of Abraham, of Isaac, and of Jacob. In the words of the Koran: "Truth emanates from God" (3:60), and it is revealed to those who love God, according to the degree of their capacity. After all, God first chooses to open dialogue with us, with humanity and the world, in many different and diverse ways. Furthermore, God only asks for our *own* hearts to be open for dialogue; God never asks that we open the hearts of *others* for dialogue.

Moreover, each of us is called to communicate "to all those who request from us a word concerning the hope that lies within us" (1 Pet. 3:15), as well as an account of the faith and experience that lies within our tradition. Again we read in the Koran: "Say: Truth emanates from your God; he who so desires, let him believe; he who does not so desire, let him remain in faithlessness" (18:29). The same freedom is discerned in the Gospels, where Christ repeatedly states: "If any want to become my followers, let them . . . follow me" (Matt. 16:24).[20] And in the Hebrew Scriptures: "When in the beginning God created the human race, God left them free to make their own decisions" (Sir. 15:19). How can we ignore and overturn all these scriptural words by daring to impose our faith on others? Racism and prejudice are choices by humans; they are neither convictions of faith nor chances of history. As religious believers, then, we must decide what we will choose: hatred or love, racism or coexistence, war or peace.

Finally, the world's monotheistic religions owe it to their common heritage to imitate their forefather, the Patriarch Abraham. Sitting under the shade of the oak trees at Mamre, Abraham received an unexpected visit from three strangers (recorded in Genesis 18; see also Hebrews 13:2). He did not consider them a danger or threat to his ways and possessions. Instead, he spontaneously and openly shared with them both his friendship and food, extending such a generous hospitality that, in the Orthodox spiritual tradition and commentary, this scene has been interpreted as the reception of three angels, who are by extension symbolic of the Holy Trinity. In fact, the only authentic image of the Holy Trinity, of God as communion, in the Orthodox Church is the depiction of this scene of encounter from rural Palestine. As a result of his selfless hospitality, Abraham was promised the seemingly impossible, namely the multiplication—literally from barrenness!—of this seed of love for generations. Is it too much to hope that our willingness to converse and cooperate as people of different and diverse religious convictions might also result in the seemingly impossible coexistence of all humanity in a peaceful world?

Moreover, in the Orthodox icon of Abraham's Hospitality, iconographers traditionally depict the three guests on three sides, allowing an open space on the fourth side of the table. The icon serves as an open invitation to each of us. Will we sit at the table with these strangers? Will we surrender our prejudice and arrogance to take our place at the table for the sake of the very survival of our world and the peaceful future of our children? The icon of Abraham's Hospitality is a powerful symbol of the presence of God among us when we welcome others without inhibition and without suspicion. It is an image of encounter and communion. It is an icon of religious tolerance, the reverse image of the fear of foreigners, or xenophobia.

RACISM AND XENOPHOBIA

From an Orthodox Christian perspective, the virtues of respect for cultural diversity and religious tolerance provide fundamental skills for life, much in the same manner as sunlight and water nurture a plant. Without either or both of these virtues, there can be no nourishment; in fact, there is spiritual deprivation. An Orthodox Christian celebrates the diversity of the entirety of God's creation, rejoicing in the infinite multitude of beauty and meaning, which can only be truly manifest in diversity. This is how we perceive the Church; and this is how we perceive the world. Such diversity is a prerequisite for a unified and peaceful world, just as it is for unity among the members of the Church. When human beings ignore the value of diversity, they actually diminish the glory of God's creation. This is precisely because, according to the Orthodox theological worldview, diversity is based on the very concept and being of God as Trinity, namely of God as communion and of all life as an expression of that very community. Regardless of religion, race, ethnicity, color, creed, and gender, all human beings are living and unique icons of God. All human beings are equally worthy of the respect and dignity that is uniquely due to God. Any attitude or conduct that undermines or overlooks this respect and dignity is an insult also to God as Creator.

Throughout the world, Orthodox Christians live side by side with peoples of other religions and Christian confessions; this has been their reality and history for over five centuries. Yet with the rapid rise of technology as well as the advancement of communication and transportation, all of us have been increasingly liberated from the tyranny of distance and the exclusive borders of nations. Today, people find themselves dwelling in a global village among new neighbors representing widely differing perspectives of the world, of history, and of culture. The reality of pluralism especially challenges each person in this global village to reflect more critically on the teachings of his or her faith with a sense of renewed tolerance in light of these different perspectives and worldviews. Learning to live in a spirit of open dialogue and mutual respect is the basis for acquiring the skills of living in community. It is the mystery of encounter. It is also the art of living together.

The opposite of this perspective of respect and tolerance is the perspective of fear and self-righteousness, which result in fundamentalism and racism. Whenever human beings react to perspectives and beliefs of others on the basis of fear and self-righteousness, they violate the God-given right and freedom of all people to know God and one another in a manner inherent to their identity and tradition. Sadly, however, many of us are easily predisposed to viewing others on the basis of fear and self-righteousness. Such tendencies may be characterized as xenophobic, a Greek term that signifies the "fear of strangers" or the suspicion of others. Perhaps the first example of this xenophobia in Scripture may be found in the Book of Genesis, when Adam moved away from the intimate communion he had originally enjoyed with his Creator, God; it was a form of estrangement and alienation. In the embrace of God, human beings see others not as strangers, whom they should fear, but as brothers and sisters, whom they must love.

Central, then, to the teachings of the Orthodox Church is the fundamental belief that Christianity, and indeed all religions, must play an active role in the effort toward the reconciliation of all peoples, in the work of breaking down barriers of estrangement and alienation. This understanding is based on the teachings of Jesus of Nazareth, the Christ, as well as the Prophets of old, who preached the commandment to "love God with all one's heart and to love one's neighbor as oneself" (Matt. 22:37, 39; Deut. 6:5; Lev. 19:18). This reconciliatory work can only be initiated and sustained by genuine tolerance, which, together with its twin virtue of respect for diversity, reflects the love of God for the world. And it is not only religions that are called to this task. Every organization of social, international, and political character should be dedicated to the pursuit of justice, advance the welfare of society, and perform the work that is pleasing to God.

HOSPITALITY AND THE SCRIPTURES

We seem to have forgotten the virtue of hospitality, which was the defining characteristic of the early Christians and remains to this day a priority in the values of authentic monasticism. Anyone visiting an Orthodox monastery—or, at any rate, a monastery that genuinely expresses the monastic ideal—will be struck by the overwhelming charity and hospitality from the moment of reception and throughout one's stay. Life in contemporary cities and secularized urban settings has encouraged isolation and increased suspicion of others, who are regarded as strangers or foreigners.

We have already considered the example of Abraham and the importance of his hospitality, which is directly related to the mercy and compassion of God. Yet Scripture underlines the importance of hospitality in many other places (cf. Lev. 19:33–34 and Ps. 146:9). Indeed, it even identifies the stranger with each of us: "Love the sojourner; for you were all sojourners in the land [of Egypt]" (Deut. 10:19). If we consider ourselves as one with every stranger and foreigner, if we identify completely with every immigrant and refugee, then we shall welcome all people without inhibition or suspicion. This is why the second-century anonymous *Epistle to Diognetus* emphasized that Christians are at home—while also seeking the kingdom—wherever they may be.

Ultimately, at least for Christians, welcoming and embracing the other is encountering and receiving Christ (cf. Matt. 25:34–45). Jesus heals foreigners (Luke 17:18); he speaks to the Samaritan woman (John 4:9); and he holds up the example of the foreigner, in the parable of the Good Samaritan, as a model for imitation: "Go and do likewise" (Luke 10:37). This means that our destiny in this world and in the age to come depends on how we have treated foreigners and strangers. The Greek word for "foreigner" (*xenos*) is exactly the same as the Greek word for "guest." Is this, however, what is reflected in our hearts? Is this what happens, especially, in our conduct? Or do we more than often separate and segregate? Do we perhaps prefer to label foreigners and strangers as enemies and evil?

THE PATRIARCHATE AND RACISM

I am able to speak in this manner because the Ecumenical Patriarchate is not a national organization; nor does it represent any particular national or local church, such as the Orthodox Church of Greece or the Orthodox Church in Turkey, where I reside and where the See of my Throne has traditionally stood. The Ecumenical Patriarchate is a supranational and spiritual institution, not characterized by the pursuit of secular authority or worldly jurisdiction, but instead embracing believers of many nationalities and maintaining a benevolent and equitable disposition toward all. Moreover, the Ecumenical Patriarchate demonstrates religious tolerance in a unique manner, bearing respect toward its neighbors of all religious persuasions, particularly Muslims. Without the slightest trace of fanaticism or prejudice on account of religious or racial differences, we have for centuries coexisted peacefully, in a spirit that honors every human being created in the image of God.

Furthermore, the Ecumenical Patriarchate has always stood and continues to stand firmly against any expression of any racist ideology. Since 1872, at a time when nationalism was rampant in Europe as well as abroad—a reality reflected in manifold chauvinistic theories and a host of Pan-Slavist, Pan-Germanic, and pan-nationalist movements—the Ecumenical Patriarchate has officially condemned nationalism and racism through a formal synodal (or conciliar) decision. By contrast, the nationalistic movements of the nineteenth century had led to the establishment of rather narrowly defined ethnic Christian churches—including Orthodox churches—throughout the world, thereby surrendering the unifying message of the Gospel to nationalistic divisions and conflicts.[21]

Three centuries earlier, Ecumenical Patriarch Metrophanes III (1565–72, 1579–80) encountered anti-Semitic attitudes in one of his provinces, namely on the island of Crete. In the late 1560s, the Jewish residents of the island, then under Venetian rule, complained of unjust treatment and even persecution by the islanders, including certain Orthodox Christian believers. The Patriarch responded with a strong encyclical in 1568, condemning and even threatening with excommunication any Orthodox Christian involved in wrongful treatment of any person on the basis of religion—the Patriarch observed that this was "injustice on the pretext of faith"—and emphasizing the importance of "not distinguishing or mistreating people of other faiths."

Centuries earlier, during a time when the latinization of all nations was being pursued by Church authorities in the West, the Ecumenical Patriarchate did not hesitate to create a special alphabet for the Slavic people through the missionary efforts of Saints Cyril (820–69) and Methodius (815–85), the apostles to the Slavs, who undertook to translate liturgical books and promote a new, non-Greek civilization with its own unique spirituality and tradition. The brothers achieved this despite fierce opposition from Latin and German missionaries, who claimed that missionary expansion could only be understood as narrowly religious and could only be carried out in the sacred languages of Hebrew, Latin, and Greek. They endeavored to transform public life generally, translating codes of law and other fundamental texts; they understood that the Spirit of God could never be confined merely to pious expressions or the four walls of a church. From this civilization of the Slavs came the likes of Saint Seraphim of Sarov (1759–1833), the most beloved of Russian saints, and Fyodor Dostoyevsky (1821–81), that remarkable novelist and author of *The Brothers Karamazov*.

Nationalist tendencies have persisted of course and continue to exist even among certain Orthodox churches; indeed, they have proved to be the bane of Orthodox growth in recent centuries. Yet they are not normative for Orthodox experience or spirituality. In perhaps the most recent institutional expression against racism, the Fourth Pre-Conciliar Pan-Orthodox Conference, held in Geneva in 1976, expressed the desire that the Orthodox Church contribute to upholding peace, freedom, reconciliation, and love throughout the world in order to dispel racial discrimination. Organized and chaired by the Ecumenical Patriarchate, this Pan-Orthodox Conference sought to replace racism with interreligious cooperation, in order to abolish religious fanaticism of every kind. For such extreme racism undoubtedly breeds religious fanaticism and fundamentalism.

So, at the Ecumenical Patriarchate, we do not fear strangers; we cherish them. We have made it our daily practice for centuries to apply the apostolic words "Do not forget to entertain strangers"

(Heb. 13:2). We insist that all humans are equal both before the law of God and before secular law, a view surely also espoused by all sensible and sensitive people, regardless of religious conviction. At every given opportunity, then, we emphasize that the religious rights of minorities must be duly respected, including and especially their right to worship and education. After all, the very term "Ecumenical" in the title of our Church seeks precisely to denote the acceptance of all people dwelling within the *oikoumene* as being fully equal and equally welcome.[22]

Saint Paul the Apostle, himself of Jewish origin as well as of both Jewish and Greek education, stated this goal succinctly: "There is neither Jew nor Greek, there is neither slave nor free person, there is neither male nor female: for you are all one in Christ Jesus" (Gal. 3:28). His words were daring and revolutionary in a time that recognized slavery and discriminated against women, when one people (the Jews) believed they were the chosen of God and another (the Romans) exercised their supremacy over the world. Paul's words remain indispensable for religious tolerance and peaceful coexistence.

RELIGION AND POLITICS

Religion is the undisputed wellspring and timeless spiritual heritage of Western society. In this respect, it is always at the center of the dialectical encounter between old and new, whether seeking restraint, encouraging moderation, or criticizing developments.[23] Today, religion can no longer be obsessed with the past or disassociated from the present. It must be inseparably connected to ideologies of modern society, attuned to the conditions of democracy, informed of the details of modern legal theory, and involved with the lives of citizens everywhere.

Disputing the role of religion in the contemporary world is a thing of the past; it reflects an old-fashioned ideology and ground-less superstition that no longer corresponds to the real demands of civil society. Even the legal separation in many countries of church and state, the constitutional provision for the independence of government from religion, is in fact a powerful means of preserving the identity and integrity of both. Ultimately, it is a way of protecting the religious freedom of citizens and communities, rather than a theoretical circumvention of religion with a view to undermining its relevance and significance. While a very sharp line of demarcation between religion and politics may have been necessary in times of turmoil, it would be an unfortunate loss for the democratic political system today if religion were to be dismissed or ignored. Neither religious values nor religious communities ever exist in isolation; rather, they always exist within a sociopolitical context and cultural setting, within which they are also vibrant and meaningful.

In many ways, the sharp distinction, even separation, between church and state—or between the sacred and the secular—derives from the Western legacy of Christianity, especially in medieval power struggles between popes and kings, as well as in the European Enlightenment of the eighteenth century. Yet in the Christian East the distinction between church and state was never quite so marked and never quite so clear. In Byzantium, the emphasis—at least in its ideal—was on a synthesis and even harmony between the two.[24]

The Byzantine theory of Christian monarchy is not, of course, something to be imitated or idealized today. Nevertheless, the Byzantines knew about the interplay of religion and politics; theirs was undoubtedly the longest experiment in church-state relations in the entire development of Christendom, spanning and enduring over a thousand years from the Edict of Milan (313) to the fall of Constantinople (1453). Moreover, it is unfair and simplistic to condemn this experiment as "caesaro-papist," namely the subordination of the church to the state. While caesaro-papism was indeed a factor in church-state relations through the Byzantine era, it was neither the only nor the decisive factor. And while there were definitely negative consequences to the coextensive nature of the church's relationship with the state, the Byzantine imperial interventions are quite different from that which would today "appear as intolerable intrusions of the secular power into the sacred precincts of the Church . . . Caesaropapism never became an accepted principle in Byzantium. Innumerable heroes of the faith were constantly exalted precisely because they had opposed heretical emperors; hymns sung in church praised Basil for having disobeyed Valens, Maximus for his martyrdom under Constans, and numerous monks for having opposed the iconoclast emperors of the eighth century. These liturgical praises alone were sufficient to safeguard the principle that the emperor was to preserve, not to define, the Christian faith."[25]

In more recent years, the growing resurgence of religion in the Iranian revolution of the late 1970s, when an essentially nonviolent religious movement was headed by a traditionalist religious figure, reminded political leaders throughout the world that religion can be a powerful part of social and political reform. The rise of Hindu nationalism in India, the second most populous nation in the world, is another case in point. Even the emergence of Christian evangelism in the West is a growing political reality in Europe and the United States. The modern mind had so completely subscribed to the fundamental message of the Enlightenment in Europe that it failed to see how history could be shaped by anything other than science and technology. By contrast, religion was privatized and marginalized from the public square, essentially perceived as backward and outdated.

The unfortunate attitude here is that religion somehow hampers or menaces progress. This mind-set creates a moral vacuum in a society that is shaped solely by economic factors in a globalized world. The vacuum is ultimately filled either by an inhuman globalization or by a religious extremism. Religion, however, must not retreat from the public space. It must be invited to address social and political issues, and especially poverty and war. In order to do this, religion must work closely with all factors and agents of civil society in order to respond to the challenge of human suffering and environmental degradation. It should also become involved in sensitive discussions about human rights and against racial intolerance.

The point here is that omitting or dismissing the crucial role of religion in social and political development is myopic in the short term, if not detrimental in the long term. Indeed, the legitimate claim of religious principles and the consistent stance of political authority coincide in the urgent need for an explicit constitutional acknowledgment of the institutional role of religion in modern society and the lives of its citizens. On the one hand, this is mandated by the historically tested and confirmed durability of the interdependent relations between religion and society. On the other hand, it is necessitated by the political realism of a visionary democracy, which recognizes the unique and significant role of religion in the contemporary intercultural dialogue. Moreover, the undeniably intimate relationship between religion and society, which is embodied in the religious values incorporated by everyday people in their everyday lives, renders fictional any fear or tendency of confusing the two detrimentally. This has proved to be the common cultural heritage of all civilizations, and particularly of Western civilization, where religion has assumed an essential responsibility and enjoyed an enriching role within society.

THE TURKISH MODEL

When I hear about the devastating effects and fatal results of terror-
ist attacks, I recall the words of the prime minister of Turkey Recep
Tayyip Erdoğan (elected in November 2002) some years ago, who
remarked after such a tragic attack in Istanbul:

> I cannot bear it when terrorism and Islam are spoken of in one
> and the same breath . . . The Religions of the Book want to pro-
> tect life, not destroy it. In Islam, those who destroy human life
> are likened to those destroying the House of God.

These words reveal an attitude that goes to the very heart of Turkish Islam, the nature of the secular state, and the principles of democracy. They reflect the profound changes that have taken place
recently in Europe and Turkey with regard to Islam.

Today, the European Union has at least fifteen million Muslims;
three million of these are Turkish. Although its history and culture
are interwoven with European developments, contemporary Turkey
faces one of its most profound challenges, namely its accession to
and acceptance within the European Union. Turkey is, after all, the
only Muslim society that has come into close contact with and
warmly embraced the ideals of the Enlightenment and the French
Revolution. In the Ottoman Empire, the state took precedence over
religion, whereas Turkish Islam remained open to the significant influence of mystical traditions. While embracing the notion of the
modern national state, it has consistently and variously resisted the
ideology of political Islam. As a result, Turkey is unique among
Muslim nations because it has always enjoyed a deeper harmony between traditional Turkish Muslim values and the secular values of

civil society. In brief, Turkey is exceptional inasmuch as it is "Islamic *and* secular" rather than "Islamic *but* secular."

The Turkish model demonstrates clearly that the interaction of Islam and the modern world need not be on a collision course; they are neither self-contradictory nor mutually exclusive. The results of Mustafa Kemal Atatürk's (1881–1938) vision for Turkey to join what he termed "universal civilization" have been impressive and striking. Turkish citizens enjoy greater opportunities and better conditions than citizens of many other neighboring countries, where government and Islam remain conjoined.

The roots of secular Turkish Islam deeply permeate the social fabric of the country. Turks themselves are committed to a secular path and a democratic future. Even if there was a period of divergence, when the state promoted Islam vis-à-vis the challenges of the Cold War, today the desire of this nation is clear and united: to fulfill the criteria of Copenhagen in order to join the European family of nations. There is no doubt that Turkey is seriously working and striving toward joining the European Union.

Like European or American cultural identity, Western civilization can no longer be perceived purely in terms of geography or even within the narrow bounds of a particular history and specific culture. It is situated within a wider context, which espouses the same set of fundamental values and principles shared by many nations throughout the world—namely, human rights, religious freedom, social tolerance, and the rule of law. Turkey readily subscribes to and closely identifies with these values; it has repeatedly proclaimed its commitment to apply them equally to all its citizens regardless of ethnic race or religious creed. In Turkey, Christians, Muslims, and Jews live together in an atmosphere—at least for the most part—of tolerance and dialogue. Over a decade ago, by way of one example, Fethullah Gülen (b. 1941) began to educate his believers about the necessity for the existence of a dialogue between Islam and all other religions. It was Gülen's firm conviction that "negative feelings and attributes often defeat people, pulling them under their domination to such an extent that even the religions that guide people to goodness and kindness are abused, as well as the feelings and attributes that are sources of absolute good."[26]

The Turkish model of Islam seeks the legitimization of all religions and the freedom to choose at all times, without any coercion from the state by means of either religious or secular pressure. In other words, the Turkish model envisages Islam as occupying within the Islamic societies the same position and privilege that religion enjoys in the contemporary Western world. It is a world far removed from the concepts of jihad and crusades.

Turkey shaped its modern—tolerant and secular—identity out of a long struggle with the new political order at the advent of nationalism. Today, this identity is being tested once again with the emergence of the post–Cold War era at the advent of a new geopolitical reality, which is quite unlike any we have known in the past. The radically new situation within which our world finds itself demands radically new answers and approaches, from which we should not shy away. Some critics express doubts with regard to my personal support, as well as the support of the Ecumenical Patriarchate, for Turkey's admission to the European Union, perceiving in this support a sort of submissiveness of our Church to the Turkish state. This could not be further from the truth. Our position is dictated not by political criteria or influences but by spiritual interests.

It is my conviction that the accession of Turkey to the European Union would benefit all of its citizens, including the minority communities of the country. For Turkey would be required to make significant, indeed substantial modifications to its legislation, adhering to the principles of the other European nations. Although it is beyond our jurisdiction to judge whether Turkey meets the necessary criteria for this accession, we are able to indicate the necessary steps that yet remain for Turkey to conform to the democratic principles of member nations of the European Union.

The incorporation of Turkey, and in particular of this Turkish model, into the European Union may well provide a concrete example and powerful symbol of mutually beneficial cooperation between the Western and the Islamic worlds, putting an end to talk of a clash of civilizations. This, in turn, would prove truly strengthening for Europe and the European ideals, which converge with the values of "the Religions of the Book" to which the prime minister of Turkey referred.

We stand before perhaps the greatest challenge of human history: namely, the challenge to tear down the wall of separation between East and West, between Muslims and Christians, between all religions of the world, between all civilizations and cultures. As stewards of this unique and exceptional historical moment, we must face the challenge of bridging the great divide and recognizing our common humanity and common values. This is surely God's model for the world.

III. WAR AND PEACE:
CONFLICT AND DIALOGUE

Acquire inward peace, and thousands
around you will find their salvation.
—SAINT SERAPHIM OF SAROV
(EIGHTEENTH THROUGH NINETEENTH CENTURIES)

CHOOSING TRANSFORMATION

As faith communities and as religious leaders, we must constantly pursue and persistently proclaim alternative ways to order human affairs, ways that reject war and violence and instead recognize and strive for peace. Human conflict may well be inevitable in our world; but war and violence are certainly not. Human perfection may well be unattainable in this life; but peace is definitely not impossible. If this century will be remembered at all, it may be remembered for those who dedicated themselves to the cause of peace. We must believe in and "pursue what makes for peace" (Rom. 14:19).

The pursuit, however, of dialogue and peace calls for a radical reversal of what has become the normative and defensive way of survival in our world. It demands a transformation of values that have become deeply seeded in our hearts and societies, hitherto determining our relationship with those who challenge our worldview or threaten our lifestyle. Transformation in the spiritual sense is our only hope of breaking the cycle of violence and injustice. For war and peace are systems that are contradictory ways of resolving problems and conflicts. Ultimately, they are choices. This means that making peace is a matter of individual and institutional choice, as well as of individual and institutional change.

Peace, then, also requires a sense of conversion, or *metanoia*—a change in policies and practices. Peacemaking ultimately requires commitment, courage, and sacrifice. It demands of us a willingness to become communities of transformation.

RELIGION AND PEACE

As guardian of a tradition spanning two millennia, I believe that the Orthodox Church has been endowed with a vast repository of wisdom. This wisdom is based on the Judeo-Christian Scriptures and rooted in the Church Fathers. These sources provide a framework that enables us to respond creatively to contemporary issues. The issues that our world faces are in some ways hardly new. History is replete with examples of violence, cruelty, and atrocities, committed by one group of people against another. However, our present situation is in at least two ways quite unprecedented. First, never before has it been possible for one group of human beings to eradicate as many people simultaneously; second, never before has humanity been in a position to destroy so much of the planet environmentally. This predicament presents us with radically new circumstances that demand of us a radical commitment to peace.

We have an ethical obligation to resist war as a political necessity and to promote peace as an existential necessity. The threat to the fabric of human life and the survival of the natural environment make this the overarching priority over all others. In choosing the alternative of transformation through peace, then, we should remember that peace always—ultimately—starts in the heart. Moreover, peace takes much time and toil. Nevertheless, it offers us our only hope of survival as individuals, as nations, and as a species.

PEACE AS THE WAY OF THE HEART

The early spiritual literature of the Christian East has consistently emphasized the heart as the place where God, humanity, and the world coincide in a harmonious—or, as the texts themselves say, "prayerful"—relationship. Nevertheless, *The Philokalia*, a remarkable anthology of texts on prayer and silence, underlines the astonishing paradox that peace is only gained through surrender and abandonment. In this context, the notions of surrender and abandonment do not imply passivity or indifference to the suffering of the world. Surrender and sacrifice mean giving up our pride, passions, and selfish desires; at the same time, they imply embracing the virtues that constitute the other side of that coin, namely love and generosity. In fact, surrender and sacrifice are ways of achieving inner peace, through which everyone and everything around us find a common serenity. "When you find yourself in silence," claim the writings of *The Philokalia*, "then you will find God and the world entire!" And for Saint Isaac the Syrian in the seventh century, "if you make peace with yourself, then heaven and earth will make peace with you."

While silence and serenity are nurtured in a unique way in the Christian East, we certainly do not have a monopoly on them. They are also found outside of the Christian world. The ancient Jewish tradition describes the great temple at Jerusalem, erected during the reign of David's son Solomon, as being constructed in silence. The place "was made of stone, finished at the quarry," according to the First Book of Kings (see Chapter 6), "so that neither hammer nor axe nor any tool of iron would be heard in the temple while it was being established." This kind of Semitic hyperbole enriches the scriptural language and conforms perfectly to the utter absence of unwanted or unwarranted noise that prevailed during prayer in the completed temple. Silence is in fact constructive, not passive. "The Lord is in His holy temple; let all the earth keep silence before Him," the Prophet Habakkuk enjoins (Hab. 2:20). "Be still, and know God" is the exhortation of the psalmist (Ps. 46:10).

Similar understandings of the way in which God and the world can coincide in the power of silence and peace are also to be found in Islam. The Arabic root of the words "Islam" and "Muslim"—literally implying submission to God and the one who submits to God—connotes a profound sense of wholeness and integrity, of peace and serenity alike. These result from correctly ordering one's relationship to God, to others, and to the world. It is the state called "salaam," which is closely related to the Hebrew word for peace, namely "shalom." One who achieves the state of inner peace in relation to God is a true Muslim. In other words, peace is the active awareness that God, and God alone, is to be held at the center of all life. If that can be achieved, then peace is closer to us, more integral to and more definitive of us than our own selves!

PEACE AS A WAY OF TOIL

Silence and prayer are themselves forms of peacemaking, not simply preparations for peacemaking. Yet if prayer and silence are the foundation of peace, peace does not rest in these alone. Resistance can never be reduced to an anxious attempt to prevent something terrible from happening around us. On the contrary, the resistance of silence can serve as a forceful "no" to everything that violates peace. When one awakens to such silence, peace flows from within, as an expression of gratitude for what God has offered the world. Peace rests in the undoing of fear and develops on the basis of love. Unless our actions are founded on love, rather than on fear, they will never be able to overcome fanaticism or fundamentalism. Peacemaking must be deeply rooted in the all-embracing love of God, who "causes the sun to rise on the bad and the good, and the rain to fall on honest and dishonest people alike" (Matt. 5:45). Only those who know—deep inside the heart—that they are loved can be true peacemakers. Our peacemaking ultimately stems from and relates to love for all of God's creation, both human and environmental.

In this form, peacemaking is a radical response; it threatens policies of violence and the politics of power. Perhaps this is why peacemakers—whether Jesus Christ, Mahatma Gandhi (1869–1948), or even Martin Luther King (1929–68)—were considered threats to the status quo of society. Sometimes, the ultimate provocation lies in an absolute refusal to engage in intimidation. The "provocative" message of religion is to "love your enemy and [to] do good to those who hate you" (Luke 6:27). There may well be those who anticipate with enthusiasm "the end of faith," casting blame on religions for all the violent aberrations from decent human behavior and the aggressive fanaticisms of our time. Yet never was the "protest" offered by religious communities more necessary than now. Never was the voice of religion more badly needed than today. Spiritual silence as the starting point of action is appropriate; silence, in the sense of indifference, as response to war and violence is sinful and reprehensible. In many ways, our time is the beginning—and not the end—of faith.

PEACE AS THE ONLY WAY FORWARD

Over the last two decades, the Ecumenical Patriarchate has made the preservation of the natural environment a central focus of its spiritual attention and a priority of its pastoral ministry. I consider peacemaking integrally linked with the survival of our planet and with the way its inhabitants relate to the natural creation. A responsible relationship between human beings and their Creator, as well as among human being themselves, inevitably implies a balanced relationship of human beings with the natural world. The way we treat each other is reflected in the way we treat our planet; the way we respond to others is mirrored in the way we respond to the air we breathe, the water we drink, and the food we consume. In turn, these directly influence and reflect the way we pray and the way we worship God.

Our goal, then, is to promote a peaceful resolution of disagreements about how to live in this world, about how to share and use the resources of our planet, about what to change and what we have to admit we can never change. It should be our commitment as religious leaders to seek solutions through open exchange without resorting to oppression or domination. In this regard, while everyone has a part to play, those of us in the faith communities have greater responsibility to influence and change those in positions of authority. We have it in our power either to increase the hurt inflicted on our world or to contribute toward its healing. Once again, it is a matter of choice.

Paradoxically, however, we can only become aware of the impact of our attitudes and actions on other people and on the natural environment when we are prepared to show vulnerability, to take risks and sacrifice some of the things we hold most dear. Unfortunately, many of our efforts toward such accommodation—whether social or ecological—are in vain because we are unwilling to forgo established ways of living and thinking as individuals or as institutions. We refuse to relinquish either wasteful consumerism or prideful nationalism. Relinquishing can sometimes mean sharing instead of hoarding, caring instead of ignoring, and seeking a greater degree of equality within society. In any peacemaking, it is critical that we perceive the immediate and lasting impact of our practices on other people (and especially the poor) as well as on the environment.[27] When will we realize the extensive and lasting detrimental effects of war on the ecological, cultural, spiritual, and social environment? When will we recognize the obvious irrationality of military violence and national conflict, which betray such a lack of imagination and willpower? When will we appreciate that the relationship between the environment and social justice is of paramount importance—not simply for a better life, but for our very survival?

Finally, if peacemaking is our only hope of transcending violence and transforming our world; if, as faith communities and as religious leaders, we must embrace and proclaim alternative ways; if we are to reject war and violence while recognizing peace as the only way forward, then we are called not just to commitment but also to cooperation. Peacemaking will stand a better chance of succeeding if we work together at many different levels: religions, governments, institutions, organizations, individuals. If we act in isolation, we shall soon be exhausted and discouraged. If we act in solidarity, then we are assured of the presence of God, whose healing grace through Christ is always "where two or three are gathered in His name" (Matt. 18:20).

CULTURES IN CONFLICT OR DIALOGUE

The various gatherings initiated or organized at the Ecumenical Patriarchate are crucial in order to prepare the way for a more peaceful coexistence and closer cooperation between the world's peoples.[28] They serve to bring cultures together in a searching encounter and assist religious believers in establishing a more meaningful form of communication with one another. The underlying principle behind any such encounter or dialogue is that all human beings ultimately face the same problems in life. I feel that it is absolutely critical for us to emphasize conversation and to affirm the importance of open, honest dialogue among religions and civilizations as the only way of achieving genuine encounter and communication. Such an interfaith dialogue draws people of diverse religious beliefs and differing cultural backgrounds out of their isolation, preparing them for a process of mutual respect, understanding, and acceptance. It is my unswerving conviction that when we truly desire this kind of encounter and communication and our hearts sincerely seek these, we will somehow find ways to coexist despite differences in our faiths and in our cultures.

The Koran, the sacred book of Islam, explicitly declares that Christians and Jews, the adherents of monotheism and children of Abraham, must not be coerced into conversion. Furthermore, it describes the Gospel as an "illuminating book" (3:184), recognizing Christians as those most disposed to love (5:82). Therefore, there is no religious ground on which the faith of Islam can be used to justify disputes between Christians and Muslims. There are of course differences in faith and conviction, but the Koran never suggests that these are unavoidable reasons for conflict.

In fact, historical conflicts between Christians and Muslims normally have their roots in politics and not in religion itself. The tragic story of the Crusades is a telling example, bequeathing a legacy of cultural alienation and ethnic resentment. Every time religion has been used to incite enmity and aggression, it has been a case of abusing the naïveté of the masses, thereby misguiding them into actions of religious intolerance and racial discrimination. Examined carefully and considered historically, these cases are clearly unjustifiable. Speaking of an inevitable and inexorable "clash of civilizations" is neither correct nor valid, especially when such a theory posits religion as the principal battleground on which such conflict is doomed to occur.[29] It may sometimes be the case that national leaders try to bring about isolation and aggression between Christians and Muslims or that politicians or demagogues mobilize religions in order to reinforce fanaticism and hostility among nations. However, this is not to be confused with the true nature and purpose of religion. Christians and Muslims lived together, sharing the same geographical region, in the context of the Byzantine and the Ottoman empires, usually with the consent or support of the political and religious authorities of these two monotheistic religions. In Andalusia, Spain, believers in Judaism, Christianity, and Islam co-existed peacefully for centuries. These historical models reveal possibilities in our own world, which is shaped by pluralism and globalization.

Moreover, it is overly simplistic to distinguish sharply between the cultures or civilizations of "East" and "West," as if the two are unrelated or can never converge in any meaningful or creative way. Of course, all generalizations from history are simplistic, whether they are cited for or against the theory of an expected "clash of civilizations." However, it may be helpful to recall a fact that is rarely acknowledged by historical commentators and political scientists. As the Byzantine historian Alexander Vasiliev (1867–1953) observes:

Perhaps the cultural influence of both the Byzantine Empire and Islam may be noted in the origin and progress of the so-called Italian Renaissance. Classical knowledge, which was carefully preserved by Byzantium, and various branches of knowledge which were not only preserved but also perfected by Arabs [and Ottomans], played an essential role in the creation of the new cultural atmosphere . . . a connecting link between ancient culture and our modern civilization. Here we have an example of the cultural co-operation of the two most powerful and fruitful forces of the Middle Ages—Byzantium and Islam.[30]

Perhaps, then, it would be more appropriate to focus our imagination not on some inevitable clash of civilizations but on the mutual enrichment that can take place between different, diverse, and distinct cultures. This is a hope expressed in a paradoxical way by a contemporary Turkish writer, Turan Oflazoglu (b. 1932): "What we need is to enrich ourselves with those aspects of foreign culture that are not congenial to our nature."[31]

This is precisely why an explicitly religious dialogue, which acknowledges differences but also suggests ways to negotiate differences, may prove helpful in mapping out appropriate avenues of communication between cultures and nations. Religious dialogue can drive away superstitions and dissolve biases; it contributes to mutual understanding and paves the way for peaceful resolution. Fear and suspicion are bad advisers; they are only exorcised when we come to know people on a deeper level and come to learn their deeper motivations. When I was a young boy, I remember seeing Ecumenical Patriarch Athenagoras (1886–1972), an extraordinary leader of profound vision and ecumenical sensitivity. He was a tall man, with piercing eyes and a very long white beard. Patriarch Athenagoras was known to resolve conflict by inviting the embattled parties to meet, saying to them: "Come, let us look one another in the eyes, and let us then see what we have to say to one another."

Of course, many people have such strong convictions that they would rather sacrifice their own lives than change their views. Nevertheless, the entirely unacceptable side to this notion of martyrdom is that the same people are sometimes also willing to take the lives of innocent victims. What this invariably tells me is that we must listen more carefully, "look one another" more deeply "in the eyes," explore more closely in order to discern the inner motivations behind outward actions. We are always—whether we like it or not, whether we know it or not, and whether we accept it or not—close to one another in more ways than we are distant from one another;

indeed, we are much closer to one another than we might ever suspect or even imagine. As the latest insights of biology inform us, the physical differences between any two human beings are very minor compared with the vast number of characteristics that they hold in common. We share far more with each other and resemble one another far more as members of the same species than we differ in terms of culture, religion, and background.

Dialogue does not imply denial of religious faith or betrayal of religious affiliation. Instead, it signifies a shift in our mind-set and a change of attitudes, what in spiritual language we call "repentance"—or, as we have already seen, in Greek, *metanoia*, which literally means seeing things through a different perspective. This is why dialogue is the start of a long and patient process of conversation, not a fundamentalist drive toward conversion or some legal exchange of ideas like a contract. It is a way of learning how to listen in order to hear, so that Muslims can feel welcome and safe in Christian countries and so that Christians can feel welcome and safe in Muslim countries; so that both Jews and Palestinians may feel welcome and safe in the Middle East; so that all minorities in all places can enjoy the same rights and privileges as their neighbors.

THE IMPORTANCE OF INTERFAITH DIALOGUE

We hear it stated often that our world is in crisis. Yet never before in history have human beings had the opportunity to bring so many positive changes to so many people simply through encounter and dialogue. The interaction of human beings and ethnic groups is today direct and immediate as a result of technological advances in the mass media and means of travel. People of diverse cultural and religious backgrounds gather in conferences to negotiate solutions.

While it may be true that ours is a time of crisis, it must equally be underlined that there has also never been greater tolerance for respective traditions, religious preferences, and cultural peculiarities.

Thus, both unofficial dialogues, conducted on a personal level between followers of the world's great religions, and formal dialogues, organized internationally by religious leaders and institutions, have struggled to clarify centuries-old misunderstandings while gradually preparing people's hearts and minds for the possibility of peaceful coexistence and cooperation among all people. Is this effort for encounter not something sacred? Can it honestly be considered anything less than mystical or sacramental? Can there be anything more precious in the eyes of God than this struggle to communicate and relate? Is there truly anything more valuable for the future of humankind?

Cohabitation between Christians and Muslims, especially in the Mediterranean region, has been the general rule for centuries. It has resulted in greater familiarity and friendship; it has facilitated discussions and exchanges and has given rise to mutual understanding and tolerance. In particular, both Arabic- and non-Arabic-speaking Christians have lived together with Muslims, while the literature and arts of both religions have benefited greatly as a result.

Moreover, in countries such as Syria (which hosts the See of the ancient Orthodox Patriarchate of Antioch in the city of Damascus), Lebanon, and Jordan, and in cities like Bethlehem and Nazareth (within the ancient See of the Orthodox Patriarchate of Jerusalem), the percentage of Christians alongside the Muslim majority has historically been higher than in cities elsewhere in the Muslim world, such as Turkey, Iran, and Iraq. In some of those places, the centuries-long experience of coexistence and cooperation between Christians and Muslims—daily cohabitation and continual cooperation between members of these communities on all levels, as well as the rise of individuals from both religions to elevated positions in government and other senior posts—has rendered people on both sides more sensitive and open to real and responsible dialogue.

Exchanges and dialogues concerning the teachings and spiritual experiences of religions have occurred throughout the centuries. However, the degree of absoluteness in the nature of faith, and especially within the three monotheistic religions, often intensifies discussion and reduces creative conversation to negative apologetics. This has resulted in a plethora of defensive works wherein the superiority of one religious claim is set over against another. When this happens, discussion tends to highlight opposition and stress differences, pursuing logical proofs instead of mutual understanding. Even so, there are always some exceptional leaders who seek to discover the deeper message of faith that unites rather than pointing up the things that divide.

This does not mean that differences on the level of doctrine are insignificant or inconsequential, for such differences lead to a different worldview and, accordingly, a different way of life. Not seeking differences does not imply indifference; nor does underlining absolute values imply minimalism; just as pursuing those elements that unite does not imply syncretism or the thoughtless abolition of difference.[32] "Syncretism" derives from a Greek word that involves a sense of comparison and competition. What I am proposing is a sense of synergism, not syncretism; the Greek derivation of the term "synergism" implies a close cooperation in order to address issues of common concern.[33] This sense of working and living together in peace and solidarity signifies a profound respect for each person and culture as unique and unrepeatable. Genuine dialogue recognizes the inviolable right of every human being to follow a personal journey of faith, hope, and love. Many centuries ago, Jalal ad-Din Rumi (1207–73) wrote a poem titled "The Religious Conflict":

The blind face a dilemma when they worship,
While the powerful on the one and on the other
  side stand established:
Every place is happy with its way.
Only love can make their conflict stop.
Only love comes to help when you call for help
  against their arguments.

Accordingly, we do not approach dialogue in order to set our arguments against those of our opponents in the framework of conflict. We approach in a spirit of love, sincerity, and honesty. In this respect, dialogue implies equality, which in turn implies humility. Honesty and humility dispel hostility and arrogance. Just how prepared are we in dialogue to receive others and to respect others? How willing are we to learn and to love? If we are neither prepared to receive nor willing to learn, then are we truly engaging in dialogue? Or are we actually conducting a monologue?

Often, conservative Christians and other religious groups are offended by the priority that the Ecumenical Patriarchate gives to dialogues with other confessions or faiths, believing that there can be no dialogue on equal terms with heretics. The word "heresy" is another term that has been misused, if not abused, in the history of religious and theological thought. I am in no way undermining the importance of theological doctrine and its accuracy; we have already dealt with this matter in detail in previous chapters. However, it may be useful to remember here that the Greek word for "heresy"—*airesis*—does not primarily signify erroneous doctrine. Rather, it implies the conscious selection of a single aspect of truth, which one absolutizes in a fundamentalist way to the exclusion of all other perceptions of truth. We must humbly admit that all of us are guilty of this sin—Christians, Jews, and Muslims alike. Moreover, I am convinced that the purpose of dialogue is precisely to reveal the fallacy and arrogance of this attitude. This is the kind of humility that is expected of all those in dialogue, including the Orthodox who believe that they retain the fullness of the Christian truth.

True dialogue is a gift from God. According to Saint John Chrysostom, fourth-century Archbishop of Constantinople, God is always in personal dialogue with human beings. God always speaks: through Prophets and Apostles, through saints and mystics, even through the natural creation itself, for "the heavens declare the glory of God" (Ps. 19:1). Whoever can listen to the words of God through people and to the silent words of creation through nature is truly blessed. The Word of God is meaningful to us when we respond in faith. And words, too, are more fruitful in dialogue than in monologue. Dialogue is the most fundamental experience of life: from childhood, through education, to maturity. Dialogue is also the most powerful means of communication for the teacher and the preacher. Dialogue promotes knowledge and science, reveals truths and emotions, abolishes fear and prejudice, cultivates bonds and broadens horizons. Dialogue enriches; whoever refuses dialogue remains impoverished. Finally, dialogue seeks persuasion, not coercion. It does not eliminate responsibility as a critical part of response.

Interfaith dialogue can only occur in a spirit of respect, responsiveness, and responsibility. The goal of dialogue is mutual understanding, but its starting point is clarification of misunderstandings, some of which have been shaped and reinforced over centuries. Moreover, dialogue resists considering a part of the truth as the whole truth. That, as we have seen, constitutes heresy. It endeavors to discern the historical context of particular traditions and beliefs rather than applying them indiscriminately to the present context. For instance, we must distinguish the universal will of God, which is valid for all people of every era, such as love and charity, from the provisional commandments of God, such as how specific acts of love and charity are to be performed. This means not that the essential will of God changes but that human beings and historical circumstances are liable to change.

Religious leaders bear a special responsibility not to mislead or provoke. Their discretion is a key factor in people's interpretation of God's will. The integrity, then, of religious leaders plays a vital role in the process of dialogue. In the mid-fourteenth century, Saint Gregory Palamas, Archbishop of Thessaloníki, conducted theological discussions with distinguished representatives of Islam. One of the Muslim leaders expressed a wish that the time would come when mutual understanding would characterize the followers of both religions. Saint Gregory agreed, noting his hope that this time would come sooner than later. It is my humble prayer that now will be that time. Now, more than ever, is the time for dialogue.

I would not be so naive as to imagine that dialogue comes without cost or danger. Approaching another person—or another belief, another culture—always involves risk. One is never certain what to expect: Will the other suspect me or my intention? Will the other perceive me as wanting to impose my own system of belief or way of life? Will I compromise—or perhaps lose—what belongs uniquely or distinctively to my tradition or values? What is the common ground on which we can converse? What, if any, will be the fruitful results of any dialogue? These questions plague the mind and clutter the heart when approaching for dialogue. Yet I believe that in the moment when one surrenders one's mind and heart to the possibility of dialogue, something sacred occurs. In the very willingness to embrace the other, beyond any fear or spite, a mystical spark is kindled, and the reality of something—or Someone—far greater than us assumes the burden and takes over. Then we recognize how the benefits of dialogue far outweigh the risks. We are convinced that despite cultural, religious, and racial differences, we are closer to one another than we could ever imagine.

RELIGIOUS DIALOGUE THROUGH THE CENTURIES

Throughout history, people have sought to resolve conflict either by means of aggressive imposition or through peaceful and meaningful dialogue. It is natural that human beings, who have diverse perceptions and opinions, will disagree; and it is inevitable that societies and cultures, with diverse philosophical worldviews and historical backgrounds, will find themselves in conflict with others who do not share the same perspectives. Cultural values and religious principles especially heighten such conflict, since people will zealously defend what has uncritically become established as tradition. As a result, it is not always easy to discern the truth in conflicting or contradictory positions. We all know how fanaticism turned people against their own co-religionists during the Crusades in Asia Minor and the Middle East, during the so-called Sacred Inquisition in Western Europe, and during the wars of the Reformation. In recent years, we have all witnessed how the same fundamentalism and fanaticism lead to torture and terrorism worldwide.

It is easy for an entire society and nation to misconstrue the basic elements of another's cultural worldview or religious outlook. It is much more difficult, through the painfully slow progress of dialogue, to dismantle the fortress of such misconceptions one stone at a time. So often, ignorance and even deliberate distortion will lead to the general public's being misinformed, in turn leading to unquestioning intolerance and uncritical condemnation.

The Orthodox Church derives its appreciation of other faiths from the early teaching of Saint Justin the Philosopher and Martyr (100–165), who spoke of a "germinative principle" or "seminal truth" discerned everywhere that sincerity and desire for the fullness of truth exist.[34] Justin rightly believed that the Word of God may be discerned and discovered in classical writers as well as in other religious worldviews that were "able to see the truth darkly, through the implanted seed of the Word dwelling in them."[35] Clement of Alexandria (150–215) spoke of classical philosophy as "paving the way for perfection and . . . containing scintillations of the divine word."[36] According to Saint Gregory the Theologian, all human cultures "desire . . . and seek God."[37] Can we not learn from this openness and sensitivity from centuries ago?

This openness and sensitivity are based on the doctrine of the Holy Trinity. For when one worships a God who entered and shared fully a particular human condition and culture, through the Holy "Spirit, which blows where it wills" (John 3:8), God becomes profoundly associated and even identified with every human condition and culture. There is no culture and no race that is unrelated or irrelevant to the divine "Word, who assumed flesh and dwelt among us" (John 1:14). A truly Trinitarian understanding of God and the world inspires the inclusion and acculturation of God in all times and all places. It is the Spirit of God that enlarges our worldview and embraces the presence of Christ in all people and all cultures. The same Spirit of God enables us to define this worldview and discern the divine Word in all people and all cultures.

The Orthodox Church as Church claims to have received the fullness of truth through the inspiration of the Holy Spirit.[38] This truth is treasured and nurtured within the community of saints. Nevertheless, for human beings as individuals, knowledge of the divine truth is a gradual process in an endless development. Each person who journeys along this way sometimes steps on unsure ground and never on an equal footing with others. Therefore, one can never accuse another of mistakes or missteps along the way. Religious leaders are responsible for reminding people that each person receives and perceives truth in accordance with one's communal experience as well as in accordance with one's personal readiness and capacity. The divine truth exists and has been fully revealed. Nevertheless, penetration into this fullness of truth will vary from one person to another. This is not a narrowly doctrinal vision of theological truth. However, it is an essentially spiritual vision for worldly reality, one that removes arrogance from authority and opens new ways of approaching believers of other religions. It presupposes magnanimity and charity, faith and hope, tolerance and reconciliation. It opposes forceful conversion and conflict, imposition and intolerance, aggression and violence.

The humble realization on our part that we understand and experience divine truth gradually and incrementally modifies our self-confidence. It also moderates our self-sufficiency when we presume to speak the mind of God and express the will of God. Moreover, it prevents us from submitting to the tragic temptation of attributing to God intentions and decisions that are purely ours, a temptation tantamount to the sin of idolatry. If we search for guidance and inspiration from the community of saints—the poets and the mystics are especially intuitive here—we shall see how they agree that God is long-suffering and merciful, passionately eager to apply divine compassion and patiently awaiting our understanding. How can Christians ever do otherwise in dialogue with our Muslim or Jewish brothers and sisters? When we disagree, we should recall the long-suffering patience of God. When we are tempted to impose our opinions or convictions, we should remember the merciful love of God. If we strive to be like the God that is preached in all three monotheistic religions, I believe that religion will undoubtedly play a positive role in the contemporary divided world.

THE PEACE OF GOD IN A WORLD OF UNREST

The numerous stories of devastation in recent years—both those told and those that remain untold by the media, both those known to the global community and those we have selected to ignore as a global community—are powerfully symbolized in the tragic events of September 11, 2001. But there are many other similar events and tragedies. The unimaginable turmoil and torture, the destruction of war and suffering of refugees, and the ethnic cleansing occurring as I write these lines require from people of religious conviction and people of humanitarian principle the presentation of a God who is merciful and long-suffering, righteous and just. And they demand that believers in that God imitate those same virtues and values. This is the only way that we can avoid further pain and bloodshed supposedly "in the name of God," no matter what name or icon this God possesses.

I have repeatedly maintained that war in the name of religion is war against religion. War in the name of God is offensive to God. Religious fanaticism and political activism must be distinguished from religious belief and political realism. It is not religion but the distortion of religious conviction into fundamentalism and fanaticism that leads to destructive and bloody confrontations, which ultimately only compete for secular and political domination.

And all religions are to blame, not so much for the violence that is carried out in their name as for the violence that they have not avoided by their silence. Even so-called pacifist religions cannot avoid the charge that some people lay against all faiths for providing a justification for violent actions and persecution in the name of God. The "inspired son" of the Bhagavad Gita addresses to Arjuna the terrifying words of Krishna: "Rise up, then, and acquire fame, through victory over the enemies; enjoy a rich kingdom; since your enemies have been already murdered by me and no one else, you alone should become the instrument" (11:33).

It is wrong, therefore, to idealize the historical role of some religions, just as it is wrong to make condemnations that oversimplify or distort the truth. No religion that truly serves God would ever approve the idea of believers becoming instruments of persecution and execution. Indeed, to the degree that churches and religions have been involved in such criminal and sinful actions, they are obliged to repent and seek forgiveness for the blood on the hands of their leaders. It is not a blood that either appeases or can ever be approved by the God whom they worship. This is why we must differentiate among the various religious teachings—not in order to excuse, but in order better to understand and avoid repetition of the same mistakes. We must, for instance, humbly and honestly distinguish between the teachings of a particular faith that have been interpreted throughout history as expressing the will of God in the limited historical context of an individual or society and those teachings of the same faith that today would be considered erroneous inasmuch as they contradict the development of the human spirit and our evolving understanding of discrimination and exclusion. We know today that there are teachings and actions in the Scriptures that must be understood in historical context and cannot be interpreted as calling for similar actions to be carried out or emulated today. To cite these—whether in the Judeo-Christian Scriptures or the sacred text of the Koran—as justifying wrongful actions in the present day is to manipulate them for personal gain and political interest, both of which are unworthy of the God we worship and undignified for the believers of that God. After all, slavery and piracy were lawful and permissible in the past; no one would openly promote these today.

War must be numbered among these unjustified—or unjustifiable—means for imposing one's way or view. While the New Testament says little about war, it says a great deal about peace and those who promulgate peace. Peacemakers are declared "blessed" and called "children of God" (Matt. 5:9). Moreover, the New Testament has a great deal to say about the uprooting of evil in our own hearts for the sake of establishing good in the world at large. Christians are admonished to maintain peace with all human beings (Rom. 12:18). God is characterized as the God of peace. Indeed, this conviction was even adopted as the early Christian expression of salutation. Likewise, the Old Testament and the Koran, the sacred books of Jews and Muslims, describe conflicts and wars, while the Book of Revelation even speaks of wars in heaven! Nevertheless, all these sacred books have much more to say about peace. There are hundreds of references to peace in the Old Testament, where it is considered a gift from God. Those who follow the law of God are obliged to adhere to the way of peace. Moreover, in the Koran, peace is characterized as the supreme good (4:127), since God explicitly invites all to the way of peace (9:26). Indeed, one who commits the murder of one individual is held to committing the same crime against the entire human race (5:35)!

As for the tradition of the Orthodox Church, Saint John Chrysostom (347–407) declares that "nothing is as valuable as peace."[39] His contemporary Saint Basil of Caesarea (330–79) in Asia Minor states that "peace is regarded as the most sublime and perfect of all blessings."[40] Indeed, their close friend and my own predecessor on the Patriarchal Throne of Constantinople Saint Gregory the Theologian (329–89) writes: "Those who strive and show themselves to embrace peace, belong to God and approach close to the divine." For Saint Basil the Great, "there is nothing as characteristic of the Christian as making peace."[41] This is why the Orthodox Church offers a supplication for peace as its very first litany of petitions at every service: "In peace, let us pray to the Lord. For the peace from above, let us pray to the Lord. For the peace of the whole world, and for the welfare and unity of all, let us pray to the Lord."[42] Nonetheless, as we have already noted, it is the conviction and tradition of the early ascetic saints that in order to attain peace with the world, one must first acquire peace in the heart. "If one does not conquer one's spiritual enemies (namely, one's evil intentions, motivations and dispositions), one can never be at peace," writes Abba Isaac the Syrian (d. ca. 700).[43] "For nothing is as capable of producing peace as the knowledge of God and the acquisition of virtue," adds Saint John Chrysostom.[44] We have witnessed all too clearly in recent decades how wars proceed from greed and selfishness, a reality of which the early Christian writers were well aware (James 4:1–2). Social and global peace presupposes spiritual and inner peace, just as respect for human beings is a precondition for the true worship of God.

This is precisely why religious leaders are obliged to take the initiative in the peacemaking process. Perhaps this is where accusation and blame are appropriate and fitting for those of us who espouse religious beliefs and especially those of us in leadership roles within the faith communities. It is not so much that religion is to blame for creating war or provoking conflict. It is, rather, that religion has so often not assumed responsibility for peace and reconciliation. For this, there can never be any excuse or justification—before our faithful followers, before our fellow human beings, and before God.

CONCLUSION: RECONCILIATION AS PEACEMAKING

The profound and powerful concept of reconciliation permeates every aspect of Orthodox theology and spirituality. It is the underlying theme behind the doctrine of a God who "assumed human flesh" (John 1:14); it inspires the celebration of Orthodox liturgy, sacrament, and prayer; it informs the preservation of the natural environment that lies at the heart of my ministry; and it empowers the mission of the Ecumenical Patriarchate in its effort to build bridges among the world's religions and cultures as well as to make peace among the world's peoples and nations.

"Blessed, then, are the peacemakers; for they shall be called children of God" (Matt. 5:9). To become and to be called children of God is to be fully committed to the will of God. This implies moving away from what we want to what God wants. It means being faithful to God's purpose and intent for creation, despite the social pressures that may contradict peace and justice. In order to be peacemakers and children of God, we must move away from what serves our own interests to what respects the rights of others. We must recognize that all human beings, and not only the few, deserve to share the resources of this world.

Making peace is difficult and time-consuming work; it is painstakingly unrewarding and slow. Yet it is the only hope for the restoration of our broken world. By working to remove obstacles to peace, by working to heal human suffering, and by working to preserve the natural environment, we can be assured that "God is with us" (Emmanuel), that we are never alone, that we shall inherit both this world and the kingdom of heaven. For then we shall be worthy to hear the words of Christ: "Come, you who are blessed by my Father. Inherit the kingdom that was prepared for you from the creation of the world" (Matt. 25:34).

EPILOGUE:
THE HOPE THAT LIES WITHIN

Always be prepared to offer your defense,
with gentleness and reverence, to anyone
who seeks from you an account for
the hope that is within you.

—1 PET. 3:15

If you do not hope,
you will never discover
what lies beyond your hopes.

—CLEMENT OF ALEXANDRIA (THIRD CENTURY)

A WORLD OF HOPE

Hope is essential for life. Just as the body cannot live without oxygen and the soul cannot live without faith, life cannot exist without hope. And there is always hope. Religious people know that hope is a divine gift. It is the affirmation of meaning in life and the resistance against despair. It is the conviction that it is never too late, that we can still make a difference as individuals and as institutions. That is surely what faith is about and what religious institutions can contribute.

We have polluted our environment; despite valiant efforts

worldwide, poverty persists; racism and religious intolerance are increasingly menacing; fanaticism and tension are rampant; human rights and the gift of freedom are being trampled in the name of national pride and religious discrimination. Yet we must refuse to believe that this world is either the only world that we have or the best that we can do. In this respect, the message conveyed by Orthodox spirituality about the kingdom of God is one of hope. When Orthodox Christians speak of the heavenly kingdom, they are expressing the hope that lies within, not as a way of escaping from reality, but as an articulation of their faith in the transformation of this world.

We need faith in order to hope. We need to believe. We need to work together toward a goal, always living in hope. That is the dignity and nobility of human life. It expresses the image and likeness of God, according to which we were created. And it is the greatest gift that we have to offer our children: that we believe and hope in a better world, a world where war is no more, where races and religions are equally respected, where the diversity of nature is celebrated, where all people have enough, and where the language of tolerance is the mother tongue of the global family in order that the God of love may be glorified. This is the world where the "kingdom has come on earth as in heaven" (Matt. 6:10).

Citizens of developed nations are often ahead of their governments on issues of social justice, such as the reduction in levels of insecurity, poverty, violence, pollution, and inequality. They have been awakened to these issues both through the inspiration of religious conviction and by their own consciences. In this respect, these citizens, both individually and collectively, have become the "conscience" of global civil society. This in itself is surely a sign of hope, a moment of optimism and promise for the transformation of our world.

THE HOPE OF TRANSFORMATION

In the spiritual classics of the Orthodox Church, transformation signifies a foretaste of the kingdom to come. It can never be fully realized or exhausted in this world; it always extends toward the heavenly world, which informs and imbues this world with sacred meaning. Christians should remember that the Church is called not to conform to but to transform this world. The ultimate goal is not compromise with this world but the promise of another way of seeing, living, and acting.

Such is the conviction of the Orthodox Easter liturgy, when the Resurrection of Christ is proclaimed as "the firstfruits of another way of life," "the pledge of a new beginning." Transformed in the light of Mount Tabor and the Tomb of Christ, we can see the same things differently; we can march to a different drum, sometimes inevitably clashing with established patterns and with unquestioned practices or accepted norms.

Transformed in this way, Christians become a grain of mustard seed, a form of yeast, a salt for the earth. They become enthusiastic, joyful witnesses to the light of the kingdom in our world. There is only one way that we shall, with the grace of God, prevail as people and communities of transformation: together! Individuals and institutions are easily exhausted and discouraged when they act in isolation. The vision of the psalmist is within our grasp: "Behold, it is a good and pleasant thing for us to dwell together in unity" (Ps. 133:1). Such is the imperative of the ecumenical vision of transformation.

JOYFUL SORROW

There is a term coined by the author of *The Ladder of Divine Ascent,* Saint John Climacus (579–649), who was also Abbot of the historic Monastery of Saint Catherine on Mount Sinai. His masterpiece on the spiritual life comprises thirty steps. With the exception of the Scriptures and the liturgical books, no other writing in Eastern Christendom has been studied, copied, and translated to the same extent as *The Ladder.* It is a text that has greatly influenced and shaped the entire Eastern world, including its faithful laity. The seventh step of the ladder is dedicated to the mystery of tears; Saint John is the first to adopt the technical terms to describe the state that combines both joy and sorrow. He speaks of *charmolype,* or "joyful sorrow," and *charopoion penthos,* or "joy-creating mourning." It is a way of underlining the bittersweet experience of yearning and failing alike in the pursuit of spiritual joy. Joyful sorrow is a mixed emotion of joy anticipating divine grace and sorrow at the fallen state of the world.

Joyful sorrow is perhaps the most characteristic ingredient of Orthodox spirituality and Byzantine aesthetics—in its art, architecture, and music. It is also an essential feature in the lives of the saints, who struggle to reconcile God's light with the darkness that fills the world. It is a sign of hope, a symbol of optimism, and a source of consolation before the reality that surrounds us and sometimes overwhelms us. The same concept of joyful sorrow is characteristic, if not definitive, of the history of the Ecumenical Patriarchate, which has struggled through difficult and dark periods to the present moment; the Phanar has undoubtedly known strength through weakness inasmuch as it has never sought to prove itself as a secular institution of worldly power. It is in fact critical of any religious institution that is organized as a worldly power, assuming the form of a secular state. For, ultimately, such a conception leads to confusion between "the things of Caesar and the things of God" (Mark 12:17).

The most vivid experience and expression of joyful sorrow occurs each year at the Feast of Feasts, namely Easter Sunday. On that night, which is brighter than any day, I exit the altar, which symbolizes the Tomb of Christ, and chant triumphantly: "Come, receive the light!" With these words, the light from my candle is distributed to the congregation and lights up the entire church, previously waiting in darkness. It is the conviction that the light of God is brighter than any darkness in my heart and in the hearts of those in church, indeed brighter than any darkness in the world.

STANDING IN PRAYER

There is a sixth-century hymn in honor of the Mother of God, possibly the creation of one of the most original poets of the Byzantine era, Saint Romanos the Melodist (d. ca. 565). It is called the Akathist Hymn, which literally means "not sitting" or "standing." Consisting of twenty-four alphabetically arranged verses—the lines of each alternate stanza beginning with the words "Rejoice!"—the Akathist is chanted on Fridays during Great Lent and has become a very popular and deeply pious devotion for clergy and laity alike throughout the Orthodox world. In monasteries, it is sometimes chanted on a daily basis through the year.

The Akathist, however, is also a hymn that is intimately connected to the life of Constantinople. According to tradition, it was sung during an all-night vigil while the faithful congregation remained standing, as an expression of thanksgiving by the people of the city for their "safety and salvation" from invasion. Devout Orthodox also use this hymn to seek protection on every occasion of personal distress or general disaster.

The Akathist Hymn is a symbol of the stance of the entire world before the problems that beset us at this time, whether these are social issues of unemployment and poverty, political issues of war and terror, or environmental issues of human pollution and natural destruction. Each of us is called to stay alert, to remain upstanding, and to retain a keen sense of awareness and prayerfulness.

LIGHT FROM THE EAST

Finally, the treasures of the Orthodox spiritual and mystical tradition remind Orthodox Christians that they are called to be "witnesses of these things" (Luke 24:48). It is from this endless spring that we draw inspiration, as witnesses of the new life that came to the world through Christ. It is as witnesses of this transformation and resurrection that we can preserve a sense of hope for the future of the world, despite the darkness and turmoil that surround us.

A contemporary Greek poet from the island of Chios, Georgios Veritis, whom I still recall from my childhood years, writes:

I am thankful to God,
that each sunset is
followed by a sunrise.

There is no doubt that without optimism, there can be no life; and without faith, there can be no future. There is a light that shines from the East, whence the "Sun of Righteousness" rises:

For you that revere my name,
the Sun of Righteousness shall rise,
with healing in its wings. (Mal. 4:2)

Even when everything around us appears to contradict the hope that lies within us, by the grace of God, the sun will always rise and the depth of the night's darkness will give way to the day's sunlight. This sense of realism enables us to live the present in all its fullness, comforted by our vision of eternity. A new dawn will arise with our trust in God's love and our reflection of that love in the solidarity with our brothers and sisters throughout the world as well as in the preservation of this wonderful planet—all of these gifts from the almighty God for our joy—for the sake of our future generations.

NOTES

FOREWORD

1. Clément, *Conversations*, p. 68.
2. See *Cosmic Grace, Humble Prayer: The Ecological Vision of the Green Patriarch Bartholomew I*, ed. John Chryssavgis (Grand Rapids, Mich.: Eerdmans, 2003).
3. Muriel Heppell, *George Bell and Nikolai Velimirovic: The Story of a Friendship* (Birmingham, U.K.: Lazarica Press, 2001), p. 32.
4. *Cosmic Grace*, p. 209.
5. Ibid, pp. 215–16.
6. Address to the environmental symposium convened in Southern California by Jean-Michel Cousteau and Bruce Babbitt, Nov. 8, 2001, *New Perspectives Quarterly* 16, no. 1 (2002) (incorporating material from earlier speeches by the Patriarch).
7. *On the Creation of the Human Being*, 11, in J.-P. Migne, *Patrologia Graeca* 44.153D, 156B, Paris, 1857–66.
8. *The Journals of Søren Kierkegaard*, ed. Alexander Dru (London: Oxford University Press, 1938), p. 372 (translation adapted).
9. For the full text of this speech, see *Yearbook of the Greek Cathedral of St. Sophia 2005*, Bishop Theodoritos of Nazianzos (London, 2006), pp. 6–11; the passage quoted is on pp. 8–9. See Martin Buber, *The Tales of the Hasidim: The Early Masters* (New York: Schocken Books, 1968), p. 282.
10. *Cosmic Grace*, p. 209.
11. Clément, *Conversations*, p. 121.
12. Ibid, p. 122.
13. Zizioulas, *Being as Communion*, p. 17.
14. Homily at the memorial service in March 2002 for the victims of the September 11 disaster.
15. *Cosmic Grace*, p. 61.
16. Ibid., p. 45.
17. Speech on receiving a doctorate *honoris causa* from the University of London, May 31, 1994, in Clément, *Conversations*, p. 237.

18. Clément, *Conversations*, p. 72. This is a saying also quoted by Saint Silouan the Athonite (1866–1938): "Blessed is the soul that loves her brother, for *our brother is our life.*" Archimandrite Sophrony, *Saint Silouan the Athonite* (Tolleshunt Knights, Essex: Monastery of St. John the Baptist, 1991), p. 371.

19. Speech on May 31, 1994, in Clément, *Conversations*, p. 238 (italics in the original).

20. Clément, *Conversations*, p. 78.

21. *Epistle to Diognetus*, 7, 4.

22. See the Bosphorus Declaration of Feb. 9, 1994, in *Cosmic Grace*, p. 117.

23. Clément, *Conversations*, p. 32.

24. *Cosmic Grace*, p. 67.

25. Here I follow the Greek Septuagint version of the Old Testament, as used in the Orthodox Church. Where most English versions say merely "it was very good," the Greek says *kala lian*; and in Greek the adjective *kalos* means not only "good" but "beautiful."

26. Some of these essays have been published as *Ektheseis tou Mathitou Dimitriou Ch. Archontoni* (Athens: Syndesmos ton en Athinais Megaloscholiton, 2000).

27. See the introduction by John Chryssavgis in *Cosmic Grace*, p. 19.

28. *Cosmic Grace*, p. 66.

29. Clément, *Conversations*, pp. 240–41, 258–59.

30. *Cosmic Grace*, pp. 305, 308. See also chapter 4, "Vocation of Love."

31. These words were spoken by the Patriarch in Washington, D.C., on March 6, 2002, with particular reference to the difficulties that had arisen at that time in the Orthodox-Catholic dialogue because of the Uniate question.

32. See, for example, his Enthronement Address (1991) and his speech at the Patmos symposium (1995), in *Cosmic Grace*, pp. 71, 155.

33. *Cosmic Grace*, pp. 309, 311.

BIOGRAPHICAL NOTE

1. Theodore Teron (or the "recruit") and Theodore Stratelates (or the "general") were both military saints of the early Church. They are often closely associated in the Orthodox Church.

2. He was later Metropolitan of Chalcedon.

3. See, for example, *When I Was a Child* [in Greek] (Athens: Kastanioti, 2003).

4. In Byzantine times, disgraced princes would be exiled to this island.

5. The Ecumenical Patriarchate is recognized simply—legally—as a Turkish institution, while Turkish law from 1936 to this day places all Orthodox Christian property under the General Directorate of Foundations, which has the authority to dismiss foundations and seize property. Moreover, according to a 1974 ruling

of the Turkish Supreme Court, the Turkish government forbids the purchase or sale of property by minority groups after 1936. For more information about efforts to reopen the Patriarchal Theological School of Halki, see the interview by George Gilson, "Vartholomeos Demands Equal Rights," *Athens News*, Feb. 22, 2002, p. 3.

6. See John Chryssavgis (ed.), *Barsanuphius and John: Letters*, vol. 1 (Washington, D.C.: Catholic University of America Press, 2006), p. 164.

7. Bartholomew has served on the World Council of Churches' Executive Committee and the Faith and Order Commission and has attended general assemblies in New Delhi (1961), Uppsala (1968), Nairobi (1975), Vancouver (1983), and Canberra (1991). He formally accepted the 1989 official statement of unity between the Eastern Orthodox and the Oriental Orthodox churches and recently restored the official theological dialogue between the Orthodox and the Roman Catholic churches. He has also revived the bilateral dialogue with the Anglican communion and laid the foundations for discussions with other churches, such as the World Methodist Council.

8. This section draws on comments by Professor John Silber, President Emeritus of Boston University, with permission. See his article titled "Patriarch Bartholomew—a Passion for Peace," at www.ecupatriarchate.org.

9. Delivered at the Foreign Correspondents' Club in Hong Kong, Nov. 6, 1996.

10. Clément, *Conversations*, pp. 48–50.

1. HISTORICAL PERSPECTIVES

1. Throughout this book, the term "spirituality" is used to describe the life in the Holy Spirit as this is understood within the experience of the community of the Church. Spirituality is not an abstract concept in the Orthodox Church; in fact, as a term, it is nowhere to be found in the theological writings of the Eastern Church Fathers, who prefer to speak of "the spiritual life" as "the activity of the Spirit." See Saint John Chrysostom, *De prophetiarum obscuritate*, 2, in *Patrologia Graeca* 56.182.

2. Throughout this book, the word "Eastern" in reference to the Church is not an exclusive or cultural term. It is more descriptive of the Church's origins than definitive of its nature. If "Eastern" implies the religions of the Asian East, then the Orthodox cannot be identified with this term. In fact, Eastern Orthodoxy is much closer to the wider historical and cultural experience that we would identify as "Western," based at least on the classical Greek, Roman, and Judaic roots of Western civilization. Moreover, Eastern Orthodox believers, who are inhabitants of Australia, the United States, and Western Europe, adopt the values of their dominant Western culture, regardless of their origins. Any critical remarks regarding Western culture are directed at all those espousing or aspiring to the

values of that culture, including those adhering to the Eastern Orthodox faith. Nevertheless, the Eastern Orthodox spiritual worldview both retains and provides a distinctive and profound alternative within the same Western culture. See Costa Carras, "The Orthodox Church and Politics in a Post-Communist World," in *The Orthodox Church in a Changing World*, ed. Paschalis Kitromilides and Thanos Veremis (Athens: Hellenic Foundation for European and Foreign Policy, 1998), pp. 15–38.

3.   The title "Patriarch" was granted to the heads of the Serbian and Bulgarian churches during the Byzantine period (tenth through fourteenth centuries), although these patriarchates later disappeared.

4.   From the Greek words *eschaton* (meaning the last time) and *logos* (relating to study or reason).

5.   On the importance and significance of icons, see the following chapter.

6.   *On the Divine Images*, 2, 12, in *Patrologia Graeca* 94.129.

7.   *Letter of the Eastern Patriarchs* (1718).

8.   *On the Deity of the Son*, in *Patrologia Graeca* 46.557B.

9.   The term "Church in captivity" was coined by Sir Steven Runciman for the title of his remarkable book *The Great Church in Captivity: A Study of the Patriarchate of Constantinople from the Eve of the Turkish Conquest to the Greek War of Independence.*

10.   "Hesychasts" translates as "those who practice stillness or silence."

11.   It should be noted here that Orthodox Christians refer to both painted images and mosaics as icons.

12.   The formal inauguration of the city was celebrated in 330.

13.   Caesarea (in Cappadocia of Asia Minor) is distinct from the diocese under the same name in Palestine. For example, in Asia Minor the most renowned bishop of this diocese was Basil the Great (330–379), while the best-known bishop of Caesarea in Palestine was Eusebius the Historian (265–340).

14.   The term "ethnarch" signifies the leader of a nation or people. An ethnarch is considered the appointed guardian of a people's historical and spiritual legacy. The origins of the word lie perhaps in the world of Hellenistic Judaism; however, in the history of the Orthodox after 1453, it is adopted to signify wide-ranging civil and spiritual responsibilities assigned to Orthodox hierarchs—and preeminently the Ecumenical Patriarch—during the Turkish period.

15.   From an address at the Scenic Hudson in New York City, Nov. 13, 2000. See *Cosmic Grace, Humble Prayer: The Ecological Vision of the Green Patriarch Bartholomew I*, ed. John Chryssavgis (Grand Rapids, Mich.: Eerdmans, 2003), p. 292.

16. Including Alexandroupolis, Veroia (and Naoussa), Goumenissa (with Axioupolis and Polykastron), Grevena, Didymoteichon (and Orestias), Drama, Dryinoupolis (Pogoniani and Konitsa), Edessa (and Pella), Elasson, Eleftheroupolis, Zichna (and Nevrokopion), Thessaloníki, Ierissos (with Mount Athos and Adramerion), Ioannina, Kassandra, Kastoria, Kitrous, Laggada, Lemnos, Maronia (and Komotini), Mithimni, Mytilini, Neapolis (and Stavroupolis), Nea Krini (and Kalamaria), Nikopolis (and Preveza), Xanthi, Paramythia (with Filiata and Giromerion), Polyani (and Kilkision), Samos (and Ikaria), Servia (and Kozani), Serres (and Nigriti), Siderokastron, Sissanion (and Siatista), Philippi (with Neapolis and Thassos), Florina (with Prespa and Eordaia), and Chios.

17. Rhodes, Kos, Kalymnos (with Leros and Astipalea), Karpathos (and Kassos), and Simi.

2. SONG AND SPACE

1. See Exod. 20:4–23; Lev. 4:16, 5:8, and 27:15.
2. "Those who smashed icons" both metaphorically and literally.
3. *On Sacred Images*, bk. 2, 20.
4. *Homily 11, On Gregory of Nyssa*, 4–5.
5. His name literally means "golden-mouthed."
6. See his *Commentary on Ephesians*, 2, in *Patrologia Graeca* 62.19.
7. See his *Homily on the Forty Martyrs*, 19, 2.
8. *Letter to Cleidonius*, in *Patrologia Graeca* 37.176–80.
9. Gregory of Nyssa, *Against Apollinarius*, 18, in *Patrologia Graeca* 45.1160; John of Damascus, *Homily*, 4, 29, in *Patrologia Graeca* 96.632.
10. *On Sacred Images*, bk. 1, 4. See also bk. 3, 6. This was a teaching espoused by East and West, as witnessed earlier by Saint Gregory of Rome in his *Letter to Germanus of Constantinople*, in *Patrologia Graeca* 98.149.
11. *On the Holy Spirit*, 18. See also Saint John of Damascus, *On Sacred Images*, bk. 1, 21ff., where Saint John cites and interprets the passage from Saint Basil.
12. Saint John of Damascus, *On Sacred Images*, bk. 1, 14.
13. See Saint Theodore the Studite, *Antirrheticus*, 12, in *Patrologia Graeca* 99.329; Saint John of Damascus, *On Sacred Images*, bk. 3, 24, and *Exposition of the Faith*, 4, in *Patrologia Graeca* 94.800.
14. Namely, "what has not been assumed [by God in the divine Incarnation] cannot be saved." See his *Letter to Cleidonius*, which became the standard for later Christological statements.
15. While the original Church of the Ecumenical Patriarchate had a dome, the present Church of St. George, fundamentally reconstructed in the eighteenth and

nineteenth centuries, does not have a dome. After the fall of Constantinople, Christian buildings could not be covered with prominent domes, while church architecture resembled more the ancient style of the basilica. Most churches in this region, especially those constructed in the eighteenth and mid-nineteenth centuries, replaced the dome with a medallion of Christ Pantokrator, or Almighty/ All-Ruling, on the ceiling. See *The Ecumenical Patriarchate: A Brief Guide* (Istanbul: Order of St. Andrew the Apostle, 2004). Comments on architecture based on Chryssavgis, *Light Through Darkness*, pp. 21–22; used with permission.

16. From the Cherubic Hymn in the Divine Liturgies of Saint John Chrysostom and Saint Basil the Great.

17. *On the Life in Christ*, bk. 4, 1, in *Patrologia Graeca* 150.584.

18. Ibid., bk. 1, in *Patrologia Graeca* 150.493.

19. Symeon the New Theologian, *Catechetical Discourse*, 13.

3. THE GIFT OF THEOLOGY

1. For his life of Saint Symeon, see Irénée Hausherr and Gabriel Horn, *Un grand mystique byzantin: Vie de Syméon*, Orientalia Christiana 12 (Rome, 1928), pp. 1–128. This chapter is based on an article that originally appeared in *Theology Today* 61, 1, and is used with permission of the publisher.

2. Symeon the New Theologian, *Catechetical Oration*, 39, 3–5, in the Classics of Western Spirituality series (New York: Paulist Press, 1980), pp. 311–13.

3. For the biography and writings of Staretz Silouan, see Archimandrite Sophrony, *Saint Silouan the Athonite* (Crestwood, N.Y.: St. Vladimir's Seminary Press, 1999).

4. From Ode 9, Canon of the Feast of the Annunciation (March 25) and the Feast of the Entry of the Theotokos (November 21).

5. The *Life* of Saint Maximos was originally composed by Theophanes Peritheorios and edited by Saint Nikodemos of the Holy Mountain in his *Neon Eklogion* (Athens: Astir, 1974), pp. 305–17.

6. Saint Joseph Vryennios, *Homily 3, On the Holy Trinity.*

7. Saint Athanasius, *Against the Arians, Homily I*, in *Patrologia Graeca* 26.49.

8. Saint Athanasius, *On the Incarnation of the Divine Word*, in *Patrologia Graeca* 25.196.

9. Saint Athanasius, *Discourse Against the Pagans*, in *Patrologia Graeca* 25.68.

10. Didymus the Blind, *On the Trinity*, 3, 3, in *Patrologia Graeca* 39.825.

11. Didymus the Blind, *On the Psalms*, in *Patrologia Graeca* 39.1429.

12. For the *Life of St. Gregory the Wonderworker* by Saint Gregory of Nyssa, see *Patrologia Graeca* 46.893–957.

13. For the *Life of St. John Chrysostom* by Palladius, see *Patrologia Graeca* 47.5–82. A later biography of Saint John Chrysostom was composed by Symeon Metaphrastes: see *Patrologia Graeca* 114.1045–1209.

14. See Hausherr and Horn, *Un grand mystique byzantin.*
15. See Philotheos Kokkinos, *Homily on Gregory Palamas, Archbishop of Thessalonika,* in *Patrologia Graeca* 151.551–678.
16. Saint Dionysius was writing in Syria, thereby providing further evidence of the universal application of apophatic theology in the Eastern Orthodox tradition.
17. See the description of Moses' vision of God's "back parts" in Exodus 32ff., and the references to the divine light in the first chapter of the Gospel according to Saint John, especially verse 18: "No one has ever seen God."
18. *The Life of Moses II,* 163 and 162 in *Patrologia Graeca* 44.377. See the translation by Abraham Malherbe and Everett Ferguson, in the Classics of Western Spirituality series (New York: Paulist Press, 1978), pp. 94–95. See also Werner Jaeger, ed., *Contra Eunomium,* 2 vols. (Berlin, 1921–22).
19. Gregory Palamas, *Triads,* 2, 3, 67.
20. See ibid., 53.
21. From the Divine Liturgy of Saint John Chrysostom; this hymn follows immediately after the faithful have received Holy Communion.
22. This is the definition formulated in the First and Second Ecumenical Councils (Nicaea in 325 and Constantinople in 381).
23. Gregory of Nyssa, *Commentary on the Song of Songs,* 6, in Patrologia Graeca 44.755–1120.
24. Vladimir Lossky, *The Mystical Theology of the Eastern Church* (Crestwood, N.Y.: St. Vladimir's Seminary Press, 1976), pp. 42–43.
25. *Saint Silouan the Athonite* (Crestwood, N.Y.: St. Vladimir's Seminary Press, 1991), p. 91.
26. Evagrius, *Chapters on Prayer,* 60. For an English translation, see Evagrius of Pontus, *The Praktikos: Chapters on Prayer,* trans. John Eudes Bamberger (Kalamazoo, Mich.: Cistercian Publications, 1970).
27. From the *Synodikon* of the Seventh Ecumenical Council. This proclamation is repeated each year on the first Sunday of Great Lent, when we celebrate the Sunday of Orthodoxy.

4. VOCATION OF LOVE

1. See Chapter 7, "Faith and Freedom."
2. *Epistle,* 207, 2.
3. More on this notion in the Epilogue.
4. For the entire text of his prayer, see Chapter 3 on the gift of theology.
5. Anthony the Great later came to be known as "the father of monasticism," according to his contemporary biographer and personal admirer, Saint Athanasius of Alexandria.
6. *The Life of Anthony,* chap. 14.

244   N O T E S

7. *Homily*, 37, 6, in *Patrologia Graeca* 36.289B–C.
8. *The Ladder of Divine Ascent*, Step 1.
9. Ibid., Step 27; Isaac the Syrian, *Ascetic Treatises*, Homily 23; and Basil the Great, *Homily on Gregory*, in *Patrologia Graeca* 32.226.
10. *Ascetic Treatises*, Homily 4.
11. Gregory of Nyssa, a married saint of the Church, is the author of an entire treatise titled *On Virginity*.
12. Gregory of Nyssa, *On the Soul and the Resurrection*, in *Patrologia Graeca* 46.61.
13. Gregory Palamas, *Triads in Defense of the Holy Hesychasts*, 2, 2, chaps. 19–22.
14. See Basil the Great, *Letter*, 207, 2, in *Patrologia Graeca* 32.761.
15. A phrase found in the Divine Liturgy of the Orthodox Church.
16. *Chapters on Prayer*, 124.
17. *Longer Rules*, 2, 7.
18. See Saint Gregory Palamas, *Life of St. Peter the Athonite*, in *Patrologia Graeca* 150.1005.

5. SPIRITUALITY AND SACRAMENTS

1. Saint John Climacus, *The Ladder of Divine Ascent*, Step 28, 6.
2. Ibid.
3. See *The Philokalia: The Complete Text*, comp. Saint Nikodemos of the Holy Mountain and Saint Makarios of Corinth, trans. and ed. G. E. H. Palmer, Philip Sherrard, and Kallistos Ware (Boston: Faber and Faber, 1979). The complete text is in five volumes.
4. *The Way of a Pilgrim*, trans. R. M. French (New York: Seabury Press, 1972).
5. J. D. Salinger, *Franny and Zooey* (New York: Little, Brown, 1961).
6. Sometimes the words "a sinner" are added at the conclusion of this brief prayer. It is a question of recognizing not that one has committed particular sins but rather that one is divided within oneself and therefore also separated from God and from others.
7. The term means "quietude" or "stillness." Hesychasm was more than a spiritual practice; in the fourteenth century, it became a spiritual movement stretching from the Ecumenical Patriarchate through the Balkans to Russia. This international current proved a uniting and strengthening force for the Orthodox Church on the eve of the fall of Constantinople to the Ottoman Empire.
8. Isaac the Syrian, *Homily*, 2.
9. *Sayings of the Desert Fathers*, Poemen 29.
10. Saint Paul adopts this phrase over one hundred times in his Letters. Comments on sacraments based on Chryssavgis, *Light Through Darkness*, pp. 124–25; used with permission.

6. THE WONDER OF CREATION

1. *The Sayings of the Desert Fathers*, Chaeremon, 1.
2. *Homily* 15, 38.
3. See the section below on "Orthodox liturgy and the natural environment."
4. Cyril of Jerusalem, *Catechetical Treatise*, 12.
5. From a prayer in the Matins service.
6. From the Liturgy of Saint James.
7. From the Liturgy of Saint Mark.
8. *Sayings of the Desert Fathers*, Anthony 36, Paul 1, and Pambo 12.
9. *Ascetic Treatises*, 48 (Wiesbaden, 1986), p. 30.
10. This phrase was used throughout the Ottoman occupation of Greece and Asia Minor. It was possibly coined by Ecumenical Patriarch Gennadios Scholarios (1453–56 and 1463–64), the first Patriarch after the fall of Constantinople in 1453, to describe the historical humiliation of the Great Church of Christ, as the Church of Constantinople is also called, as well as to define the spiritual vigor of the Ecumenical Patriarchate that persisted through the centuries.
11. This story from Genesis is a powerful symbol of interfaith relations, as we shall see in Chapter 8. Nevertheless, since Genesis is a scriptural book accepted by all three monotheistic religions—Judaism, Christianity, and Islam—this story also becomes one of the first ecological lessons of the Bible; it is a passage to which we should pay closer attention, both theologically and spiritually, as revealing the ways of recognizing God's presence in our world as well as the ways of responding to this divine revelation.
12. See Lester Brown, *Plan B 2.0: Rescuing a Planet Under Stress and a Civilization in Trouble*, updated and expanded ed. (New York: Norton, 2006).

7. FAITH AND FREEDOM

1. *Ascetic Treatises*, 18.
2. "On Faith and Knowledge," in *Special Ceremony of the Aristotle University of Thessaloníki*, Oct. 1997, p. 76.
3. Karl Jaspers, *Way to Wisdom*, trans. Ralph Manheim (New Haven, Conn.: Yale University Press, 1979), p. 65.
4. See for example, Ps. 119:5: "O that my ways may be steadfast in keeping your statutes!" See also verse 12: "Blessed are you, O Lord, teach me your statutes."
5. See Saint Maximus the Confessor, *Chapters on Theology*, 2, 71. Cf. *The Philokalia: The Complete Text*, comp. Saint Nikodemos of the Holy Mountain and Saint Makarios of Corinth, trans. and ed. G. E. H. Palmer, Philip Sherrard, and Kallistos Ware (London: Faber, 1981), vol. 2, p. 154.
6. *Macarian Homilies*, 15.
7. Cf. Saint Basil, *On the Holy Spirit*, 20, in *Patrologia Graeca* 32.160–61.

8. Cited in *Episkepsis*, Dec. 15, 1986.
9. *Oration*, 38, 11.
10. Literally, "of the Godhead." Cf. *On the Holy Spirit*, 18 [45].
11. Zizioulas, *Being as Communion*, p. 17.
12. *Epistle to Diognetus*, 7, 4.

8. TRANSFORMING THE WORLD

1. See Katherine Marshall and Lucy Keough, *Mind, Heart, and Soul in the Fight Against Poverty* (Washington, D.C.: World Bank, 2004), p. 1, quoting Charles Kimball, a scholar of religion.
2. See his *Homily 19, 5 on Matthew*, in *Patrologia Graeca* 57.280.
3. It was the Feast of the "Leave-Taking" of the Transfiguration (August 13), when the Orthodox Church celebrates the conclusion of the Feast of the Transfiguration (August 6).
4. Euripides, *Suppliants*, 407.
5. Aristotle, *Politics*, 4, 8, 1294A.
6. J. R. R. Tolkien, *The Return of the King: Being the Third Part of the Lord of the Rings* (Boston and New York: Houghton Mifflin Company, 1994), p. 861.
7. In January 1920, the Ecumenical Patriarchate issued a historical encyclical "unto the churches of Christ everywhere," inviting Christians throughout the world to overcome the spirit of mistrust and bitterness in order to demonstrate the power of reconciliation and love by establishing a *koinonia* (or "communion") of churches. The covering letter proposed a "League of Churches" in accordance with the establishment of the League of Nations. This is a fine example of the prophetic voice of the Ecumenical Patriarchate on issues of unity and peace.
8. The phrase "Oriental Orthodox churches" is used to distinguish from the Orthodox churches and describes those churches that refused to acknowledge the Fourth Ecumenical Council of Chalcedon in the mid-fifth century. Informal conversations began in the 1960s, while the official dialogue commenced in 1985 and culminated in a formal statement in 1989, which was formally accepted in 1992 as one of the earliest acts of reconciliation in my tenure.
9. November 30 is the Feast of Saint Andrew, also known as the "first-called" of the Apostles and elder brother of Saint Peter the Apostle, as well as the founder of the Church in Constantinople.
10. For further reading, see Constantin Patelos, ed., *The Orthodox Church in the Ecumenical Movement* (Geneva: World Council of Churches, 1978). International dialogues are also held with the Lutheran Church, and conversations have be-

gun with the Methodist Church. Theological dialogues are also carried out on a regional level with these and other churches throughout the world.

11. They are listed here not to demonstrate a particular dimension of my ministry but rather because, at a time when so much turmoil and controversy reign over interfaith and interracial issues, so little is advertised about efforts made on an international level to bring representatives of religions together.

12. See Leopold Labedz, *Solzhenitsyn: A Documentary Record* (Harmondsworth, U.K.: Penguin, 1974), p. 314.

13. See Saint Gregory of Nyssa, *On the Creation of Man*, 18, in *Patrologia Graeca* 44.193.

14. On the sacramental vision of the world, see Schmemann, *For the Life of the World*.

15. On the concept of freedom and human rights, see Chapter 7 above.

16. On several misconceptions about the problem of fundamentalism, see R. Scott Appleby and Martin E. Marty, "Fundamentalism," *Foreign Policy* 128 (Jan.–Feb. 2002).

17. Literally, "in the form of man."

18. The word "fanaticism" derives from the Latin *fanaticus*, meaning "inspired by a god." The word "assassin" comes from an Arabic word for a Muslim order that attacked Christians during the Crusades. How unfortunate that these words, which we normally identify with extremism, may be traced to religious roots and contexts.

19. For the names of God in Islam, see, for example, M. R. Bawa Muhaiyaddeen, *Asma'ul Husna: The 99 Beautiful Names of Allah* (Philadelphia: Fellowship Press, 1979). For the Eastern Orthodox tradition, see, for instance, the Liturgies of Saint John Chrysostom and Saint Basil the Great; in particular, the latter refers to God as "without beginning, invisible, incomprehensible, indescribable, and without change."

20. See also Mark 8:34 and Luke 9:23.

21. See Chapter 7, "Faith and Freedom."

22. The term "ecumenical" was established in the sixth century. See Chapter 1, "Historical Perspectives."

23. See Peter Berger, *The Desecularization of the World: Resurgent Religion and World Politics* (Grand Rapids, Mich.: Eerdmans, 1999).

24. See Justinian's Sixth Novel, or Decree, in *Social and Political Thought in Byzantium*, trans. and ed. Ernest Barker (Oxford: Clarendon, 1957), pp. 75–76.

25. See John Meyendorff, *Byzantine Theology: Historical Trends and Doctrinal Themes* (London: Mowbrays, 1974), pp. 214–16. See also John Meyendorff, *The Byzantine Legacy in the Orthodox Church* (Crestwood, N.Y.: St. Vladimir's Sem-

inary Press, 1982), pp. 43–66; and Francis Dvornik, *Early Christian and Byzantine Political Philosophy* (Washington, D.C.: Dumbarton Oaks Center for Byzantine Studies, 1966), pp. 610–850.

26. See his *Essays, Perspectives, Opinions* (Somerset, N.J.: Light, 2002), p. 26.

27. It was most fitting that the 2006 Nobel Peace Prize was awarded to Dr. Muhammad Yunus of Bangladesh, the pioneer of microcredit, and his Grameen Bank (or, "Bank of the Villages") "for their efforts to create economic and social development from below" in an effort to alleviate poverty.

28. For a historical overview of the Orthodox dialogue with Islam through the centuries, see Archbishop Anastasios, *Facing the World*, pp. 103–26. The Byzantine interest in understanding Islam was later transferred to Russia by Maxim the Greek (1470–1556), who authored three treatises on Islam in Russian.

29. See Samuel Huntington, *The Clash of Civilizations and the Remaking of World Order* (New York: Simon and Schuster, 1997). How ironic that religion proves to hold a more liberal position in this regard than the realism of a political scientist. The starting point of religion in recent decades has been the pursuit of dialogue to demystify and understand the "great religious divide . . . between the Eastern and Western churches" (ibid., p. 160). Although I am not exploring here the pioneering ecumenical efforts that the Ecumenical Patriarchate has initiated in recent years to bridge that divide, instead of passively accepting the inevitable consequences of the schism that has divided the two churches since the eleventh century, it is important to recall the recent visit, in November 2006, of Pope Benedict XVI to the head offices of the Ecumenical Patriarchate in Istanbul, which was historic not only in terms of relations between the Eastern and the Western churches but also with regard to Christianity and Islam. The newly elected Pope was continuing a tradition established by his predecessor, the late John Paul II, who visited the Phanar immediately after his election in 1978.

30. "Byzantium and Islam," in *Byzantium: An Introduction to East Roman Civilization*, ed. Norman H. Baynes and H. St. L. B. Moss (Oxford: Clarendon Press, 1949), p. 325.

31. "Making Use of Traditions," *Türk Dili*, no. 475 (July 1991), pp. 1–10.

32. The term "syncretism" is sometimes used in conservative religious circles to signify the combination of different doctrines into a single philosophical or cultural system.

33. Indeed, "synergy" (or *synergeia*) is sometimes used as a technical term in theological circles to denote the sacred relationship between God and the world.

34. Justin spoke of *logos spermatikos*—namely, of the "seed of the divine Word." For an Orthodox theological approach to understanding other religions, see Archbishop Anastasios, *Facing the World*, pp. 127–53.

35. *Apology*, 2, 13 and 46, in *The Apologies of Justin Martyr*, ed. A. W. F. Blunt (Cambridge, U.K.: Cambridge University Press, 1911).

36. See his *Stromata*, 1, 5, in *Patrologia Graeca* 8.728, and *Exhortation to the Heathen*, 7, in *Patrologia Graeca* 8.184.

37. *Second Theological Oration*, or *Homily*, 28, 15, in *Patrologia Graeca* 36.45.

38. See John 16:13.

39. *Homily 36 on Genesis*, 2–3, in *Patrologia Graeca* 53.335.

40. *Commentary on the Prophet Isaiah*, chap. 3, in *Patrologia Graeca* 30.305.

41. Cited in Basil, *Epistles*, 114, in *Patrologia Graeca* 32.528.

42. From the Divine Liturgy of Saint John Chrysostom, which is celebrated in Orthodox churches throughout the world on a daily and weekly basis.

43. *Oration*, 68.

44. *Commentary on Psalm 4*, 15, in *Patrologia Graeca* 55.57–58.

FURTHER READING

Anastasios, Archbishop (Yannoulatos). *Facing the World: Orthodox Christian Essays on Global Concerns.* Crestwood, N.Y.: St. Vladimir's Seminary Press, 2003.

Bulgakov, Sergius. *The Orthodox Church.* Crestwood, N.Y.: St. Vladimir's Seminary Press, 1988.

Chryssavgis, John. *Light Through Darkness: The Orthodox Tradition.* Maryknoll, N.Y.: Orbis Books, 2004.

Clément, Olivier. *Conversations with Ecumenical Patriarch Bartholomew I.* Translated by Paul Meyendorff. Crestwood, N.Y.: St. Vladimir's Seminary Press, 1997.

Geanakoplos, Deno. *A Short History of the Ecumenical Patriarchate of Constantinople (330–1990): "First Among Equals" in the Eastern Orthodox Church.* Brookline, Mass.: Holy Cross Orthodox Press, 1990.

Istavridis, Vasil. *History of the Ecumenical Patriarchate: Bibliography.* Vol. 2 [foreword in Greek; sources in Greek and English]. Thessaloníki: Kyriakidis, 2004.

Maximos, Metropolitan of Sardes. *The Oecumenical Patriarchate in the Orthodox Church: A Study in the History and the Canons of the Church.* Thessaloníki: Patriarchal Institute of Patristic Studies, 1976.

Meyendorff, John. *The Orthodox Church: Its Past and Its Role in the World Today.* Crestwood, N.Y.: St. Vladimir's Seminary Press, 1981.

Paliouras, Athanasios, ed. *Oecumenical Patriarchate: The Great Church of Christ* [collected essays in Greek]. Athens: E. Tzaphere, 1989.

Pelikan, Jaroslav. *The Christian Tradition: A History of the Development of Doctrine.* 5 vols. Chicago: University of Chicago Press, 1971–89.

Runciman, Steven. *The Fall of Constantinople, 1453.* Cambridge, U.K.: Cambridge University Press, 1990.

————. *The Great Church in Captivity: A Study of the Patriarchate of Constantinople from the Eve of the Turkish Conquest to the Greek War of Independence.* London: Cambridge University Press, 1968.

Schmemann, Alexander. *For the Life of the World: Sacraments and Orthodoxy.* Crestwood, N.Y.: St. Vladimir's Seminary Press, 1973.

Walker, Andrew, and Costa Carras, eds. *Living Orthodoxy in the Modern World.* Crestwood, N.Y.: St. Vladimir's Seminary Press, 2000.

Ware, Kallistos (Metropolitan of Diokleia). *The Orthodox Church.* 2nd rev. ed. London: Penguin Books, 1993.

Zizioulas, John (Metropolitan of Pergamon). *Being as Communion: Studies in Personhood and the Church.* Crestwood, N.Y.: St. Vladimir's Seminary Press, 1985.